Russia's Road to Democracy

*Canst thou draw out leviathan with
an hook? or his tongue with a cord
which thou lettest down?*

— *The Book of Job*

STUDIES OF COMMUNISM IN TRANSITION

General Editor: Ronald J. Hill
>*Professor of Comparative Government*
>*and Fellow of Trinity College,*
>*Dublin, Ireland*

Studies of Communism in Transition is an important series which applies academic analysis and clarity of thought to the recent traumatic events in Eastern and Central Europe. As many of the preconceptions of the past half century are cast aside, newly independent and autonomous sovereign states are being forced to address long-term, organic problems which had been suppressed by, or appeased within, the Communist system of rule.

The series is edited under the sponsorship of Lorton House, an independent charitable association which exists to promote the academic study of communism and related concepts.

Russia's Road to Democracy

Parliament, Communism and Traditional Culture

Victor Sergeyev
Analytic Centre,
Russian Academy of Sciences

and

Nikolai Biryukov
Moscow State Institute
for International Relations

Edward Elgar

Published by
Edward Elgar Publishing Limited
Gower House
Croft Road
Aldershot
Hants GU11 3HR
England

Edward Elgar Publishing Company
Old Post Road
Brookfield
Vermont 05036
USA

British Library Cataloguing in Publication Data
Sergeyev, Victor
  Russia's Road to Democracy: Parliament,
  Communism and Traditional Culture. –
  (Studies of Communism in Transition)
  I. Title II. Biryukov, N.S. III. Series
  320.947

ISBN 1 85278 851 8

Electronic typesetting by Lorton Hall

Printed and bound in Great Britain by
Hartnolls Limited, Bodmin, Cornwall

Contents

Preface

Preface

This book is an attempt at understanding a post-totalitarian society. The phenomenon we are going to discuss is far from clear. It is, moreover, somewhat surprising. Numerous observers of totalitarian societies, both insiders and outsiders, including those who studied its past and those who have analysed its present or tried to look into its future, have proceeded from the assumption that the phenomenon is, indeed, unnatural, while, on the contrary, subscribing to the hypothesis of natural human rights violated by totalitarian regimes. This hypothesis of natural human rights makes one think of totalitarianism as a kind of fetter societies have been forced to wear. Once this fetter has been cast off, so the reasoning goes, societies would regain their freedom and immediately restore to their citizens all their natural rights. Seen from this perspective, the transition from totalitarianism to representative democracy appears a simple and easy matter, something to be achieved almost spontaneously as soon as the artificial obstacles have been removed.

Recent political developments in Eastern Europe (since the autumn of 1989), however, make one wonder if this has not been but wishful thinking. These developments have brought about a new phenomenon, namely a post-totalitarian phase, with features so surprising that one is almost compelled to conclude that standard political and economic recipes based on the intent to restructure and reorganize these societies by implanting in them 'the basic achievements of world civilization' fail to work. It would be pointless to blame the failure on the recipes. Years of totalitarianism have transformed the society. They have created a type of mentality, as well as institutional structures and social groups, that resist the transformation. All recipes for rapid transition to the state of harmony with the 'civilized world' are rejected by the very social forces that alone are able to undertake the necessary reforms. The result is an ever deepening social, economic and political crisis.

It is not our intention here to go into generalities. Ours is a more modest task. We would like to see whether our analysis of the rise and fall of a particular social institution, namely the USSR Congress of People's Deputies, might not help us understand how political systems operate in the post-totalitarian phase of social development.

This study is based on a detailed analysis of the available primary sources, particularly the proceedings of the five Congresses of People's Deputies of the USSR to have taken place between May 1989 and September 1991. However, it has been clear to us that the task calls for a comparative approach. Our research has taken us to the very foundations of the political system that developed in Soviet society after the revolution of 1917, and this, in turn, has made us turn to the pre-revolutionary Russian political culture, without which it would have been impossible to understand what was going on in the country's political life during the last two or three years. To answer this question one needs a system of 'landmarks' against which recent developments can be viewed and assessed.

Institutions of representative power tend to focus on the major national political problems. And, equally important, their activities are, as a rule, well documented. Moreover, the sessions of the Congresses were broadcast on national television, which in a way allowed the authors to witness what was going on at the Kremlin Palace of Congresses.

It is the fate of the Congress that its history has absorbed the whole spectrum of conflicts and contradictions that have afflicted Soviet society. This makes it a good model for analysis. The Congresses have brought to the foreground and made visible to independent observers the set of processes that constitute our present crisis: the failure of the economic reforms, the collapse of the old ideological dogmas, the dismantling of the totalitarian political structures. And, perhaps most important of all, they have made apparent the states of mind, which have proved totally unprepared for the radical changes to come. They have demonstrated the deep-rooted inability to grasp the scope and gravity of problems that the collapse of totalitarianism is bound to raise. The devastating combination of the insouciant 'historic optimism' and the ruthless censorial control over any kind of independent and honest social research has achieved its aim: not only the man in the street, but the intellectual elite, too, fail to understand the society they live in.

The present study is a modest attempt to clarify certain features of this society based not so much on speculative argument - our daily, weekly and monthly publications are full of this kind of stuff - as on the available documents. Our approach is also based on a study of the evolution of political ideas that influenced the fate of Russia, for any attempt to introduce representative institutions into its political life was bound to run against the suspicious attitude toward representative democracy embedded in the national political culture. New forms of political life cannot exist without the appropriate political culture: for it is the soil without which the transplanted exotic flower will fade. This interdependence of political institutions and political culture is the focus of our study.

It was a hard time for our country when this book was being written. (What country, by the way? The Soviet Union? The Russian Federation? Even now it is not easy to answer this question.)

The uncertain and difficult political situation (to say nothing of the everyday hardships) could not help leaving its mark on the book. We are, therefore, all the more grateful to those institutions and fellow scholars that helped this book come into being.

We express our most sincere thanks to the Analytical Centre of the Russian Academy of Sciences and its Director, Professor Dmitry Piskunov, for providing both financial support and favourable conditions for our research. The authors are likewise grateful to the members of the Department of Philosophy of the Moscow State Institute of International Relations for their patient and undemanding assistance.

The authors would like to express their profound gratitude to the Swedish Collegium for Advanced Study in the Social Sciences (SCASSS) and its Director, Professor Bjorn Wittrock, for giving Viktor Sergeyev the opportunity to spend a few weeks in the summer of 1991 working on the present project in the capacity of collaborator of SCASSS, and also for their kind invitation to discuss the main findings at the seminar on 'Democracy and Societal Development' in Uppsala in October 1992.

Our deepest gratitude is to the Department of Politics of the University of Leeds, its Head, Professor Lionel Cliffe, and Dr Jeff Gleisner for the opportunity for each of us to spend a term (in spring

1992 and spring 1993) at their University working on the book, and to Dr David Beetham for a fruitful discussion of the authors' basic ideas at his seminar at the same university.

The authors thank Academician Ivan Kovalchenko for the chance to discuss their main findings at his seminar at Moscow University and for the constructive criticism they met there.

Special thanks are due to Professor Robert Tucker of Princeton University whose penetrating comments proved most helpful both at the early stage of this research and for the final presentation of the results.

The authors would also like to thank all their colleagues, both in Russia and abroad, for their stimulating remarks and the interest shown in our work. We are particularly pleased to mention among them participants in the seminar on 'Problems of Interdependence' sponsored by the American Academy of Arts and Letters and the USSR Academy of Sciences, held in Moscow in June 1991, especially Professor Hayward Alker, Professor Daniel Druckman, Professor George Lakoff, Dr Paul Stern, Professor Philip Tetlock, Professor Charles Tilly, Dr Lee Walker and Dr Stephen Walker. The seminar gave us a rare chance to present the preliminary arguments of this book to an audience that was interested, competent and objective. We are also grateful to Professor Donna Bahry and Professor George Breslauer for extensive and fruitful discussions of some of our most cherished ideas.

The authors thank Professor Paul Chilton and Dr Mikhail Ilyin, who read the original versions of some of the chapters and made valuable comments. We also thank SAGE Publications and Verlag Volk und Welt in Berlin, and also Professor Paul Chilton and Michael Harms and Peter Linke as editors, for the opportunity to present some of our findings to the public in Great Britain and Germany (in *Discourse and Society* **4**, 1 (January 1993), and *Ueberall Klippen: Innen- und Aussenpolitische Gegebenheiten Russlands*, respectively).

Our special thanks are to Dr Jeff Gleisner and Paul Chaisty of the University of Leeds who helped us through the depths of English grammar and made the English of this book appear less outlandish than it might otherwise have been.

Needless to say, none of the persons mentioned above is responsible for the contents of this book and its possible shortcomings or inaccuracies.

And, last but not least, this book would have never been finished without the unfailing and considerate support of our wives, Marina Sergeyeva and Svetlana Biryukova, whose efforts in creating the atmosphere of domestic peace and confidence in the future can scarcely be exaggerated.

V.S.
N.B.

1 Introduction: Parliamentary Activity and Political Culture

> ... *What entitles us to characterize the being as the presence? The question comes too late. For this cast of being has been decided on long ago and without us.*
>
> — M. Heidegger, *Time and Being.*

REPRESENTATIVE DEMOCRACY IN THE WESTERN WORLD

The problem of representative democracy emerged on the eve of modern history as a part of a larger task: the rational organization of society. Inspired by the conspicuous success of mathematics and the natural sciences, the greatest thinkers of the seventeenth century tried to understand not only the interrelations of human mind and nature, but the nature of human society, as well. Thomas Hobbes's *Leviathan* (1651), John Locke's *Two Treatises of Government* (1690), the political writings of Gottfried Leibnitz, *Letters to a Provincial (Les lettres à un provincial)* by Blaise Pascal (1657) and - in the following century - *The Spirit of the Laws (De l'esprit des lois)* by Charles Montesquieu (1748) and *The Social Contract (Du contrat social)* by Jean-Jacques Rousseau (1762) rivalled the great classical works by Plato (*The Republic*) and Aristotle (*Politics*) in the significance and originality of their ideas.

The history of science bears witness to the close relationship that exists between human attempts to understand nature and efforts to rationalize social relations through giving *sense* to forms of social life. Just as the development of science and philosophy in the Golden Age of Pericles was followed by waves of revolutions in Greek *poleis* that brought direct democracy into being, so the outstanding intellectual achievements of modern times gave birth to new forms of statehood: representative democracy and the separation of powers.

Of the various topics that are related to the problem of understanding the nature of society and inventing a rational system of its government, based on the ideas of 'natural' human rights and the initial equality of human beings, some appear to be of primary importance.

The first is the source of state sovereignty and the development of cooperation between self-centred individuals. If people are born equal and free, how can the human commonwealth with its inherent hierarchy and relations of power emerge out of the initial chaos of egoistic individual drives? What was the beginning of civil society? The question was asked by Hobbes who drew the following conclusion: civil society had been created by a *social contract* between individuals who had renounced their rights in favour of a *sovereign* in order to put an end to the natural state of *war of all against all*. This idea of a social contract became the main topic of political debate in the next century - up to the Great Revolution - and formed the theoretical basis of representative democracy, that is, a political system in which citizens invest their elected representatives with the legislative powers that belong to them by right of nature. A powerful and dynamic statement of this interpretation of democracy is to be found in the treatise by Rousseau with its constant emphasis on the necessity to represent and express *the will of the people*.

This served to introduce the next theme: how to prevent tyranny on the part of the new, 'elected' sovereign? Its theoretical aspects had been discussed by Montesquieu who had proposed the celebrated principle of the *separation of powers* later to be implemented in the constitution of a new North American state.

Both principles - democratic representation and division of powers - proved insufficient, however. This was made apparent by the tragic events of 1793–94 in revolutionary France where the democratically elected Convention operating formally under conditions of divided powers and declared human rights established and maintained a state of bloody terror. Many leaders of the democratic revolution, including members of that sovereign assembly, fell victims to it.

Political mechanisms that could safeguard society and its members against abuse of power on the part of those they had themselves elected emerged as the third main problem of democratic political theory. The solution came as a demand for *free political activity*, that is, freedom to create political organizations that might express and defend the interests of various social groups.

These three ideas – political representation through free election, division of powers and freedom of political activity – may be said to form the basis of modern democracy.

DEMOCRACY AND TOTALITARIANISM

However clear these principles may have appeared to be after the debates of the enlightened seventeenth and eighteenth centuries, a problem of profound complexity has since been encountered, namely, *transition to democracy*. Unlike theoretical interpretations of the *nature* of democracy – and we may still witness impressive insights here[1] – the problem of transition to democracy calls for descriptive[2] rather than prescriptive studies. For differences both in the initial conditions in which various societies find themselves and in their subsequent development are so great that speculations (like Russia's recent debate on the need for an authoritarian phase in the transition from totalitarianism to democracy) will hardly yield anything more reliable than prophecies by an oracle.

Part of this problem is the close relationship between totalitarianism and the mass culture that developed in the course of the industrial revolution and its accompanying process of 'human standardization', the mentality of that 'man of the mass' to which José Ortega y Gasset first drew our attention.[3] Although totalitarianism appears to be an

---

1 See the classic works by Robert Dahl (1982, 1985). Studies of institutional aspects of democratic rule are one of the leading branches of political science in Great Britain and the United States. For studies of political culture within which democratic institutions operate, see Verba 1987, Putnam 1976, and Aberbach *et al.* 1981.

2 See, for example, *Transition* 1991.

3 Ortega y Gasset 1932. The problem was later discussed by the social philosophers of the Frankfurt School: see Marcuse 1964 and, especially, Adorno and Horkheimer 1972, a work that was written during the Second World War but profoundly influenced contemporary 'post-modern' theories of society.

outcome of a unique constellation of circumstances peculiar to modernity, 'the man of the mass' in whose psychology it is reputedly rooted is by no means a 'new' man – he is essentially a man of the traditional, 'pre-mass' culture. This makes one wonder in what relation the traditional culture and the phenomenon of totalitarianism stand to each other.

Twentieth-century totalitarianism has always been at odds with the idea of parliamentary rule. It would be easy to rationalize this as a natural outcome of the conflict between the irrational 'mass consciousness', on the one hand, and the rational cooperation of the 'best' members of society, on the other. But this interpretation raises a series of uncomfortable questions, including, perhaps, the most 'awkward' one, namely, in what sense may one regard elected representatives of the populace as indeed the 'best'? It would also involve a sound scholarly description (and conceptualization) of the process of their collective legislative activity.

REPRESENTATIVE INSTITUTIONS AS ARTIFICIAL INTELLIGENCES: THE ROLE OF PROCEDURES

Why should we think that 'one mind is good, but two minds are better', as a Russian proverb has it? And what about a few hundred minds that usually constitute a parliament? It is a point of common knowledge, well supported by personal experience, that a crowd tends to be less rational than the individuals it consists of. This would make one doubt the validity of the proverbial assumption. Why should an assembly of elected representatives of the populace be more reasonable than a crowd of ordinary citizens? And if it is to be, what are the necessary conditions? And, finally, what does the expression 'a wise decision' mean when it is applied to a group?

It seems clear that for a great number of people to behave more or less reasonably, they must interact in a rational, orderly way. They need some kind of organizational structure and an associated set of rules of behaviour, that is, a *procedure*. When parliamentarians discuss their problems they interact, they argue, they exchange opinions and knowledge. This entitles us to treat parliamentary decision-making as essentially the same process of altering the structure of knowledge as takes place in the human mind, according to the latest findings of cognitive science and artificial intelligence studies, when it contemplates and makes a decision.[4] The difference is that in collective decision-making the transformation of knowledge is externalized. The 'program' that determines the process of contemplation is projected 'outside' and takes the form of procedures regulating the activities of the organization and the behaviour of its members. All organizations may indeed be viewed as some kind of 'artificial intelligences', except that their 'minds' are embodied in procedures, statutes and regulations rather than in computer processors.[5] The bulk of the work is done in human minds, of course, but the stricter the rules, the more predictable (and the more manageable) the outcome.

With the help of this metaphor of artificial intelligence one may venture to examine in what sense the activity of a parliament may be called 'rational'. Is a group of individuals cleverer than a single individual? Why do we need (if, indeed, we do) collective decision-making? While no group probably can be cleverer than a very clever person, when it comes to parliaments the stakes are different. An assembly of ordinary ('average') persons can, in certain circumstances, be cleverer than any one of them taken alone. The function of procedures is to provide for these circumstances. But what is, perhaps, even more important is the fact that the public character of debates makes the 'working' of this collective intelligence comprehensible to outside observers and hence subject to the conscious control by those who delegate powers to the deputies. This can hardly be the case if a single leader, however democratically elected, contemplates his decisions, more competent though they may be, in the silence of his office after a private exchange of opinions with his advisers.

The parliamentary idea thus has to withstand attacks on both 'populist' and 'aristocratic' quarters, the proponents on both sides favouring, more or less consciously and more or less openly, authoritarian rule.

The problem is, of course, that parliaments often fail to meet the criteria of 'collective intelligence'. They may become but crowds

---

4 It is worth noting here that the metaphor of a 'community' of individuals has proved fruitful in building models of intellectual activity (see Minsky 1985).

5 See Sergeyev 1985.

guided and manipulated by skilful demagogues.[6] Or they may split into factions capable only of fighting one another and blocking any reasonable decision on any significant issue, and thus grow impotent, undermine the very principles in which they are based, and give rise to authoritarian sentiments.

Analysis of the circumstances that cause these failures, and of means to prevent them, might prove a vital contribution to our understanding of representative democracy. The subject has been broached by K.J. Arrow in his pioneering studies.[7] His main goal was to determine the circumstances that make voting ineffective as a way of arriving at a decision. Arrow was able to formulate the celebrated paradox that, when there happen to be more than two alternatives, the availability of a 'dictator' who directs the voters how to vote is the only means of ensuring a definite decisional outcome in all circumstances. Though decision-making by collective bodies has been the subject of intensive research and is discussed in numerous published works,[8] the relationship between the discovered theoretical probabilities of ineffectiveness and the given political realities remains an open question.

PARLIAMENTARY STUDIES AND THE SCIENCE OF MANAGEMENT

The main assumptions of the 'voting' approach to the study of representative political institutions are the independence of the voters' wills and the ensuing 'atomistic' vision of voting behaviour. In actual fact, however, parliaments are complex political institutions that consist of great varieties of internal structures, both formal and informal. These structures, as well as parliaments' interrelations with other political institutions of society, have been described and analysed in numerous works, both in case studies and in theoretical syntheses, based on the precepts of traditional institutionalism. This

6 For a discussion of the limits of 'rationality' in collective decision-making, see Artyushkin *et al.* 1990.
7 See, for example, Arrow 1951.
8 For a classic work that had a profound impact on subsequent research in the field, see Alker and Russett 1965.

kind of research has been conducted for individual countries, and also in comparative perspective.

The limitations of the purely institutional approach to the study of parliaments arise from its inability to account for the differences in the functioning of apparently similar institutions in different socio-cultural contexts. Thus, representative bodies of Latin America and the United States, structurally almost identical, are strikingly different in the way they function. This is not the place to dwell on this point. Suffice it to say that the representative bodies of the so-called 'people's democracies', such as the East German *Volkskammer* (People's Chamber), the Polish *Sejm*, the Yugoslavian *Skupshtina*, or the *Federal Assembly* of Czechoslovakia, as well as the numerous *Supreme Soviets* of the USSR and its constituent republics, were, from the *formal* point of view, political institutions of exactly the same type as the parliaments of the Western democracies. In reality, however, they were entirely different: both in the Soviet Union and in Eastern Europe organs of representative power operated as plebiscitary bodies subject to severe ideological control.

Institutional analysis is doubtless an indispensable element of the study of representative institutions, but in itself it proves insufficient. How are we to make up for its limitations?

A parliament is not only a 'social mechanism' created and operating along certain lines or according to certain rules. It is an *organization*, that is, a cluster not only of structures and rules of interaction, but also of living minds that constitute its corps of deputies and its apparatus as well. The knowledge, habits, patterns of behaviour, ideas and social preconceptions of those who work in it have a profound impact on how it functions. This approach – which lays stress on the informal socio-cultural factors and the organization's 'internal environment' – has been the dominant trend in managerial science since the pioneering writings of Herbert Simon.[9]

We believe that analysing representative institutions along these lines will considerably improve our understanding of them, particularly if we deal with cultural environments that differ from those in which the idea of parliamentarianism was originally conceived.

In the meantime one should not neglect the structure of the

9   Simon 1957; see also his autobiography (Simon 1991). For further development of these
    ideas, see March and Olsen 1989.

organization's activity. Absorption with voting as the deputies' main occupation is indicative of a gross misunderstanding of the nature of the decision-making process. From this perspective the collective decisional outcome is viewed merely as the sum total of a number of individual decisions made by persons who constitute the collective body. This approach could be justified only if the deputies were denied any opportunity to communicate and had to cast their votes from isolated chambers. In real life it is precisely this communication – in various commissions and committees, as well as during the sessions, both in and outside the conference halls – that forms the background, not to say the foundation, of parliamentary activity. The complex process of working out the resulting documents – involving the 'compiling' of the text, the generation of ideas, debates and arguments – is the very stuff that a student of parliament must deal with.

But what is most important about parliament is, of course, its status as an organ of representative power.

THREE FUNCTIONS OF REPRESENTATION

In his book *Representation*, Anthony Birch distinguishes three main meanings of the word: (1) representation as delegation of authority; (2) representation as 'typicality', that is possession of features 'typical', 'average' or 'ordinary' for a group of persons; and (3) representation as a symbol.[10]

Parliament embodies all three functions. Its members are elected representatives to whom the voters' authority has been delegated. The parliament as a whole 'represents' the nation; it may be seen as the nation in miniature. And, last but not least, it serves as a national symbol. As an organization, its functions are determined by these three meanings of 'representation'. Voting is a partial discharge of only the first one of them, as is the MPs' other main activity – negotiations.

In certain circumstances the parliament implements the second meaning of representation. It acts as if it were the nation itself, albeit in miniature. This function becomes vital in situations of national

10 Birch 1971, p.15.

crises. Thus, it is to their respective parliaments that most democratic constitutions assign the right to declare the state of war. This is done on the assumption that in such situations parliaments will voice the national feelings. But to serve as a true mouthpiece for the nation, the parliament, or for that matter any other agency, must not lose touch with the society. The crucial factors here will be the effective exchange of information and the free media to maintain it.

The word's third meaning – symbolic representation – is also important if we are to understand the role of parliaments in social life and their political functions. Parliament symbolizes democracy, and when democracy is in danger it is the parliament as a symbol of democratic order that first comes under attack by its opponents and is the first object of concern for its defenders, as we witnessed in Vilnius and other Baltic capitals in January 1991 and in Moscow seven months later.

Reference to this symbolic function will play a significant role in our account of the crisis and the final fiasco of the USSR Congress of People's Deputies. The legitimacy of democratic regimes rests on the efficiency of their representative institutions. A feeble parliament may fail to play its role of symbol and hence undermine the legitimacy of the political system within which it has been established. The Soviet political culture being what it was, the symbolic role of the Congress proved of paramount importance.

If the representative institutions the social scientist deals with operate within social milieux with political cultures considerably different from the one that gave birth to the classic parliamentary system, it will not be beside the point to inquire how each of the three functions of representation is affected by the political culture of the society in question. Their relative value may vary markedly, depending on the cultural tradition to which the representative institution belongs. To answer this question, it is necessary to consider the notion of political culture.[11]

11 The notion of political culture as it is developed and applied in the present volume is based on philosophical premises that differ considerably from those customarily adopted by American political science. By and large, it may be said to remain within the European tradition, marked, as far as the problem in question is concerned, by the writings of Max Weber, Karl Mannheim, Martin Heidegger, Michel Foucault and, to turn to more recent writings, Anthony Giddens and Pierre Bourdieu.

POLITICAL CULTURE AND ITS BASIC ELEMENTS

Political culture is defined here as the basic knowledge about or vision of social life shared by a relatively large section of society that determines for those who belong to it their understanding of particular political situations and their behaviour in them.[12] This kind of knowledge may be and usually is unconscious. That is why it works 'without fail' – not because it is adequate to the situation it is used for coping with, but because there is no alternative to it: no other patterns of interpretation or behaviour are known and hence available. This knowledge is structured into a set of highly generalized conceptual schemes that can be neither verified nor refuted by experience for the simple reason that they themselves are used to interpret all kinds of experience, as well as the world behind it. Particular interpretations may fail, of course, but this can always be blamed on the failure to allow for one of the apparently innumerable circumstantial factors, rather than on the limitations of the interpretative scheme itself.

A good example of the kind of interpretative scheme we have in mind is provided by cosmic dualism, a doctrine which holds that whatever happens in the universe is an episode in and a result of the unceasing struggle between two opposing principles, Good and Evil. The scheme is irrefutable because any particular situation may be reinterpreted to confirm it, the more so as the agents of Good and Evil are not named in advance. The political culture that has formed in the Soviet Union is prone to this type of dualism: the world was once seen as a battlefield of Socialism and Imperialism; it came to be viewed as an arena of struggle between Democracy and 'Partocracy', the State and the Mafia, and so on.

To describe the political culture of a society one must determine the basic types of knowledge used to evaluate situations and to make

12 Compare this to the standpoint taken by Karl Mannheim (1956, p.3):

> Strictly speaking it is incorrect to say that the single individual thinks. Rather it is more correct to insist that he participates in thinking further what other men have thought before him. He finds himself in an inherited situation with patters of thought which are appropriate to this situation and attempts to elaborate further the inherited modes of response or to substitute others for them in order to deal more adequately with the new challenges which have arisen out of the shifts and changes in his situation.

decisions.[13] We have found it expedient to divide knowledge of this kind into three categories, namely, social ontology, values and operational experience.

Social Ontology as Patterns of Pre-Understanding

In order to act one must have an idea of the present situation. However, since the diversity of situations is infinite, this means that one must have a set of rather broad categories in order to classify them, form one's judgement and work out a scenario of future actions. The system of categories used to classify social situations is here called *social ontology*.[14] If you come across a statement such as 'The will of the Soviet people foiled the wicked schemes of Imperialism', this means that the speaker assumes, first, that there exists something called 'the Soviet people' that can take political actions (which further means that 'things' of this kind are capable of action in general); secondly, that there is something that may be defined as 'the will of the people' (thereby again applying to the people the metaphor of 'agent'); third, that there is something called 'Imperialism' that also possesses a will since it is capable of devising 'wicked schemes'; and, finally, that these two agents can interact in a direct way. Displayed in this manner, it sounds grotesque, of course, but when words like these are backed by a military intervention (as, for example, in Hungary in 1956), they somehow grow real.

Social ontologies (that is general conceptual models of social reality) are backed by what we call 'patterns of pre-understanding': complex systems of knowledge, usually unconscious, that make these

13 For the initial version of the typology used in this book, and also for a discussion of problems faced when developing typologies of this kind, see Sergeyev and Tsymbursky 1990.

14 For the role basic ontological assumptions play in interpreting historic reality, see Sergeyev 1987, where the principal distinction between the procedural (based on the metaphor of 'steps') and the processual (based on the metaphor of 'organism') understanding of political development is introduced. The former depicts social reality as created exclusively by the interaction of political actors and political institutions: that is, it is entirely 'man-made'; the latter views political development as either a 'stream of history' governed by laws that are independent of the human participants, or some kind of 'life of a social organism'. Both may be subject to external influences, of course, which cannot, however, affect their 'basic nature'. For application of this distinction to a particular situation, see Parshin and Sergeyev 1990.

schemes applicable.[15] The use of social ontology as a theoretical construct will be demonstrated later in the course of our analysis of the continuity of the Russian political culture of the pre- and post-revolutionary epochs.

Values

Next on our list of the kinds of knowledge that form a political culture are *values*. These are highly complex constructs directly related to the social ontology. Whereas the ontology serves to describe and classify situations, the values are used to single out certain types of them and to ascribe to these some degree of 'acceptability' or 'unacceptability'. To make the point clear let us consider for example the value of *justice*, which plays such an important role in political life in general and in the life of a parliament in particular.[16]

There are two main interpretations of justice: 'distributional' justice, and justice as administration of law. The notion of 'distributional' justice is based on the (socio-ontological) assumption that there exists a 'resource' that is to be distributed by some agency – the Distributor – among a number of Recipients (to whom the Distributor may belong, too). The distribution is to follow some 'principle', and following that 'principle' is what we call 'Justice'.

The alternative interpretation – administration of law – can be reduced to the first type if it is assumed that courts (or whichever state institution administers the law) are to reward everyone according to their deserts, that is, to 'distribute' prizes and penalties, 'the Law' becoming the 'principle' of distribution.

With values structured in this way, we are able to distinguish among various interpretations of them adhered to by different political actors. The context will allow us to determine, for instance, who is

15 The notion of 'pre-understanding' as a basis of subjective ontology, as 'life inside language' was put forward by Heidegger (1971). For its relation to 'post-modern' social science, see Habermas 1987, pp.131–60. In a paper delivered at the 1991 ISA Annual Convention in Vancouver one of the present authors has analysed various types of pre-understanding of social reality and formulated semantic principles for the development of a typology of pre-understanding (see Sergeyev 1991).

16 For a discussion of the role of values in political discourse and the related typology of argumentation, see Sergeyev 1986. For an interpretation of the linguistic structure of values, see Baranov and Sergeyev 1988.

supposed to be the Distributor and who are the Receivers, what kind of 'resource' is to be distributed and according to what 'principle'. A similar interpretative scheme based on the semantic deconstruction of the notion can be applied to other values.

The structure of values is of particular importance in studies of representative power, since values are the basis of argument in all political debates, and political debates form the substratum of all parliamentary activities. Each party to a political debate usually seeks to demonstrate that the action in question will lead to a situation that is good (or bad) and is therefore to be adopted (or rejected). Since parties to the debate may and usually do appeal to different values, their ability to maintain the discourse depends on whether they can work out and adhere to a mutually acceptable hierarchy of values.

The structure and hierarchy of values are essential elements of the political culture. Conflicts that occur at historic crossroads often take the form of a drastic change in the structure and hierarchy of values. In our case the whole period of *perestroika* can be seen as a revolution in the hierarchy of values, involving a change-over from 'social justice' and 'order' – that is the ideal of an all-powerful state attending to the distribution of resources and the administration of law – to 'human rights' and a 'market economy' – that is to the ideals of a free individual and a free economy.

It is easy to observe that every political debate of the *perestroika* period was pivoted on this change in the hierarchy of values. From this perspective *glasnost'* may be seen as an education project on a grand scale aimed at changing the political culture of the country. However, the debates seldom touched upon other elements of the political culture – the social ontology and the operational experience – that were left practically unaffected.

But hierarchy of values is the least stable element in a political culture. As will be seen from the analysis below, the internal structure of values and the social ontology are far more conservative. Changes in the hierarchy of values are indicative of a social transformation on the 'macro-level', as it were. On the 'micro-level', that is, in everyday life (and hence in the long perspective), the social ontology and the structure of values appear much more significant.

That is why *perestroika* may be viewed as a kind of 'macro-shift' in the political culture, as a *re-construction* in the literal sense (*pere-stroika*): its initiators found quite a perfectly appropriate name for the policy they had in mind. Speaking metaphorically, it might be said that they have managed to destroy the cohesion between the blocks of the structure, turning it into a pile of broken brick but leaving the properties of the material untouched. However, if their intention was to put an end to the state of 'stagnation', they had to change the nature of the society on the 'micro-level', that is cause a change in the properties of the 'social material'. For a task like this, polymerization would prove a far better analogy.

Operational Experience

Let us now turn to the last element of a political culture: operational experience. Operational experience is the complex of means that have been developed within a political culture in order to deal with problems typical of it. It may be seen as a collection of standard scenarios for standard situations.

To turn to the parliament, let us consider the problem of coalitions, for example, which often have to be formed in order for a decision to pass – hence the importance of operational experience in forming such coalitions. The following is an illustration of the point.

On the very eve of the French defeat of 1940 Charles de Gaulle had a conversation with Paul Reynaud. At that moment Reynaud was desperately trying to form a cabinet for 'decisive actions', and de Gaulle was surprised to hear that Pétain was to be included, since he could hardly be reckoned among the supporters of that policy. Asked by de Gaulle why he did it, Reynaud answered that he preferred an opponent inside rather than outside.[17]

The story is interesting in its demonstration of a substantial difference in the operational experience of, on the one hand, a military commander with a broad political outlook who is chiefly concerned about the efficiency (and hence the unity) of the future government and, on the other hand, a parliamentary politician whose primary concern is for the stability of that government and hence the parliamentary support it may count on and for whom the problems faced by the government are sometimes overshadowed by the need to secure its very existence.

17 See de Gaulle 1954, p.43.

The history of *perestroika* shows similar examples. In a way, relations between Mikhail Gorbachev and Boris Yeltsin between 1987 and 1991 mirrored the story told by de Gaulle. Whereas Gorbachev, whose operational experience consisted mainly of the manoeuvring and alliance-building skills acquired in the Politburo, was inclined to place the stability of leadership above all other considerations (which probably accounts for his persistent calls for consensus in situations where apparently no consensus could have been reached), Yeltsin was guided by operational experience of a totally different nature – the one he had acquired in trying to cope with the everyday problems of a large industrial province – and was, therefore, more likely to favour strong and consistent measures befitting a crisis situation. Despite the fact that his experience was accumulated elsewhere, Gorbachev may be regarded as a parliamentary type. It was not, perhaps, accidental that it was Gorbachev who sought to introduce parliamentary government into the USSR. Yeltsin is, by contrast, a crisis leader prone to tackling grave problems by tough administrative means. From this perspective, Gorbachev's ultimate failure was due to the fact that the type of operational experience he had gained proved totally inadequate to the severity of the crisis. The same was true of Paul Reynaud.

Unlike social ontology, operational experience varies: a political culture may incorporate many different types of it. It also can be said to depend on personal psychology. This is easy to explain. Standard ways of settling problems are different in different spheres, as are the problems themselves. But personal careers depend on the particular skills and traits: a person capable of a brilliant military career can hardly expect to do as well on the diplomatic field, where flexibility and willingness to compromise are valued above strictness and straightforwardness. Nevertheless, it would be wrong to assume that operational experience is conditioned entirely by the sphere of one's activity. Much will depend on the cultural traditions, as the differences in the national styles of diplomatic behaviour described by Harold Nicolson suggest.[18]

It is hardly necessary to dwell at length on the significance these aspects of political culture have for parliamentary activity in general. But it would not be out of place to observe that cultural traditions

18 See Nicolson 1942, pp.127-54. For styles of diplomatic behaviour, see also Fisher 1980, and Binnendijk (ed.) 1987.

appear particularly important when societies that hitherto have lacked parliamentary institutions seek to create them.

Social and political innovation is, by and large, a complicated and painful process. The story of the USSR Congress of People's Deputies might serve as an impressive illustration of the point, whose significance extends beyond the immediate political future of Russia and other heirs to the Soviet Union and which may also prove relevant to our understanding of the processes of democratization that now seem to be acquiring global importance.

It is our intention to demonstrate in this study the way in which the conceptual framework outlined above may help us analyse the complicated process of setting up a democratic society and the obstacles encountered on the way.

Part I

The Soviet Leviathan

> *Because the major part hath by consenting voices declared a Soveraigne; he that dissented must now consent with the rest; that is, he contented to avow all the actions he shall do, or else justly be destroyed by the rest.*
>
> — Thomas Hobbes, *Leviathan, or The Matter, Form, and Power of a Common-Wealth Ecclesiastical and Civil*

2 The Roots of Bondage

You are an ass. You are an ass because you are lazy. You've never bothered about general ontology.

— S. Lem, *The God's Simple.*

THE PARADOX OF STABILITY

The Soviet political culture was formed under a variety of influences, of which political reality in the Soviet Union itself was, of course, the most important single factor. That was a paradoxical reality. The Soviet Union managed to create a kind of political system for which the ideological justification was borrowed from outside but which, nevertheless, remained alien to the society that originally developed and supplied the theoretical sanction. Although imported, the system struck root in Russian soil, having demonstrated, moreover, a surprising degree of stability. It was maintained for decades without major malfunctions despite appalling failures on both domestic and international scenes. One would think that any of the social disasters such as the famine of the early 1930s or the defeats in the early 1940s would have been more than sufficient to bring about the fall of any government, democratic or despotic alike. Yet the Stalin regime stood firm. How could that be?

The question was asked by everyone who had a chance to ponder over the nature of Soviet society and the Soviet political order. The answers can be divided into two main varieties. Some hold that it was a totalitarian regime upheld first and foremost by violence.[1] Inefficient in itself (except, perhaps, in a number of emergency situations), the totalitarian regime managed to delay its otherwise inevitable and

---

1 For a classic exposition of this position, see Arendt 1958; see also journal publications of the early *perestroika* period: for example, Gozman and Etkind 1989.

immediate collapse by painstakingly searching for and removing well in advance whatever might have threatened it. In real life that meant that ruthless extermination awaited not only those who dared to oppose the regime, but anyone who happened to hold an opinion that 'deviated' from the one that was officially approved of and imposed. In that way, whatever discontent there might have been felt in some sections of the society, it was not allowed to assume the form of a political action and develop into direct confrontation with the authorities, because any feeble impulse in that direction would have been stopped long before an organizational structure could have been created that might have been capable of active resistance. Expedient though it might be from the standpoint of the ruling elite, the country had to pay much for this preventive self-defence, for it robbed it of both stimuli and means of development.

According to the above interpretation, the stability of the Soviet regime is to be explained by its ability to use violence in any place and at any time. We have no wish to defend Stalinism, of course; but we would suggest that reference to violence alone is not enough. For, in the first place, in order to use violence in an efficient way one must be strong, and it is precisely the question of how to account for that strength that we are discussing here: from what source was it derived? In the second place, violence on the scale that would warrant this point of view was exercised only until the mid-1950s, that is, during the regime's first thirty-five years. The second half of the seven Soviet decades passed without Stalin-style mass repressions. One might object, of course, that to crush all resistance, however slight, and even the very will to resist was precisely the point of the Great Terror. But the objection would amount to recognition that the regime succeeded in creating a political culture congruous to itself and thus acquired legitimacy. In the third place, evidence of the intrinsic stability of the Soviet political system is provided by the inertia it displayed when subjected to transformation.

An alternative explanation of this stability alludes to some peculiar features of the Russian national character. According to this, their tragic history had taught the Russians to submit to authoritarian power and even to cherish it as their only chance for survival.[2] This assertion

---

2 This standpoint is popular with Soviet historians, who tend, however, to treat it in an apologetic manner. See, for example, Nesterov 1980: '"To be or not to be?": this

of 'the servility of the Russian soul' is bound to arouse extreme irritation and indignation on the part of those who style themselves Russian patriots, but there is at least one point on which the 'patriots' agree with their opponents: both parties would subscribe to the opinion that there exists a mysterious entity called 'the Russian soul' which somehow migrates between individuals and generations. We would prefer to speak not so much of the 'soul', especially a 'mysterious' one (this is after all nothing but a common metaphor), as of the traditional political culture, of which mechanisms of translation can, in principle, be described and explained in a rational way.

---

question that no West European nation has ever faced arose for Rus' [ancient Russia], menacingly simple and inevitable' is Nesterov's starting-point (p.20). 'What was it that enabled the Russian state to loosen up twice and then to break the vicious ring that was tightening around it? In other words, what was Moscow's response to the historic challenge the Russian people had perforce to take up?' he proceeds to ask (p.30). His answer runs as follows: 'Centralization and discipline – that was the response of Moscow to the challenge thrown to the Russian people. That was a stern response, but it was the only true one in the unequal struggle that the people had to wage for its very existence, for the national independence' (p.59). Citing a number of touching examples, the author feels obliged to add, however (p.60):

> But was it only to them, that is to state centralization and political discipline, that [Russia] owed its decisive victories? In our opinion, it would be both contrary to the facts and singularly unfair to that heroic nation to confine ourselves to considering only these two factors. Throughout our age-old history there was also a third major factor of Russia's grandeur in action: the power of the national patriotism. [Original italics]

A critical variation of the above standpoint is also known in Russian social thought. This may be traced to the radical criticism of Russian culture in the first of Chaadayev's *Philosophic Letters* (for the French original, see Chaadayev 1991, p.96):

> Alone in the world, we have given the world nothing, we have taken nothing from the world; we have not added a single thought to the mass of the human ideas; we have contributed nothing to the progress of the human mind, and whatever fell to our lot of that progress, we have distorted.

This interpretation of national history and political culture has been applied to many latter-day problems. It underlined the criticism of the Russian revolutionary movement in the celebrated collection of essays, *The Stakes* (*The Landmarks*) (for publication data, see Bulgakov 1991). Compare this with a later work by one of the contributors (Berdyaev 1972, p.140):

> ... Only bolshevism could control the situation. It only corresponded to the instincts of the masses and their real attitude to things, and it, like a true demagogue, turned everything to its own use. ...
> It made use of the Russian traditions of government by imposition, and instead of an unfamiliar democracy of which they had had no experience it proclaimed a dictatorship which was more like the old rule of the Tsar.

Of course, there is no need to choose between the extremes. That extreme standpoints are deficient is, however, a platitude: it is the burden of many a script, no matter what its subject.[3] In our opinion, 'a golden mean' is of little use as a methodological principle unless it is based on a sound substantial theory of the subject of research.

We thus come back to our basic methodological assertion: without analysis of the traditional political culture and its constituent pre-understanding patterns our account of the political development of Russia, both before and after *perestroika*, will remain at least incomplete.

'POPULISM' IN THE RUSSIAN POLITICAL TRADITION

The People as the Repository of Truth

The political rhetoric of nineteenth-century Russia put great emphasis on the notion of *narodnost'*, which can be translated – somewhat inadequately – as 'populism'. *Narodnost'* is derived from *narod*, which stands for both 'nation' and 'people', the latter almost invariably understood as 'the common people' and opposed to 'the higher' or, as Leo Tolstoy would have put it, 'the educated' classes.

That interpretation might have belonged to the common stock of the European egalitarian or democratic ideology, but what formed a peculiar feature of the Russian political culture, as it developed towards the end of the last century, was the fact that the catchword of populism was to be read on the banners of both reactionaries and revolutionaries. Political forces might have differed in their attitude toward the other two elements of the political doctrine officially

---

3 To cite an example from within our field (Medvedev 1989 **4**, p.20):

> I am convinced that the truth lies between these extremes. History cannot be interrupted even by a most radical revolution and, although by nature a social revolution signifies a decisive rupture from the former structures and the order of the old society, the character of the revolution and its consequences are related to the character and features of that old society. In revolution there is negation of the past, but there is also continuity, which is why it would be erroneous to take into consideration only one side of this interrelation of the past and the present and ignore the other.

preached by the government of Nicholas I, namely, autocracy and Orthodoxy, but would invariably swear allegiance to the people. It may be objected, of course, that their interpretations of populism were different, as were their opinions concerning who constituted the people, to say nothing of their understanding of the people's interests. But the appeal was significant in itself, whether it issued from the court of Nicholas I or the future *narodniks* (populists). That attitude was based – or at least seems to have been based – on the implicit belief that the people were not just 'our suffering brothers', of whom their more prosperous fellow citizens ought to take care and whose burden they were to relieve (if they were 'honourable men', that is); 'the people' stood for something immeasurably greater: it was a source, or rather *the* source, of ultimate truth and ultimate wisdom denied to representatives of the 'educated' classes despite the finesse of their lifestyles and their superior knowledge.[4] Leo Tolstoy's

4 Compare Berdyaev 1947, pp.101–2:

> *Narodnichestvo* is a phenomenon which is peculiar to Russia just as Russian nihilism and Russian anarchism are peculiarly Russian phenomena. It had many different manifestations. ... **But all the while at the root of it was a belief in the people as the guardian of truth and right.** ... In religious *Narodnichestvo* the people is a sort of mystical organism which goes deeper into the soil and deeper into the spirit, than the nation, which is **a rationalized, historical organization** in connection with the body politic. The people are a concrete community of living persons, whereas the nation is a more abstract idea. But even in religious *Narodnichestvo*, among the Slavophils with Dostoevsky and L.Tolstoy, the people meant especially the peasants and the working classes of society. While to the *Narodnichestvo* which was non-religious and revolutionary the people were identified with the social category of the working class, and their interests were identified with the interests of labour. The spirit of the *narodniks* and the spirit of democracy (in the social sense) were mingled together. The Slavophils thought that among the simple people, among the peasantry, the spirit of the Russian *narodniks* and the Orthodox faith were preserved to a greater extent than among the educated and the ruling classes. ... The people is not the only complete constituent part of the historical nation. **For over [and] against the people stands on the one hand the Intelligentsia and the educated classes, and on the other hand the nobility and the ruling classes.** As a rule the *narodnik* who is a member of the Intelligentsia does not feel himself an organic part of the whole mass of the people or that he fulfilled a function in the life of the people. **He was conscious of the fact that his position was not normal, not what it ought to be, and even sinful. Not only truth was hidden in the people but there was also hidden a mystery, which it was necessary to unravel.** *Narodnichestvo* was the offspring not of the organic [of the non-organic' would be a more appropriate translation – V.S. and N.B.] character of Russian history of the Petrine period, but ['but' is unnecessary in view of the above correction – V.S. and N.B.] of the parasitic character of the mass of the Russian nobility.... [Italics in the English translation; emphasis added]

Confessions would provide a glaring example of that attitude,[5] while his Platon Karatayev has developed into a textbook illustration of a common man, a man of the people, from whom that intelligent aristocrat, Pierre Bezukhov, still has something to learn.[6]

The Problem of *Sobornost'*: Popular Wisdom and Democratic Procedures

Applied to politics, however, this appeal to popular wisdom was indicative of, or bound to create, a specific pattern of pre-understanding to be distinguished from the notion of popular sovereignty as it had evolved within the European democratic tradition. The classical teachers of democracy had not based their arguments on the belief in *demos* as the repository of some specific political wisdom. The notion of a sovereign as the ultimate source of legitimacy would constitute a natural point of departure for any theory of delegated authority, while attribution of that status to the people, rather than to some other body social, would be justified by the people's natural right to choose their own destiny. The line of argument used to substantiate this view can be traced to the nominalistic roots of the philosophical tradition to which the majority of the classical democratic thinkers belonged. Most of them, it will be recalled, shared a common, if broadly defined, empirical outlook. Within this tradition any question concerning whether this or that particular choice is 'true' or 'false' is utterly pointless, although it certainly makes sense to distinguish between 'right' and 'wrong'. The traditional Russian political outlook is, by contrast, realist (in the sense implied by scholastic philosophy): it would identify a 'right' decision as the one that is objectively justified ('true' or 'correct') and

---

Compare also Lossky 1991, p.282:

> ... The Russian intelligentsia has always displayed heightened interest in social justice and concern about improvement of the conditions of the peasantry as the most hapless estate. In the nineteenth century a movement arose among the intelligentsia which was called *narodnichestvo*. **With some persons, it consisted in a selfless service to the people, with others, moreover, in an extreme idealization of the people and the ensuing desire to learn from the people, to master the 'truth' it was carrying.** [Emphasis added]

5 Tolstoy 1904a, pp.59–61, 79–80.
6 Compare Tolstoy 1904b **8**, pp.66ff: 'No, you cannot understand what it is I learned from this illiterate, foolish man', Pierre would later say to Natasha (ibid., p.323).

it would expect a political actor to aspire to such a decision. This outlook is based on the ontological assumption that there is some ultimate reality, some objective social order to back up a 'correct'- and therefore 'right' - decision.

Classical democratic theory is pivoted on the idea of the people's will because it finds it appropriate for the right to choose to belong to those who are to be affected by the choice. There can be no other authority above the people to which legitimate appeal against their decisions might be made, which might reveal them as either true or false, and even less replace them with its own judgement. The conceptual model we attempt to analyse here belongs to a political culture moulded in a different fashion, a culture that strives for 'correct' answers. If it turns to the people, rather than to anyone else, it is because it assumes that they possess the appropriate knowledge, not because it believes in their 'rights' or even attributes rights to them.[7]

Regarded in the procedural perspective, the difference becomes crucial. If your primary concern is to know the people's *will*, you will seek to ensure that the will is really theirs, that it has not been distorted, falsified or misinterpreted in any way. You will try to invent and introduce a set of measures that would protect your sovereign people from being bullied or deceived. You will do your best to prevent any abuse of power over their bodies and minds. And you will ask for opinions not because you are looking for the correct one and believe that the more you have to choose from, the better your chances of finding it. You will do that because there is no other way to arrive at a solution that would be acceptable to all, and the reason it has to be acceptable to all - or at least to as many as possible - is that it is to be binding on all.

But if you are concerned with finding the one correct decision, rather than simply a generally acceptable one, just any opinion will not do: it will have to be the opinion of the best available expert. Turning to 'the people' for that expertise is of tremendous consequence, both ideologically and politically.

---

7   Consider, for example, the following passage: 'When a law is proposed in [the people's] assembly, what is asked of them is not precisely whether they accept or reject the proposal, but whether it is in conformity with the general will that is theirs' (Rousseau 1974, p.88).

In the first place, strange as it may sound, 'the people' gain very little from it as far as practical matters are concerned. They may be praised as 'masters of life', but they are not allowed to become 'masters of their fate'. They are not free to choose, for experts are asked for advice, not for their choice. But 'the people' are not even experts in the literal sense of the word. It would be more appropriate to call them 'oracles', for the origin of their superior wisdom remains somewhat mysterious. The practical implications of this apparently 'demophilic' position have little in common with what is generally considered genuine democracy. In such circumstances, not only is every dissident minority to be treated as a gang of heretics deserves, which in itself would be a violation of one of the fundamental principles of democratic community, but the majority itself is not expected to exercise any particular 'rights'. On many occasions this 'people-loving' attitude has failed to ward off repressions against those who would conventionally be regarded as 'the people', to cite but La Vendée of 1793 and Tambov of 1921 as the most impressive examples of such repression in modern European history.

In the second place, it is evident that anyone can make mistakes. Whoever you choose to classify as 'the people' will be no exception. Moreover, if you go and ask people for their opinions, you are sure to find them different. And if you still insist on retaining your belief in the people's wisdom, it will have to take the irrational form of an appeal to the people *en masse*. In that case the people will no longer be 'they' but 'it'. And the decision will have to be *its*, not *theirs*. The resulting outlook is paradoxical. 'The people' taken as a single whole does know 'the truth', while the empirical people, that is the social agglomerate that consists of (and hence is divided into) particular groups and individuals, lack that knowledge.[8] Within this outlook and, it would not be out of place to observe, in full accord with the spirit of scholastic realism, 'the people' as a whole acquires independent

---

8 A striking parallel is presented by Rousseau: 'It follows from what has been said above that the general will is always well-meaning [*droite*, right - V.S. and N.B.] and always tends toward the public good; but it does not follow that all decisions made by the people are equally sound' (Rousseau 1974, p.26). ('Il s'ensuit de ce qui précède que la volonté générale est toujours droite et tend toujours à l'utilité publique: mais il ne s'ensuit pas que les délibérations du peuple aient toujours la même rectitude': *Du contrat social* (Paris: Editions Seghers, 1971), p.82. For further parallels between Rousseauist social ontology and ontological patterns of the Russian traditional culture, see below.

and peculiar ontological status to be distinguished from those of empirical individual human beings, social groups or even those very people regarded as a concrete socio-historic formation, for example, the population of a given country at a given time. The unity of 'the people' pervades space and time and is considered a primary bond, not to be doubted or denied, whatever the (empirical) circumstances.

It would constitute a lengthy and, perhaps, unnecessary digression to consider in detail various attempts at a 'rational' justification of this postulated unity. Suffice it to say that, owing to the impracticability of the task, all such attempts have invariably assumed a pseudo-rational character and tended to produce some kind of militant nationalistic ideology.

In the third place, this type of political culture has no use for democratic procedures, if by that name is meant a set of rules whose primary function is to help find out and implement the will of the people. Interests differ, and it takes much time and great effort to negotiate an acceptable compromise. But it would be a waste of time and effort to enter a debate if the result is already known. And it certainly would be ridiculous, not to say immoral, to compromise over matters of truth and falsehood. This would pose no particular problem as long as one were dealing with objective reality, for objective reality does not need to be recognized, nor does objective truth depend on whether people agree to accept it or not. But when it comes to matters of public concern, it is not easy to justify a decision by reference to people's will if that will remains ambivalent. Hence the need for procedures that ensure the unanimity of decisions, rather than their universal acceptability.[9] In order to qualify for this task, a representative institution must be something different from what stands for it in the Western political culture, that is, the parliament.

The problem is somewhat analogous to the scholastic debates over God's will. Some philosophers have argued that God is not free if His decisions are motivated by His knowledge, if that is independent of His will. Others would object that He is not wise if He goes against His better judgement. The solution would come in the form of some

---

9 'The more agreement there is in the assemblies, that is, the closer opinions come to being unanimous, the more the general will is dominant; but long debates, dissension, and tumult herald the ascendancy of private interests and the decline of the state' (Rousseau 1974, p.87).

mystic harmony between His will and His knowledge. The populist myth calls for a similar harmony, and Russian political philosophy has a name for it: *sobornost'*.[10] If this harmony does not come spontaneously, it has to be created; if it cannot be created, it has to be faked.

Work and Grace: the Anti-Intellectual Bias of the Russian Political Culture

Another important element of the traditional Russian political culture is its peculiar understanding of the nature and value of work and particularly of the relation between physical and intellectual efforts. This part of the social ontology is best explained by reference to the traditional Orthodox attitude towards spiritual activity, especially to its superior forms.

In the conceptual framework of Christianity one of the central positions has invariably belonged to the notion of *grace*. The contribution of the Eastern Orthodox Church to the development of that notion was of particular importance. What interests us here is interpretation of spiritual endowment as a direct gift of grace and the consequences thereof. According to this view, all abilities, talents and skills are distributed by the will of God. Therefore, it would be arrogant for those who possessed such talents to consider whatever results their exercise might produce as being due to their own merit. Such self-appraisal would verge on mortal sin and certainly deserves to be censured. We have no reason to believe, of course, that people who had merits were never proud of them. However, it is not with isolated facts that we are concerned in this study, but with mass beliefs. The medieval Russian attitude towards creative activity seems to have been based on the assumption that all such activity was indeed the activity of the Holy Spirit, and the particular human being involved in the process was to be regarded as Its instrument or Its agent. In that case the artist had certainly no reason to feel proud of himself: such feelings would have been utterly inappropriate. The anonymity of medieval art attests to the authenticity of this description.[11] Icon-

10 The notion of *sobornost'* is discussed below.
11 For Byzantine roots of this attitude, see Averintsev 1977, and Kazhdan 1968; on the medieval artist's attitude to his work, see Lotman 1973.

painters would not sign their works: even if some of them believed in their own authorship, which is doubtful, they would not risk claiming it in public; the reason, apparently, was that such a claim would have been indignantly rejected.

That appraisal led to a surprising conclusion: personal merits were recognized only where a particular activity could not be directly attributed to grace, be it for its insignificance and worthlessness, or because it appeared dubious from some moral or religious standpoint, or for some other reason. In that way a scale of deserts was introduced which would perhaps appear distorted to a modern mind, but which seemed perfectly logical from the standpoint outlined above.[12]

According to that scale, in secular life a high appraisal would be given to precisely those deeds and achievements that would have no value from the superior religious (spiritual) point of view. For the dualistic mentality there was no contradiction in this. We do not wish to assert that secular appraisals did not count: in real life they would probably mean what they do today. Our argument is somewhat different: genuine spiritual merits would be of a kind that called for no secular recompense – indeed, such recompense would degrade them. Hence it was inferred, logically enough ('*render unto Caesar things which are Caesar's*' – Matthew, 22: 21), that worldly goods were to be distributed according to their deserts in those fields that had no spiritual meaning or value. Ordinary manual work was commonplace enough to qualify for such a prize. (Manual work could have spiritual value, too, if it was related to some specific service; but that had to be a specific case, for which no worldly reward was expected: as an example the work of monks can be cited.) As far as spiritual (or intellectual) work was concerned, it was not to be regarded as work at all, if by work one means something that must be paid for – a striking resemblance to a less remote doctrine based on entirely different principles!

The subsequent secularization removed the initial dualism and with it the double scale of appraisals. Rewards would no longer be divided into the worldly and the spiritual – the former alone were to remain. That meant a radical change in the structure and hierarchy of values.

12 On the moral appraisal of physical work in medieval society, see Gurevich 1984, pp.268–81, and 1990, pp.36–42.

Intellectual activity has not ceased, of course, but it assumed the character of something dubious, inferior, almost unnatural.

Western culture has on the whole managed to avoid that trap, because religious emancipation was preceded in Western Europe by scholastic rationalism and the Reformation. The Reformation extended the sphere of grace to include all fields of activity – even (or, should one rather say, above all) the most profane. It started to regard worldly deeds as a means to achieve private confidence in one's salvation (state of grace) – on a level with the spiritual achievements – and in that way sanctified them.[13] That was followed (or facilitated) by the ever growing individualization and personalization of the *Weltanschauung*. By the time religious indifferentism and a secularized mentality were firmly engrained, that mentality had already become quite individualistic, on the one hand, and had managed to fill the initial abyss between the profane and the sacred and grown accustomed to the idea of their fundamental homogeneity, on the other. In the course of that process creative spiritual activity became emancipated from the purely religious interpretation and acquired its own independent value. In Eastern Europe the Reformation's emancipatory and individualizing role remained unplayed, and secularization of the conscience paved the way for the triumph of the most vulgar form of materialism.

It would be interesting to observe that Marxist political economy has inherited that medieval interpretation of work, contradictory though it is to its definition of social labour. The two basic elements of that definition, it will be recalled, are expenditure of physical and mental energy and social recognition of the results in the act of market exchange. There is nothing in that definition that would prevent us from considering as work any kind of activity (organizational, mental and so on) as long as there are prospective buyers for its product. Nevertheless, the followers of Marx persist in using the term in an exclusive sense and apply it to production of only 'material values'. 'Materiality' is also interpreted in a way that would be more appropriate for the 'old' (pre-Marxist) materialism: work is what produces 'things', 'physical objects'. As a philosopher, Marx would probably have shunned this interpretation, but as an economist and a political thinker he failed to do so. His disciples, less versed in

13 See Weber 1958.

philosophy, did not consider the contradiction at all. And when the idea finally reached the 'masses', it was in the vulgar form of a belief that, besides workers and peasants, all are parasites and live by exploitation. Let all these teachers, scholars, writers, artists and so forth live, if that is necessary, but let them know their place. Timid objections to the effect that these people work, too, and earn their own living, would be met with disdainful comments on the negligible results of that 'work'. Failures in industrial ('material') production, however, would be also blamed on the intelligentsia, this time in their capacity as managers, engineers and scientists.

What was an outcry of guilty conscience with Leo Tolstoy became social narcissism when applied by workers and peasants to themselves. The workers' and peasants' narcissism is easy to understand, but what about Leo Tolstoy? Are we to understand that, born into a rich and noble family, Leo Tolstoy was able to live in luxury, though he did not have to earn his living, and therefore had every reason for remorse? Perhaps. But it would be ridiculous to call him idle (incidentally, those who were idle hardly ever felt remorse). Why would he not value the work of a writer? If he did not, who would? And Tolstoy was not alone: his attitude was shared by a large portion of Russian intelligentsia. If that was what intellectuals thought, one need not be surprised by the attitudes of workers and peasants.

It is hardly necessary to demonstrate that this attitude is both erroneous and harmful. Somehow, invective appears singularly out of place in this age of science. It is, moreover, not our task to criticize, even less to refute, mass patterns of pre-understanding, but to identify them, trace them to their roots and find out how they affect political behaviour. Hyperbolization of manual work and invectives against intellectual work have been of tremendous political importance: they have influenced employment policies and expectations of both blue- and white-collar workers, and they have affected the status of political activity itself.

Let us now consider another vestige of medieval dualism that is also relevant to the subject of work. Since in our case religious emancipation meant little more than 'amputation' of the spiritual sphere, it did not (and could not) help change the low status of the secular sphere. On the one hand, the value patterns that had previously been applied to intellectual activity were now valid for manual work, too, although they had been transformed to fit its specific nature. But the principal point remained as before: manual work did not come to be valued for its own sake, nor judged by its own intrinsic criteria. It is not the work as such, the exertion, that is valued, but the socially acceptable and socially approved activity. That is why it may be morally possible to disapprove of a work that is too effective. That is why the nickname of *miroyed* (extortioner or blood-sucker) may sound natural when applied not only to the idle landowner, but to a fellow-peasant if he works harder and lives better than you.[14] The transformation of value beliefs initiated by the secularization of the dualistic mentality has legitimated the negative attitude towards worldly activity, although for different reasons. This has brought about a strange symbiosis: a combination of the vulgar materialistic cult of manual labour with an ascetic attitude to its results. Efforts must be physical; rewards must be moral. Translated into the language of the Third Programme of the Communist Party of the Soviet Union (CPSU), this would sound like 'transformation of work into a major necessity of life'.

While the social roots of economic materialism can be traced to the major role that industrial production and economic activities in general play in the bourgeois society, the paradoxical combination of economic fetishism with the scathing condemnation of business is a peculiar feature of Soviet mentality.

SOBORNOST' AND MARXISM

In the previous section we approached the idea of *sobornost'* from the populist perspective. It is now time to elucidate its relationship to Russian Marxism.

Sobornost' in the Russian Political Tradition

The word *sobornost'* alludes to the *Sobor*, a representative institution of sixteenth- and seventeenth-century Russia.[15] Throughout this work, therefore, it is used to refer to a model representative institution,

14 On this point, see also Chapter 4, Section 2, below.
15 For the latest survey of historic data, see Cherepnin 1978.

analogous to the British parliament and its various counterparts in other Western countries. Whether historic reality will eventually justify this use of the term seems, from our perspective, irrelevant, since it is models – or what Max Weber might have called 'ideal types' – that we deal with when we study political cultures, rather than actual institutions that exist or existed on the political scene. Still, the choice of names should not be entirely arbitrary; ours is not, as the following effort to trace the ideal of *sobornost'* to its medieval roots will show.

To begin with, the *Sobors* of medieval Muscovy were originally ecclesiastical institutions. The word is still used in modern Russian to refer to Ecclesiastical Councils and, more significant still, it translates the Greek *ekklesia*: both words mean 'assembly', and this, incidentally, accounts for the word's other meaning: 'cathedral'. Its connotations are thus peculiarly religious to the Russian ear. But what is relevant to the present argument is the fact that representative political institutions cannot be modelled on ecclesiastical councils without certain consequences, for, underlying whatever polemics and arguments might take place at them, there is the notion of the ultimate truth to be attained. They are not convened to reach a balanced opinion that would be acceptable to everyone (or even the majority), and it makes little sense to negotiate a compromise over an issue before them or put it to a vote of the participants. Neither procedure is appropriate, for what an ecclesiastical council, or for that matter a scientific symposium, is seeking is the objective truth. Neither of these gatherings is expected to take account of the participants' personal interests, or the interests of those they may be considered to 'represent'. Hence, neither will qualify as a 'representative' institution, especially a genuinely democratic assembly, for both are bound to fail in meeting the egalitarian standards of modern democracy.

A Russian medieval *Sobor* never presumed to do so, of course. Nor did any other European representative assembly, whether the parliament of England, the *Etats généraux* of France, or the *Cortes* of Castile. If only as a remnant of an age-old tradition, the House of Lords bears sufficient witness to that lack of genuine democracy, as the latter is understood nowadays, that was characteristic of the time the institution came into existence. Nevertheless, our present argument stands, for it was not only their original form, but also their subsequent evolution, that made the European parliamentary institutions what they are today. The Russian *Sobors* were never given the chance to evolve. One reason was that their history was too short compared with that of their European counterparts: indeed, it is confined to little more than a century.[16] And throughout that century they remained an irregular, *ad hoc* institution. It was only at times of severe crises - little short, perhaps, of national catastrophes - that they were allowed to play a significant political role.

The latter circumstance was of major importance. Convened primarily to solve issues of an extraordinary nature and with little or no experience of 'normal' operation under stable conditions, the Muscovy *Sobors* were not considered assemblies whose members were expected to represent their electorate, their parties, or even their social strata - regardless of the particular procedure used for their nomination. A *Sobor* was meant to represent civil society as a whole. It was a symbolic deputy of the People in its intercourse with the government. Its primary function was to re-establish the union between the two, lost through the hardships of fortune. As such, the *Sobor* would consider it most improper to attempt to play the role of opposition, and particularly to tolerate any factions within its ranks.

The subsequent evolution towards unlimited autocracy left no niche for a representative institution in the political life of the Russian Empire. *Zemskie Sobory* (secular assemblies) fell into total disuse, and it was not until the nineteenth century that the idea of *sobornost'* began to play a significant role in Russian political philosophy. It was put forward by Slavophiles, a peculiar band of philosophers who managed to combine a liberal outlook with a fervent idealization of medieval Muscovy, and later elaborated by the great idealistic thinkers of what came to be known as the Russian Renaissance. It stood for some mystic union of humanity and was opposed to the individualism believed to be a characteristic feature of the Western (unorthodox) culture: *sobornost'*, by contrast, was exemplified by the collectivistic totality of the Russian Orthodox *mir*, or self-governed village community.

16 The first *Sobor* met in February 1549; the last was convened at the end of 1683 and, having held no session, was dissolved next March (Cherepnin 1978, pp.382–4).

The Adaptation of Marxism: Why did it Prove Attractive in Russia?

The philosophers did not 'invent' the idea of *sobornost'*, of course. It would be more appropriate to say that they 'elicited' it from the fundamentally religious culture of the masses. It was this culture that the triumphant victors of October would have to deal with and, in the long run, to rely on. One may wonder, however, how that culture could 'stomach' - moreover, so soon and so easily - what appeared to be the entirely alien ideology of Marxism. The adaptation was doubtless facilitated by a number of similarities and a partial identity of political rhetoric, but it also owed much to some ideological intermediates and to the ideological genealogy of Marxism in general.

The Russian Marxists' attitude to the religious thinkers responsible for the notion of *sobornost'* was invariably hostile, of course. The latter were regarded as ideological and class enemies - a grave accusation for a follower of Marx and Lenin. But although no manifest reference to the pre-revolutionary idealistic philosophy would be tolerated by the thoroughly materialistic Bolsheviks, and although the word *sobornost'* had never come to be uttered by any one of them, the idea of *communion* - another possible translation of the word - proved singularly consonant with their own political rhetoric. It became more or less their motto, and it gave the name to both their movement and their party.

It would not be out of place to observe that, although the Marxist tradition in social thought is justly associated with the ideas of social stratification and class struggle, stratification itself was invariably regarded by Marx and his followers as a social evil to be eliminated, while the much celebrated struggle between the bourgeoisie and the proletariat was expected to pave the way to a homogeneous (classless) society.[17] It is not difficult to discern in this goal the ideal of *sobornost'* that has formed the basis of a peculiar national political Utopia.

Taking this into account, it should not be surprising to find many traditional features in the political system that the self-professed grave-diggers of the old Russian society created on its charred ruins. The political triumph of Bolsheviks would, indeed, hardly have been

17 See Marx 1983, pp.62-5.

possible had not their leaders' slogans touched familiar chords in the souls of their potential followers. For, strictly speaking, the emergence of Marxism as Russia's dominant ideology was surprising enough – if, that is, Marx's theory and political ideas were to be taken seriously. The social and political situation in Russia at the time when Marxism began to spread there differed significantly from the situation in Western Europe before, during and after the revolutions of 1848, the time when Marxism had been conceived and born. From this point of view, the Russian 'social being' had little to contribute to the evolution of 'social consciousness' towards Marxism. (By this we do not mean, of course, the ideology of small, clandestine or semi-clandestine groups, which can be borrowed from anywhere, but the consciousness of broad masses of the people.) The Marxist conquest of Russia is least of all explained by the fact that Marxism had something important to say concerning Russia's troubles.[18] To account for its success we must turn to other factors: to structural parallels between Marxist ideology (or certain aspects of it, to be more precise) and the political mentality of the Russian intelligentsia. It is hardly necessary to add that Marxism emerged from this adaptation process as something unrecognizable in the place of its birth and had to be 're-exported' there in a new form. What were those structural parallels? What aspects of Marxism made it so attractive initially to the Russian revolutionary intelligentsia and then to the broad masses of the Russian people?

First among them was certainly the rhetoric of popular rule, so dear to the future Russian Marxists. That rhetoric admittedly played no important role in Marx's theoretical legacy. Marx seems to have taken certain pride in the fact that his ideas were not the outcome of some particular sympathy for the proletariat, but resulted, rather, from his purely dispassionate analysis of social facts. He would speak with irony, if not contempt, about those who derived their political ideas

18 As Berdyaev would put it (1972, p.106)

> [Lenin] brought about the revolution in Marx's name, but not in Marx's way. The Communist revolution was brought about in Russia in the name of totalitarian Marxism – Marxism as the religion of the proletariat, but it was a contradiction of everything that Marx had said about the development of human society. It was not revolutionary *narodnichestvo*, but orthodox totalitarian Marxism which succeeded in achieving the revolution, in which Russia skipped that stage of capitalist development which to the first Russian Marxists had appeared so unavoidable.

from their compassion for the 'working man's burden'. But that was for the most part a mere pose: the political attitudes and political rhetoric of Marx himself were sufficiently emotional, too. But this was precisely what made the theoretical part of Marxism, disguised as politically and emotionally 'neutral', 'objective science', a minor point in its popularization and propaganda. In the meantime, Marx's political bias and his fervent support for whatever he believed to be a revolutionary movement (from the Sepoy Revolt in India to the Civil War in the United States with its abolition of slavery, to say nothing of the Garibaldians or the Polish and Irish freedom fighters – no matter how these might fit into his sociological schemes or how remote their ideologies might be from his own doctrine) were very much to the liking of the Russian revolutionary intelligentsia.

It is important, therefore, to distinguish in the nineteenth-century Marxism between two distinctly different elements: its sociological doctrine, which may be considered Marxism in the proper, narrow sense, and the 'Jacobin spirit', which it shared with a variety of political and ideological movements of the time. This common element made Marxism appear relevant and attractive even to those revolutionary movements that were alien to it in their genesis, social base or ideology. It made it easy, for instance, for the Russian revolutionary culture to assimilate Marxist ideas, in spite of the fact that Marx had little or nothing to say on the substance of problems that faced Russian society.

This is not to say that Marxism proper (in the sense outlined above) had no influence on the subsequent development of political thinking and political culture in Russia or the Soviet Union. It certainly had, and we shall have further opportunity to consider it. But the way for that influence to be manifest was cleared by the fact that Marxism incorporated pre-understanding patterns that were, if not truly identical, then, at least, consonant with those of Russian political thinkers. And it is worth noting that this assimilation of Marxism into Russian revolutionary ideology was further facilitated by their common roots.

The Influence of Western Philosophy and the Triumph of Marxism

Both Russian philosophy (above all, *social* philosophy) and Marxism descended from classical German philosophy, although in both cases the major role belonged to different leading figures. That Marx owed much to Hegel and Feuerbach is an established fact, acknowledged by himself and confirmed by Engels, and needing no further proof. Schelling's influence on the early Russian thinkers is also taken for granted.[19] For all that separated them later, both Schelling (a recognized authority for *Lyubomudrys*[20] and Slavophiles) and Hegel had a common background, and their respective systems' starting-points were definitely related. In both cases the dominant theme was the totality of existence, dialectically interpreted. The theme was entirely absent from the ontology and epistemology of Kant, emerging only in his aesthetics. It is noteworthy that Kant's influence had never been particularly strong in Russia and was, moreover, characteristically limited to his aesthetics, interpreted in the spirit of romanticism. Marxism and Slavophilism were thus related on the system-building level.

On the other hand, the direct influence of Hegel (on Bakunin and Belinsky, for example) and Feuerbach (on Chernyshevsky) made Russian social thinkers, if not ready to immediately adopt, then, at least, sensitive to Marxism on the theoretical level.

Another channel of influence was related to the 'Jacobin spirit' of Marxism. It is hardly necessary to enlarge on how much the Jacobin political ideology owed to Rousseau and particularly to his theory of the social contract. Related to the English political thought of the seventeenth century, notably that of Hobbes and Locke, Rousseau's doctrine contained a point that would have been totally alien to the British thinkers. Indifferent to epistemological problems so dear to the British empiricists, and certainly not sharing their nominalistic bias, Rousseau introduced a significant amendment into the theory of the social contract elaborated by Hobbes a century earlier. This was his

19 For a general survey of the early Russian philosophic thought, see Zenkovsky 1953 1; for Schelling's influence, see Kamensky 1980b.
20 A loan word for 'philosophers' (literally, wisdom-lovers). The name was assumed by a small group of young thinkers active in Moscow in the 1820s: see Kamensky 1980a.

notion of *general will* (*la volonté générale*). For Hobbes, the people's will, alienated for the benefit of the future sovereign, is common only inasmuch as the interests of the individuals involved are the same. The sphere of this agreement is limited to their common concern for their individual safety. It is this concern, indeed, that makes them bend their sovereign will to an outside authority.[21] In other respects Hobbes seems to have found the unity of that will at least problematic. This would incidentally account for his recurrent emphasis on the subjects' implicit obedience to legitimate authority: Hobbes apparently did not expect them to welcome every single decision that issued from that authority. He would not, therefore, presume to deduce that decision from the will of the people and would assert only that, since the people have agreed to put that authority above them, they have undertaken to obey it and must keep their promise.[22]

This call for 'consistency' and 'conscientiousness' sounds somewhat sophistic, to tell the truth. Certainly, Rousseau would never consent to it. Not only could Hobbes's argument serve (as it did in his case) as an ideological excuse for absolute monarchy; it stood in irreconcilable contradiction with Rousseau's social ontology. His naturalism would account for his realism. For Rousseau the general will could not be indeterminate: it had to be determined by the nature of the society. Hobbes would have maintained that the only natural beings were individual beings, while society was a monster, a leviathan, that could at best be regarded as an artificial organism, a quasi-organism. For the sake of self-preservation, this quasi-organism had to follow the law of organisms, but he could not secure this lawfulness by natural means. For Rousseau, on the contrary, society was a genuine organism, from which he would infer, quite logically, that this organism must have its own natural interests and that these interests refer to it as a single whole.[23] The general will is the

21 See Hobbes 1980, pp.223-8.
22 Ibid., pp.231-2.
23 Rousseau 1974, pp.17-18:

> Each of us puts his person and all his power in common under the supreme control of the general will, and we collectively receive each member as an indivisible part of the whole.
>
> In place of the individual persons of the contradicting parties, the act of association immediately creates a collective, artificial body [literally, a moral and collective body:

expression of these interests. The metaphor of the organism would allow him to liken individual citizens (or groups thereof) to members and organs of this social body.[24] These 'members' and 'organs' (or individuals and groups) may have their own specific 'interests', of course, but these 'interests', natural though they are, are secondary and subordinate to the general interest.[25] Granted this interpretation of the general will as *the will of the whole*, its priority over individual wills would remain valid even if it were opposed to the sum total of

---

un corps moral et collectif - V.S. & N.B.], composed of as many members as the assembly has voters, and the same act gives this body *its unity, its collective self, its life and its will.* [Italics added]

24 Rousseau was not the first to discover this metaphor of the organism, of course: it was already popular with the classical authors of antiquity. A striking example is Menenius Agrippa's address to the rebellious plebeians to be found in Livy's *History of Rome* (II:32:8-12, quoted from Livy 1965, pp.125-6):

The senatorial party accordingly decided to employ Menenius Agrippa as their spokesman to the commoners on the Sacred Mount - he was a good speaker, and the commoners liked him as he was one of themselves. Admitted to the deserters' camp, he is said to have told them, in the rugged style of those far-off days, the following story. 'Long ago, when the members of the human body did not, as now they do, agree together, but had each its own thoughts and the words to express them in, the other parts resented the fact that they should have the worry and trouble of providing everything for the belly, which remained idle, surrounded by its ministers, with nothing to do but enjoy the pleasant things they gave it. So the discontented members plotted together that the hand should carry no food to the mouth, that the mouth should take nothing that was offered it, and that the teeth should accept nothing to chew. But alas! while they sought in their resentment to subdue the belly by starvation, they themselves and the whole body wasted away to nothing. By this it was apparent that the belly, too, has no mean service to perform: it receives food, indeed; but it also nourishes in its turn the other members, giving back to all parts of the body, through all its veins, the blood it has made by the process of digestion; and upon this blood our life and our health depend'. This fable of the revolt of the body's members Menenius applied to the political situation, pointing out its resemblance to the anger of the populace against the governing class; and so successful was his story that their resentment was mollified.

The metaphor's anti-democratic (totalitarian) potential is obvious.

25 Compare Rousseau 1974, p.19:

The sovereign, being formed only by the individuals who compose it, neither has nor can have any interest contrary to theirs; consequently there is no need for the sovereign power to give guarantees to the subjects, because it is impossible for the body to want to harm all its members, and as we shall see later, it cannot harm any one of them in particular. Merely by virtue of existing, the sovereign is always what it should be.

This, however, is not true of the subjects in relation to the sovereign, which, despite the common interest, could not count on them to fulfil their obligations unless it devised means of making sure of their fidelity.

them. Hence the general interest would be set off not only against particular interests *per se*, but against all of them taken together.[26] Hence also the 'community' spirit, the emphasis on the common rather than the particular, that would become so characteristic of the rhetoric of Rousseau's future disciples and would prove so devastating when they came to power.[27]

Marx's vision of society was different. The metaphor of the organism seems to have been alien to his social ontology, and his interpretation of the 'common interest' is well known: since (and so long as) society is split into different classes, some particular interests assume the form of an *illusory* common interest.[28] This sober (for some, cynical) outlook was consistently applied in his social analysis. Marx insisted that all social problems are class problems and their solutions are pivoted on class interests, but he would not presume to present the latter as general interests. Still, our exposition of Marxism would be one-sided if we failed to go beyond this assertion. For it would be hard to contend that Marx shared with Rousseau and his followers their negative attitude towards particular interests. Marx would not condemn a particular interest just for being particular: proletarian interests, after all, are also particular interests. But the fact is compensated for in his eyes by the greatness of the proletariat's historic mission. Marx emphasized on numerous occasions that while

26 Compare Rousseau 1974, p.27:

> There is often a great difference between the will of all and the general will. The latter looks only to the common interest, while the former looks to private interest and is only a sum total of individual wills. But take away from those same wills the pluses and minuses that cancel each other out, and the general will remains as the sum of the differences. ('Il y a souvent bien de la différence entre la volonté de tous et la volonté générale; celle-ci ne regarde qu'à l'intérêt commun; l'autre regarde à l'intérêt privé, et n'est qu'une somme de volontés particulières: mais ôtez de ces mêmes volontés les plus et les moins qui s'entre-détruisent, teste pour somme des différences la volonté générale': Rousseau, *Du contrat social*, op.cit., p.129.)

27 The following is an illustrative example (Rousseau 1974, pp.19-20):

> In order, therefore, that the social pact shall not be an empty formality, it tacitly includes one stipulation without which all the others would be ineffectual: that anyone who refuses to obey the general will shall be compelled to do so by the whole body. This means nothing else than that *he shall be forced to be free*, for such is the condition which gives each citizen to his country and thus secures him against all personal dependence. This condition is essential to the functioning of the social machine, and *it also legitimizes civil obligations, which would otherwise be absurd, tyrannical, and subject to the most outrageous abuses.* [Italics added]

28 See Marx and Engels 1976, pp.46-7.

they perform their mission, the proletarian masses, who, it will be recalled, 'have nothing to lose', rise above their particular interests and commit themselves to a goal that is of tremendous importance to all mankind. But this would mean that in the long run the particular class interest of proletariat is, indeed, as general as the will of Rousseau's social organism. Incidentally, the class interest of the bourgeoisie was interpreted by Marx in a similar way: in certain stages of historic development it was an expression of mankind's general interest.

Although their arguments were different, as were their social ontologies, Rousseau and Marx would sometimes move in similar directions. Marx's vision of society was not as a natural organism, but he would certainly view it as a specific whole, subject to laws that are responsible for successively pushing its various classes into the foreground of history. This would in a singular way parallel Hegel's philosophy of history with its notion of *historic nations*.[29] Marx did not speak of historic nations, but he did certainly speak of historic – in his language, 'historically progressive' – classes.

This appraisal of a social class's (or a nation's) historic role would seem arbitrary to those who fail to subscribe to Marx's (or Hegel's) philosophy of history. A nominalistically oriented critic might ascribe it to a personal preference. But Marx was no nominalist. Aimed at 'tearing off all and any masks', he sought to expose (to use a latter-day expression of Lenin) any starry-eyed statement as a manifestation of some egoistic class interest. But his philosophy of history made him attribute universal significance to class interests. For all his criticism of 'idealistic interpretations of history', 'the meaning of history' was not a meaningless problem for Marx. He did see some objective meaning and some objective purpose in it. Whoever doubts this conclusion should read his bitter attacks on human essence lost in the alienated bourgeois society.[30]

This attitude sometimes made Marx draw paradoxical inferences. Reading his *Eighteenth Brumaire of Louis Bonaparte*, one might discover that Marx was a better expert on the bourgeoisie's class

29 '... World history represents the Idea of the spirit as it displays itself in reality as a series of external forms. The stage of self-consciousness which the spirit has reached manifests itself in world history as the existing national spirit, as a nation which exists in the present' (Hegel 1975 p.152).
30 Marx 1976, pp.275-7, 294-6.

interests than the bourgeoisie itself, whose members could lack foresight or class solidarity.[31] Marx generalized this standpoint in his
notions of classes 'in themselves' and 'for themselves'. According to
him, it is not for social classes to decide on their interests and their
historic missions; these are determined by the objective course of
history.[32] That is why class attitudes and class policies are to be based
not on the personal preferences of the individuals that comprise a
particular class (they would then remain a socially impotent class 'in
itself'), but on a scientific analysis of historic development. Since it
was logically impossible to address this demand to the illiterate
masses (nor to those who were literate but unversed in the Marxist
philosophy of history), Lenin found it necessary to develop a whole
theory of 'revolutionary vanguard' that would enlighten proletarians
about their true interests and lead them to fight for them.[33] The
Rousseauesque counterposing of the *general* will and what might be
called the *common* will – that is, the sum total of empirical individual
wills – thus finds a parallel in the Marxist tradition.

For all the differences in their *Weltanschauungen*, therefore,
Rousseau, Marx and Russian ideologues of *sobornost'* agreed on one
significant point, at least: the wills of social agents were believed to
be objectively determined – 'prescribed' – and those wills would
often fail to coincide with the actual aspirations of individuals who
comprised those collective agents. It is not surprising, therefore, that,

31 See Marx 1979, p.171.
32 'Men make their own history, but they do not make it just as they please...' (Marx
1979, p.103).
33 See Lenin 1961 (*What Is To Be Done?*). The question is discussed at somewhat greater
length in Chapter 3, below. The discrepancy of this attitude was stressed by Bulgakov
(1991, p.75):

> In its attitude towards the people, the service to which the intelligentsia sets as its
> task, it invariably and inevitably hesitates between two extremes: people-worship and
> spiritual aristocratism. The need for people-worship in this or that form (whether in
> the form of the old *narodnichestvo* that goes back as far as Herzen and is based on
> the belief in the socialist spirit of the Russian people, or in its latest, Marxist form,
> which attributes the same qualities to a part of the people, namely, to the proletariat,
> rather than to the whole of it) arises from the very foundations of the intelligentsia's
> creed. But from it also and necessarily arises the opposite: the supercilious attitude
> towards the people as an object of salutary influence, as to a minor that needs a nurse
> to be brought up to 'consciousness', unenlightened in the intelligentsia's peculiar
> sense of the word.

The subject is discussed at greater length in the next chapter.

different though these thinkers' social ontologies were, they tended to work in a similar manner, when it came to political behaviour. And this, in turn, would account for the paradoxical syncretism created by superimposing the revolutionary outlook of Marxism upon the religious culture of traditional Russia.

3 The Brilliance and Poverty
of Soviet Power

BOLSHEVISM AND TRADITION

Criticism of Representative Democracy in Russian Political Thought

A contemporary Russian's peculiar attitude towards representative democracy may be viewed as the key to understanding the relation between traditional political culture and political ideas of Russian Marxism. The question is, however, which Russian is to be taken as a model? We would strongly advise against choosing a humanist, versed in both national and world history (West European for the most part, of course) and reading in foreign languages, since his consciousness has been formed under a variety of influences, of which Western political culture was by no means the least important. The Soviet *homo politicus*'s group portrait must naturally include an individual like him, but he would not be representative of the majority.

The majority is suspicious of democracy, to put it mildly, and this suspicion can be traced to the invectives hurled at it by Russian Bolsheviks early in this century. Their arguments can be drawn from Lenin's numerous writings. To Lenin, parliament was but a screen that served to cover the political supremacy of the bourgeoisie that was based on its economic power. A class that is dominant in the economic sphere, he maintained, would have no problems in getting its deputies through any election, since it possesses all the necessary resources, above all financial, that proletarians are denied. As a last resort, the bourgeoisie would bribe the deputy after the election. Hence, all this may look democratic, but it is indeed a mockery of popular rule.

This argument certainly sounds logical, although much of its persuasiveness is lost through refusing to consider counter-arguments.[1] We shall not present the counter-arguments here, since our goal is not to refute this criticism of parliamentary democracy, but to understand it. Rather than discussing the arguments themselves, therefore, we shall consider the pre-understanding patterns that lie behind the arguments in order to appreciate why something that fails to convince us today appeared so cogent to both the Bolsheviks and those to whom they addressed them.

But before this, we must ward off a possible objection based on doubt as to the sincerity of the above argument, often dismissed as purely demagogic. The objection is characteristic of certain rationally-minded intellectuals inclined to attribute their own mentality to members of all other social groups. For people of this mould logical flaws are unmistakable signs of either stupidity or insincerity. But for the personal abuse involved, this judgement could be accepted if applied to individuals. But what may be demagogy in an individual (particularly an intellectual) is a social fact as far as mass consciousness is concerned.

The Bolsheviks' anti-democratic rhetoric was a regular feature of their policy, which means that it was effective. Had the Bolsheviks been mere demagogues who did not care whether their propaganda clichés were true or not, they would have renounced or forgotten them as soon as they saw that the clichés had lost their appeal. They did not renounce them, so either they believed in what they were telling the people or the people believed in it. Otherwise, their persistence would be incomprehensible. But if the Bolsheviks' rhetoric proved convincing to their audience, or even a part of it, is it inconceivable that it could have been equally convincing to them-

1 See Russell 1920.

selves? In politics words must be taken seriously in any case: if they fail to express the political reality in a way that would meet the criteria of science, they may nevertheless be instrumental in creating or altering that reality.

Why was the Idea of Representative Democracy Rejected?

Why did (and, indeed, does) Lenin's argument against parliamentary democracy prove so persuasive? Our answer is that it fitted into the traditional Russian mentality and conformed to the pre-understanding patterns that it comprised. The Bolsheviks were not the first to criticize democracy, of course. This criticism is as old as democratic institutions and democratic procedures themselves. The great philosophers of Athens were known to indulge in it.[2] It has often been heard in modern times. And although this criticism sounded more natural when offered by those who opposed the kind of reorganization the Bolsheviks, among others, stood for, it was by no means entirely alien to Russian revolutionaries, including those who have come to be referred to as 'revolutionary democrats'. Even Herzen, for all his liberalism, levelled criticism at the parliamentary system from time to time.[3] As for the 'Jacobin' branch of the populists, their attitude

2 Criticism of democratic institutions by ancient thinkers - Socrates, Plato, Aristotle and others - is well known, although, in our opinion, sometimes misunderstood these days. This is mainly because concepts of the ancient political culture are easily identified with our own if they bear the same names. Analysis of their arguments against democracy would show, however, that the object of their criticism was not so much (or, perhaps, not at all) the political system we now call 'representative democracy' as *direct popular rule*. It would not be easy to interpret Socrates's doubts concerning the wisdom of popular assemblies or the advisability of election of officials by lot, or Plato and Aristotle's indications concerning the danger of democracy's degenerating into tyranny should the will of the crowd be placed above the law, and so on, in any other way (see Plato, *The Republic*, 563e-565d in Plato 1966 pp.155-7; Aristotle, *Politics*, 1279á, 1292á in Aristotle 1952, pp.476, 491). Polybius's attitude was essentially the same (*History*, VI, 57, in Polybius 1984, p.350), as was Cicero's (*De rep.*, I, 43-5): both counterposed 'mixed' forms of government to the 'pure' and unstable, on the grounds that they were considerably more stable. Translated into modern political jargon, 'mixed government' would be equivalent to 'separation of powers', as V.S. Nersesyants has correctly pointed out (Nersesyants (ed.) 1985, p.270).

3 Compare Herzen 1924-28 3, pp.143-4:

All parties and shades of opinion in the petty-bourgeois world have gradually divided into two camps: on one hand the bourgeois property-owners, obstinately refusing to abandon their monopolies; on the other the petty-bourgeois who have nothing, who

towards representative democracy was frankly disdainful. To anarchists, parliament was an agency of state violence like any other government institution, although perhaps more disguised and hence, from the point of view of the real masters of life, more convenient, but then also more hypocritical.[4] As for that apologist for revolutionary

---

want to tear the wealth out of the others' hands but have not the power - that is, on the one hand *avarice*, on the other hand *envy*. Since there is no real moral principle in all that, the part taken by any individual on one or the other side is determined by external conditions of fortune and social position. One wave of the opposition after the other triumphs - that is, attains property or position - and passes naturally from the side of envy to the side of avarice. **Nothing can be more favourable for this transition than the fruitless swing backwards and forwards of parliamentary parties** [literally: parliamentary *debate* - V.S. and N.B.] - it gives movement and sets limits to it, provides an appearance of *doing something*, and an external show of public interest in order to attain their private ends. [Original italics; emphasis added]

Herzen then commented with irony on holding a plebiscite to determine the form of government (ibid., p.145):

Full of confidence in their victory, [the French petty-bourgeois] proclaimed *universal suffrage* as the basis of their new regime. This arithmetical standard suited their taste; the truth is determined by addition and subtraction, it could be reckoned up and put down in figures [literally: it could be calculated on abacuses and marked by pins].
    And what did they put to the decision of *the votes of all* in the present state of society? The question of the existence of the republic. They wanted to crush it by means of the people, to make of it an empty word, because they did not like it. Is anyone who respects the truth going to ask the opinion of the first stray man he meets? What if Columbus or Copernicus put America or the movement of the earth to the vote? [Original italics]

Liberal-minded Herzen did not seem to believe in direct democracy, either: his last argument sounded quite Platonic. Still, on another occasion he wrote with enthusiasm about self-governing village communities and *artels* (see Herzen 1956, pp.183-4).
4 Compare Bakunin 1972, p.329:

This fiction of a pseudo-representative government serves to conceal the domination of the masses by a handful of privileged elite; an elite elected by hordes of people who are rounded up and do not know for whom or for what they vote. Upon this artificial and abstract expression of what they falsely imagine to be the will of the people and of which the real living people have not the least idea, [the Marxists] construct both the theory of statism as well as the theory of so-called revolutionary dictatorship.

And further on (ibid., p.330):

By the people's rule, they mean the rule of a small number of representatives elected by the people. The general, and every man's right to elect the representatives of the people and the rulers of the State is the latest word of the Marxists, as well as of the democrats. That is a lie, behind which lurks the despotism of the ruling minority, a lie all the more dangerous in that it appears to express the so-called will of the people.

(For the complete text of *Statism and Anarchy*, see Bakunin 1989 pp.291-526). As Walicki has correctly pointed out, conservatives and socialists 'would compete with each other in discrediting liberalism, in reducing its ideals to mercenary deception or self-deception' (Walicki 1991, p.28).

violence and the anarchists' most bitter opponent, Pyotr Tkachev, he restricted the function of the representative assembly to legitimizing the power of the revolutionary conspirators.[5]

This restrained enthusiasm or hostility towards parliamentary democracy was motivated mainly by the Russian revolutionaries' firm conviction that parliament was a purely bourgeois institution. The Russian democrats did not like capitalism; therefore they shunned parliamentary democracy which they believed to mean nothing but the political dominance of the hated bourgeoisie.[6] If they criticized parliamentarianism it was not to defend autocracy and perpetuate the existing political system. The latter had to be changed, of course; but it was not a parliamentary republic of the kind known to Western Europe that was to replace the autocratic monarchy, but a totally different type of political system that would befit a true revolutionary concerned for the suffering masses and would better conform to his notion of genuine popular rule. This was *direct democracy*, an idea that was popular with many revolutionaries in the West, too, although all attempts to implement it there had invariably failed. The Russian revolutionaries, however, were not discouraged. They seemed to believe that the unique constellation of circumstances in Russia was more promising: the Russian bourgeoisie was weak, both economically and politically, and Russian peasants were still organized into communes. However convincing these arguments may have appeared to Russian socialists, the notion of direct democracy was rooted in the

5 On Tkachev, see Weeks 1968 and Hardy 1977. Tkachev never attacked democracy in a direct way, but the role he assigned to representative institutions in political life is clear from the following (Tkachev 1976b, p.96):

> ... Notable for its inexorability in the struggle against the conservative and reactionary elements of society, [the revolutionary state's] constitutional activity, on the contrary, must be noted for elasticity, for a capacity to adjust itself to the existing level of popular needs and popular development. In order not to depart from this level, not to lapse into utopias, in order to give life force to its reforms, it must surround itself with bodies of popular representation, a *Popular Duma*, and **to sanction its reformist activity by their will**. [Original italics; emphasis added]

In itself this statement could be interpreted in a number of ways, perhaps, but confronted with what Tkachev had to say on the necessity of dictatorship of the 'revolutionary minority' (see Tkachev 1976a, especially pp.215-16), its meaning is manifest.

6 'The socialist *narodniks* were afraid of political liberalism on the ground that it brings in its train the triumph of the bourgeoisie' (Berdyaev 1947, p.100). 'It was this premature passion for socialism that afterwards proved one of the main obstacles to stand in the way of legal culture in Russia' (Walicki 1991, p.28).

type of political mentality that was, by no means, their exclusive possession.

The Russification of Marxism

It has been observed on many occasions that pre-revolutionary Russian and post-revolutionary Soviet political cultures are typologically related. We shall not dwell on the thesis here: it is well known and does not seem to call for further substantiation or illustration.[7] Our task is to look into 'heredity mechanisms' that might account for this continuity. In summary, ideological stereotypes or theoretical concepts were not borrowed and adopted: the process unfolded on a deeper level that involved patterns of pre-understanding and models of social reality, which both theoretical considerations and experience show to be more stable than ideological beliefs. Models of social reality, it will be recalled, consist for the most part of non-verbalized or scarcely verbalized 'primary axioms'. These are seldom, if ever, rationalized or even stated explicitly – still less consciously chosen – but they nevertheless constitute the conceptual framework that serves as a net of adaptation and transformation filters. All mental or physical acts must fit into it, or else they are rejected. Any attempt to inculcate a thesis that contradicts a pre-understanding pattern is likely to fail: on a conscious level the contradiction is easy to detect, but the simplest way to settle it is to discard the contradicting thesis. The alternative would be to reject or restructure the pre-understanding pattern itself, but this would involve its implicit definition and rational reassessment, which is doubtless a more complex and more complicated task. In this mental controversy the new idea appears a far more likely victim. By contrast, the idea that fits into the ontological framework is easily incorporated. If this is true of individuals, it is still more true of mass consciousness.

7 To quote from just one of the writers (Berdyaev 1972, p.107):

> Lenin turned anew to the old tradition of Russian revolutionary thought. He pronounced that the industrial backwardness of Russia, the rudimentary character of its capitalism, is a great asset for the social revolution.
>
>   There will be no need to deal with a strong, organized bourgeoisie. There Lenin was obliged to repeat what Tkachev had said, and by no means what Engels had said. *Bolshevism is much more traditional than is commonly supposed. It agreed with the distinctive character of the Russian historical process. There had taken place a Russification and orientalizing of Marxism.* [Italics added]

The purpose of this analysis is to find out how Marxism came to be incorporated into Russian political culture and what form it chose or was obliged to assume in the course of this adaptation, or, to put it differently, which aspects of the doctrine were to come to the fore for the particular result to be achieved. It is hardly necessary to demonstrate that Russian Marxism (that is, Leninism) was different from classical Marxism as this had appeared and developed in Western Europe. The difference was responsible for the eventual rupture between Russian Bolsheviks and their West European teachers: mutual recriminations and accusations of having distorted the theoretical foundations of Marx's doctrine would bear sufficient evidence to that. The fusion of Marxism with the traditional Russian political consciousness would hardly have been possible on the basis of 'pure' Marxism. But this is not to say that, from the theoretical point of view, Russian Marxism was nothing more than the traditional ideology of Russian tsarism translated into the language of 'the materialist interpretation of history'; that would be a gross oversimplification. The revolution of 1917 brought about a thorough transformation of the Russian political culture, but what emerged as the result of that transformation was linked by numerous bonds to what had existed before the revolution. On the one hand, only to the extent that this continuity was not impossible was revolution under the Marxist banner able to succeed. On the other hand, that would account for the fact that substantial elements of the old culture were allowed to survive under the new circumstances. But those elements were utilized to construct a new system, and the Soviet political mentality was by no means a mere copy of the political culture of pre-revolutionary Russia.

Let us now turn to those elements of present-day Russian political culture that it owes to the influence of Marxism.

Three features draw our attention here, one of which appears, at the present time, at least, to be of a purely ideological nature while the other two are rooted deep in social ontology. The first is the notion of 'vanguard', a socio-political role the Bolshevik (later Communist) Party claimed for itself since early in this century.[8] Although there are

---

8 The vanguard as *conditio sine qua non* for the victory of the proletarian revolution, as well as the claim of what was to become the Bolshevik Party to that role were the main subjects of Lenin's *What Is To Be Done? Burning Questions of Our Movement*, written

good reasons to believe that identifying the 'vanguard' with the party
is anachronistic nowadays and further persistence in that direction
would indeed appear ridiculous, and although there do not seem to be
any new claimants to the role, we would not claim that the 'vanguard'
ideology is obsolete in itself. Lenin's technocratic doctrine of a 'progressive intelligentsia' that, having mastered the science of social
development, is thereby entitled to govern the society (even if society
would not consent to this) has been thoroughly discredited by both
the poor results and the disreputable practices of that government, far
removed from what would be conventionally regarded as 'scientific'.
Today's aspirants to leadership roles are unlikely to back their claims
by doctrines of that kind. We may therefore assume that in its present
form this element has been forced out of the set of ontological beliefs.
Still, this does not mean it cannot revive in a different form. Any
definitive judgement would appear premature, and the realist bias of
our political culture may still give rise to some new kind of
technocratic Utopia.

Economic Determinism in the Russian Political Culture

Another element of the present-day Russian political mentality, which
seems to have struck deeper roots, is related to the place and role of
economics. The belief in the latter's priority over all other spheres of
social life appears almost universal. If there are any segments in
Russian society that do not share it, they are not very large. Radical
democrats and both orthodox and reform-minded communists,
lobbyists for the military-industrial complex and champions of the
market economy, fighters for whatever locality's sovereignty and
defenders of the Empire display a touching agreement on the issue. It
is true that an idea has been circulating among the ranks of the
democratic opposition that there can be no economic reform without
major political changes, and hence political matters must be attended
to first. But, even then, political strife would be regarded by
democrats as basically a means to secure sound economic decisions –
or that, at least, has been the logical structure of their argument.

---

in 1901–02 (see Lenin 1961). On the cultural effect of Lenin's argument, see Tucker
1987, pp.33–50; on institutional consequences, see Section 2 of the present chapter.

There can be little doubt, of course, that to democratically-minded persons political democracy is an end in itself. It would be odd, indeed, if members of liberal professions regarded freedom of speech or freedom of the press as simply a means to improve their material well-being. In most cases the personal motivation of democratic leaders and their followers is undoubtedly a reverse one: private property and a market economy are advocated as economic safeguards against totalitarianism. Still, it is noteworthy that the safeguards are seen as primarily economic in nature: separation of powers and other elements of state organization are evidently considered secondary or, at least, not particularly reliable.

It would be hard indeed to overlook the influence of Marxist social philosophy here. The materialist interpretation of history, taught for decades in every educational institution of the country, has apparently gained a firm foothold in the mass consciousness. In this respect a question may be asked which is similar to the one discussed above in connection with the Bolsheviks' political triumph in 1917: why? Much has been taught at schools and universities, besides historical materialism and Marxist political economy, with equal persistence but less effect – the CPSU's leading role, to cite but one example. There was a period in Soviet history, and not a short one at that, when mass consciousness would accept that role with due respect, but that has long gone. Slogans such as 'the Party is the wisdom, honour and conscience of our time' are sneered at, while Marxist economic determinism is very much alive.

A number of explanations can be offered. They would lie on different planes, and hence need not exclude each other. However, this does not mean they are of equal strength. In the first place, it may be assumed that, as a theoretical hypothesis, economic determinism (we say 'economic determinism', since this component of political thinking apparently transcends the boundaries of historic materialism, although it is based on it) was fortunate in having a greater number of faithful supporters among teachers than did other ideologies, and hence the teaching proved more effective. But this would hardly be sufficient to account for the phenomenon. Economic determinism is, after all, not wholly indisputable, and high-level teachers, at least, would have been acquainted with objections (those of lesser skills need not concern us here, since they would hardly have qualified for the argument). In other words, even if we assume it was all a matter of the teachers' conviction, the question would remain, but applied to a particular social group. In other words, we should have to explain why a considerable majority of teachers, if not all of them, would subscribe to this controversial theory. And if, in the long run, this conjecture proved justified (and it appears to be at least partly true) that would mean only that we have discovered a gear-wheel, albeit an important one, in the transmission mechanism of a particular pre-understanding pattern, but not the origin of the pattern itself.

An alternative explanation might refer to the peculiar character of the Soviet social process that would presumably account for the extraordinary preoccupation with economic problems, rationalized as economic determinism. In other words, constant economic disorders of 'developed socialism' would naturally become a focal point of public concern, on the principle that 'he who is ill talks of his ache'.[9] It may be the case that somewhere else (or at some different time) economics might not be the key sector of social life, but the Soviet Union was not that place.

It is beyond dispute that the Soviet economy has been in a sorry plight and certainly deserves whatever attention it may get: that statement is a banality. But that is precisely why it would explain nothing. Many spheres of Russian life, if indeed not all, cause no less anxiety, and there have been constant attempts to draw public attention to them. Thus, many people are genuinely and rightly concerned about the state of national culture: who would dare to say there is nothing to worry about in this respect? Many people are alarmed by environmental problems and the dangers of nuclear power engineering. All these people are leaders of public opinion. Their voice is loud but it seems to cry in the wilderness. It might be objected, of course, that the country has more immediate and graver problems, and that ecology and culture can wait. But that is the point! What makes the Russian public believe that economic troubles are both more immediate and more imminent than say, ecological disaster? Generally speaking, the latter would appear to have a better claim for the top priority. If the Greens are right in their assertions, the ecological danger is immeasurably greater and ecological mistakes are both more difficult and more expensive to correct (if indeed it is

9 A Russian proverb.

possible at all), while the people of Russia have in the past survived years of economic hardships and there are economies inferior to theirs. And if it should be objected that ecological problems are considered secondary because people are for the most part ill-informed or not educated enough to comprehend the danger, that would again serve to elaborate the question rather than answer it. Why should they be ill-informed? Is not the issue talked or written about? And, come to think of it, when did the Soviet public wait for additional information in order to start worrying about something? It is rather the opposite. It appears that the Greens' argument fails to convince the public in Russia not because it is not convincing in itself, but because the logic of current ecological thinking, despite the fact that certain attitudes incorporated in the traditional Russian culture sound singularly consonant with it,[10] has proved by and large alien to the Soviet mind, while the logic of economic determinism is close to it and is clearly understood. For all their political and ideological disagreement, almost everyone in Russia seems to believe that whatever problems exist can be traced to the economy. Some see the market as a panacea, while others would rely on strengthening labour discipline. The logic of economic determinism is applied to ethnic conflicts ('if people lived better, there would have been nothing to quarrel about'), cultural stagnation ('everything would change for the better if market mechanisms replaced ideological control') and environmental problems ('in this country it is unprofitable to care about nature').

We do not intend to question the validity of the above arguments. Whether they are right or wrong is for experts to decide. But we would like to note that they have proved singularly effective in present-day Soviet and Russian political discourse, presumably because they fit the mental framework of a contemporary Russian.

But it is also noteworthy that these pre-understanding patterns are not limited to thinking. They may and do affect the practical actions of whoever shares them. In the present book, which aims to deal with representative institutions and legislative power, it is important to emphasize that the widespread belief that law is but a 'superstructure' on the economic 'basis'[11] is bound to affect all aspects of legislative

10 This subject is discussed in more detail in Chapter 4, Section 2, below.
11 Even though some modern Marxist philosophers insist on distinguishing between

activity, from the contents of particular bills to the understanding of the purpose and function of legislation in general.

Economic Determinism and the 'Populist' Bias

To return to the roots of economic determinism, it is worth noting the intrinsic, if unexpected, relationship that exists between this explanatory pattern and the cult of the people and the traditional attitude to work discussed in the previous chapter. The concept of 'the people', if it is not limited to the purely ethnic interpretation, has no definite sociological meaning. Numerous examples of arbitrary and mutually contradictory uses of the term, both in recent times and historically, could be cited in support of this statement. Depending on the context, 'the people' may stand for: (1) the population of a given country, which makes sense only in contrast to other countries; or (2) only a portion of that population set off against some kind of 'non-people' (the neologism may sound misleading in English, but would make perfect sense in Russian in which it would be a collective singular noun), implicit but undefined since definition is possible only within the framework of the implied dichotomy.[12] This makes 'the people' an ambivalent concept. A Russian mind would overcome the difficulty by identifying 'the people' with the sum total of social groups whose members do manual work in order to provide for themselves. Speaking in Marxist jargon, these would include 'peasants' (a professional group ranked as a social class despite the fact that it would not fit the Marxist definition of the latter) and 'proletarians'

'relations of production' and 'economy', everyone, apart from them, still seems to take it for granted that whenever 'the basis of society' is referred to by historical materialists, it is 'economy' that is implied.

12 Compare a modern Russian poet:

> The people - it divides into non-people
> And people in the literal sense.
> The former is no monster and no cripple,
> But it's a mongrel - in a higher sense.

> But who is people is not exactly people,
> But it expresses people. So you can't just drop:
> 'Look, here is people' (for it is not that simple),
> But you may say: 'There is a people!' Full stop.

> – *D. Prigov* (translated by N. Biryukov; for the Russian original, see *Mirrors* 1989).

('the working class'). As for other social groups, including those that earn their own living, their status would remain undefined. The ambivalence thus re-established would be a great convenience, since it allows us to interpret 'the people' as either a sociological concept to be used in frameworks claimed to be 'scientific' or as a moral-political category. Shifting between the two would be an effective manipulatory device and make the word a perfect ideological 'label'.

But the focal point would still be some element related to work, almost invariably manual, thus establishing a striking parallelism between the theoretical Marxist dichotomy of 'base' ('material production') versus 'superstructure' (all other kinds of activity and institutions) and an ideological, moral–political dichotomy of 'people' (those engaged in 'material production') versus 'non-people' (those otherwise engaged).

In this way, economic determinism gains unexpected support from the traditional culture and, instead of remaining a mere theoretical postulate, has emerged as an axiom of mass consciousness. Thus, populism (*narodnost'*), economic determinism and a typically medieval understanding of the meaning and value of intellectual work have merged into a single set of ontological beliefs, all the more tight and stable as its components fit, supplement and support one another.

THE SOVIETS AND THE PARTY

The Allure of the Soviets

'The workers' and peasants' revolution, about the necessity of which the Bolsheviks had always spoken, was accomplished'[13] under the slogan 'All Power to the Soviets!'. The new regime would come to be known as 'Soviet', and the word would be incorporated in the official state designations, first of the Russian Soviet Federal Socialist Republic[14] and then of the Union of Soviet Socialist Republics established on 30 December 1922.

---

13 A slightly adapted quotation from Lenin's famous speech at the meeting of the Petrograd Soviet of Workers' and Soldiers' Deputies on 25 October (7 November) 1917, the day the Provisional Government was overthrown and the Bolsheviks came to power (see Lenin 1964g, p.239).

When one knows what fate awaited the Soviets after the revolution, one cannot help being surprised at the Bolsheviks' insistent demands that all state power be vested in the Soviets and their solemn attitude towards the slogan itself. They would advance or withdraw it, depending on the situation, and in all seriousness would discuss the issues involved. It is as if in 1917 the demand to transfer power to the Soviets had some specific meaning, subsequently lost. For it is an open secret that after the Bolshevik revolution had been won, the power that they would still call 'Soviet' was vested elsewhere.[15]

To understand better the political meaning of the slogan 'All Power to the Soviets!' and to comprehend the October leaders' political ideal – unless, that is, the slogan was but a tactical trick on their part – we must compare it to alternative slogans and programmes. There were basically two of them: the traditional programme of autocratic monarchy, and the liberal one which was modelled after Western standards that had come to be acknowledged as more or less classical by that time. If we leave aside the somewhat anachronistic call to restore autocratic power to the tsar, which had been undermined by years of ineffectual rule and, as the February events had already shown, was of little appeal even to those whom it believed to represent, two programmes remain: the liberal and the Bolshevik. The difference between them and between their respective slogans – 'All Power to the Constituent Assembly!' and 'All Power to the Soviets!' – can be reduced to the difference between two models of government: representative democracy and direct popular rule.[16] From

14 See 'Declaration of Rights of the Working and Exploited People' (adopted by the Central Executive Committee on 3 (16) January 1918 and approved by the Third All-Russia Congress of Soviets on 12 (25) January, later to constitute the preamble to the first Soviet Constitution passed by the Fifth Congress of Soviets on 10 July 1918): 'Russia is hereby proclaimed a Republic of Soviets of Workers', Soldiers' and Peasants' Deputies. All power, centrally and locally, is vested in these Soviets' (Lenin 1964c, p.423).

15 See, for example, Carr 1950, pp.214–32.

16 'Not a parliamentary republic – to return to a parliamentary republic from the Soviets of Workers' Deputies would be a retrograde step – but a republic of Soviets of Workers', Agricultural Labourers' and Peasants' Deputies throughout the country, from top to bottom': that is how Lenin formulated the Bolshevik policy in his 'April Theses' (Lenin 1964i, p.23). The idea of a Constituent Assembly was not rejected outright, but its convocation and success were said to depend on the victory of the Soviets: 'And the view is attributed to me that I am opposed to the speedy convocation of the Constituent Assembly! I would call this "raving", had not decades of political struggle taught me to regard honesty in opponents as a rare exception' (ibid., p.25).

the standpoint of practical politics, the matter was more complicated, of course. Throughout 1917, as mentioned above, the Bolsheviks advanced and withdrew their slogan several times, depending on which political forces dominated (or expected to dominate) the

---

Still, the Constituent Assembly's political future did not seem particularly inspiring. In an article published a few weeks later Lenin answered the question of whether the Constituent Assembly should be convened in the name of different political parties, including his own. The Cadets' (Constitutional Democrats') view is presented by Lenin in the following form: 'Yes, but without fixing a date. As much time as possible should be spent consulting professors of law; first, because, as Bebel said, jurists are the most reactionary people in the world; and, second, because the experience of all revolutions has shown that the cause of popular freedom is lost when it is entrusted to professors' (Lenin 1964e, p.99). The Bolsheviks' answer runs as follows: 'Yes, and as soon as possible. But there is only one way to assure its convocation and success, and that is by increasing the number and *strength* of the Soviets [of the Workers', Soldiers', Peasants' and other Deputies] and organizing and *arming* the working-class masses. That it the only guarantee' (ibid., original italics; words in square brackets, absent from the edition quoted, are added from the Russian original: see Lenin *PSS* **31**, p.197).

That was written in April 1917. In July (August by Gregorian calendar) Lenin confirmed his position: 'If the Soviets were to win, the Constituent Assembly would be certain to meet; if not, there would be no such certainty' (Lenin 1964b, p.197). That this 'patronage' meant the Constituent Assembly's total submission to the Soviets the Bolsheviks did not even try to conceal (Lenin 1964j, p.144):

> With the Soviets of both capital cities in their hands the Bolsheviks would be reducing all their propaganda for the Power-to-the-Soviets slogan to empty phrases and, politically, would be covering themselves with shame as a party of the revolutionary proletariat if they refused to carry out this task [of preparing an uprising], **and if they became reconciled to the convocation of the Constituent Assembly** (*which means a faked Constituent Assembly*) **by the Kerensky government.** [Italics in the *Russian* original; emphasis added]

That became obvious after Bolsheviks seized power in October. The 'Draft Decree on the Right of Recall' promised (Lenin 1964d, p.337):

> The Soviets of Workers' and Soldiers' Deputies and the Soviets of Peasants' Deputies of each electorate district *shall have the right to appoint re-elections to all* city, Zemstvo and all other *representative institutions in general, not excluding the Constituent Assembly.* [Italics added]

And when the elections to the Constituent Assembly were eventually held and brought an overwhelming majority to the Socialist Revolutionary Party, the Bolsheviks' main rival, Lenin wrote in 'Theses on Constituent Assembly' (Lenin 1964k, p.383):

> The only chance of securing a painless solution to the crisis which has arisen owing to the divergence between the elections to the Constituent Assembly, on the one hand, and the will of the people [*sic*] and the interests of the working and exploited classes, on the other, is for the people to exercise as broadly and as rapidly as possible their right to elect the members of the Constituent Assembly anew, and for the Constituent Assembly to accept the law of the Central Executive Committee on these new elections, to proclaim that it unreservedly recognizes Soviet power, the Soviet revolution, and its policy on the questions of peace, the land and workers' control,

Soviets at the given moment.[17] In any case, the Second All-Russia Congress of Soviets, whose first sitting opened in Petrograd when the Provisional Government was still besieged in the Winter Palace and closed when it was already under arrest, proclaimed all power to transfer to the Soviets. Two months later the Council of People's Commissars, established by the Congress, was to dissolve the Constituent Assembly, which would be allowed a single day for its work, and thus put an end to all hopes for representative government in the future.[18]

---

and to resolutely join the camp of the enemies of the Cadet-Kaledin counter-revolution. Unless these conditions are fulfilled, the crisis in connection with the Constituent Assembly can be settled only in a revolutionary way, by Soviet power adopting the most energetic, speedy, firm and determined revolutionary measures against the Cadet-Kaledin counter-revolution, no matter behind what slogans and institutions (*even participation in the Constituent Assembly*) this counter-revolution may hide. Any attempt to tie the hands of Soviet power in this struggle would be tantamount to aiding counter-revolution. [Italics added]

January 1918 was to sum the story up.

17 The Bolsheviks were so proud of Lenin's tactics in this respect that the story of this slogan was made the focal point of the official account of 1917 events in the standard (compulsory) university course of *The History of the CPSU*; for that reason it is not recounted in detail in this book. Readers outside the former Soviet Union unfamiliar with the subject are addressed to Carr 1950, pp.70-101 (especially pp.79-84, 91-3); Rabinowitch 1976 (especially pp.59-62, 169-72); and Slusser 1987 (especially pp.55-6, 163-4).

18 'Declaration of Rights of the Working and Exploited People', read out by Ya.M. Sverdlov at the first sitting of the Constitutent Assembly on 5 (18) January 1918, demanded that the Assembly proclaimed the following (Lenin 1964c, pp.424-5: 'Declaration of Rights of the Working and Exploited People' in Lenin, *Collected Works*, vol.26):

Having been elected on the basis of party lists drawn up prior to the October Revolution, when the people were not yet in a position to rise *en masse* against the exploiters, had not yet experienced the full strength of resistance of the latter in defence of their class privileges, and had not yet applied themselves in practice to the task of building a socialist society, *the Constituent Assembly considers that it would be fundamentally wrong, even formally, to put itself in opposition to Soviet power*.

In essence the Constituent Assembly considers that now, when the people are waging the last fight against their exploiters, there can be no place for exploiters in any government body. *Power must be vested wholly in the working people and their authorized representatives – the Soviets of Workers', Soldiers' and Peasants' Deputies.*

Supporting Soviet power and the decrees of the Council of People's Commissars, the Constituent Assembly considers that *its own task is confined to establishing the fundamental principles of the socialist reconstruction of society.* [Italics added]

That was, indeed, an ultimatum, a shameless demand for unconditional surrender. The

The Failure of the Soviets

'This victorious, triumphal advance of the Soviet power' (as latter-day textbooks called it[19]) was soon checked, however. The new power proved utterly impotent and was one of the major factors that brought about the rapid disintegration of the country. It is hardly necessary to argue that the Soviet system failed to meet the requirements of democratic rule: this is evident enough. It is no less evident, though, that it was never meant to do so: all Lenin's writings dealing with matters of the state and power bear witness to that.

We have noted above the Bolsheviks' negative attitude towards parliamentary democracy. As to the concept of Soviet power, Lenin's major work *The State and Revolution*, written in semi-clandestinity in the late summer of 1917, is of particular interest.[20] A startling feature of this book - intended, after all, to be a kind of programme - was a total lack of any attempt on the author's part to summarize and analyse the experience acquired by the Soviets in 1905 and 1917. Nor did he theorize about how the institutions of Soviet power had functioned or should function. His main emphasis was on contrasting the Soviets, as a form of the dictatorship of the proletariat, with the representative institutions of the parliamentary type, as a form of the dictatorship of the bourgeoisie.[21] He would repeat his central thesis - endlessly and without fear of appearing tedious - that state power always was and could not but be a dictatorship, and that the only question to be asked was whose dictatorship (of what particular class) it was in each particular case, but he remained totally indifferent to problems of practical government. His interest was in the *fact* of power, not its 'mechanisms'. Not only did *The State and Revolution* fail to answer how the future proletarian power was to be structured:

Constituent Assembly was to denounce its legal status, fawn on the victors and dissolve itself. Its fate was predetermined and whether it would accept the 'Declaration' or reject it was of no importance. The Assembly rejected it and was dissolved that very day. As Lenin put it, 'the development of the Russian revolution has overcome the bourgeois parliamentary system' ('Draft Decree on the Dissolution of the Constituent Assembly' in Lenin *PSS* **35**, p.232).

19 Lenin's expression from his 'Report on Ratification of the Peace Treaty' delivered at the Extraordinary Fourth All-Russia Congress of Soviets on 14 March 1918 (see Lenin 1965d, p.175).

20 Lenin 1964h.

21 Ibid., especially pp.422-7.

the book failed even to ask the question. The author seems to have found it immaterial. If government structure was discussed at all, it was to substantiate his thesis that the old 'state machine' had to be 'smashed'. Inability or reluctance to 'smash' it were qualified as a grave political error, if not betrayal. The techniques of power interested him only inasmuch as they could be exposed as the exploiters' tricks used to deceive the working masses: they were subject to criticism, but they were not matters of concern for the future. Lenin sought mechanisms of power that would secure the dominance and interests of the proletariat. But he seemed to believe that the goal would be attained if representatives of the workers were ensured superior numbers in institutions of power: that would settle the question for him. Since the Soviets were to be elected by industrial workers, Soviet power was proletarian by definition. As a matter of fact, the argument is based on the traditional pattern of *sobornost'* amended to suit a new understanding of 'the people'. As Berdyaev has correctly pointed out, the Bolsheviks substituted 'proletariat' for 'the people'.[22] And within that pattern of thought it was natural to assume that proletarians had but to take counsel together for all their problems to be solved and all their needs satisfied.

It may, indeed, appear surprising that the pattern was followed in 1917 by the man who had strenuously objected to being guided by a 'spontaneous' working movement in 1902. If we go by *What Is To Be Done?*, we must conclude that fifteen years before he sat down to write *The State and Revolution*, Lenin had not expected the illiterate and impoverished workers to see an inch beyond their noses. He had argued then that the proletariat, left to its own resources, and deceived moreover by bourgeois propaganda, had not been able to rise above their momentary concerns and comprehend their genuine class

22 Compare Berdyaev 1972, pp.106-7:

> At that time the illusions of revolutionary *narodnichestvo* had already been outlived; the myth about the [peasantry] had collapsed. The people had not accepted a revolutionary intelligentsia. A new revolutionary myth was needed. And the myth about the people was changed into the myth about the proletariat. Marxism broke up the conception of the people as an integral organism; it analysed into classes with opposed interests. But in the myth of the proletariat, the myth of the Russian people arose in a new form. There took place, as it were, an identification of the Russian people with the proletariat, and of Russian messianism with proletarian messianism.

interests. The type of consciousness they would have developed 'spontaneously', Lenin had maintained, would have been 'trade-union consciousness', that is a consciousness aware of only 'limited' and 'particular' interests, such as higher wages, shorter working hours, improved conditions of work, and so on.[23] If workers fought their employers, it was not for political power, although that would have solved their problems once and for all time. Proletarians lacked a true understanding of their historic mission: it took the revolutionary intelligentsia to develop a revolutionary theory and teach it to the workers. Thus, proletarians needed a teacher. And as we know, that was to be the 'vanguard party of the working class', which Lenin had sought and which he eventually managed to create and bring to power.[24]

We may thus assume that the revolutionary power was always meant to be the power of the Bolshevik party. As for the Soviets, they were the simplest way to seize and retain it. The Bolsheviks were to become those 'workers' deputies' who would exercise power on behalf of the workers and secure their interests. Other parties were apparently not fit for the role and, as workers were soon to understand, had to resign or be ousted.

The Bolsheviks' Attitude towards Parliament

If the Bolsheviks counted on having a majority in the Soviets, why would they not attempt to win it in the parliament? The answer was determined by the balance of forces, of course, and the attitudes of the voters. The Bolsheviks' influence was stronger in urban areas and among industrial workers than in the countryside and among peasants. Peasants were more likely to support the Socialist Revolutionary Party, the Bolsheviks' main rival. That is why the Bolsheviks stood a better chance if elections were held at factories, rather than in territorial constituencies. Renunciation of equal suffrage and proportional representation was also to their advantage, since the proletariat, on whose behalf they were supposed to act, was much less numerous than the peasantry.

But it was not just a matter of tactics. The Bolsheviks might stake

23 See Lenin 1961, pp.375ff.
24 Compare Chapter 2, Note 33, above.

their fortunes on the Constituent Assembly, of course, if the voters' sympathies promised them a majority. They seemed to entertain certain hopes, otherwise why would they allow the election to take place (it was held in November, *after* the October coup). From the standpoint of political manoeuvring, it would have been more convenient to postpone or cancel the election under any pretext and thus leave open the question of who enjoyed greater voter support, rather than to lose it and face the unpleasant task of dissolving the supreme and legitimate organ of government. But the heart of the problem was different. The Bolsheviks did not favour parliament not merely because it would have been difficult for them to hold a majority in it, but rather because they did not like parliamentary practice and procedures. And the reason they did not like them was that parliamentary methods would not let them 'lead the masses' in their own way. The whole plan of socialist construction was bound to fail if it depended on the outcome of this or that election or this or that vote. That is why there are good reasons to believe that even if the Bolsheviks had managed to win a majority in the Constituent Assembly or any other representative body, they would have done their best to reduce it to the kind of decorative institution they reduced their cherished Soviets to.[25] The Constitution of 1936 would eventually alter the electoral system and reorganize the Supreme Soviet into a bicameral parliament-like body with a complete set of attributes for becoming a representative institution, without raising its rank within the Soviet political system to the slightest degree. The Bolsheviks wanted no parliament, they wanted a *Sobor:* a parliament's function is to *exercise* power, a *Sobor's* to *symbolize* it.

---

25 The role assigned to the Soviets by the leader of the revolution is made explicit in the *Theses* that he wrote for the October Conference of the Petrograd Party Organization (Lenin 1964j, p.143:

All the experience of both revolutions, that of 1905 and that of 1917, and all the decisions of the Bolshevik Party, all its political declarations for many years, may be reduced to the concept that *the Soviet of Workers' and Soldiers' Deputies is a reality only as an organ of insurrection*, as an organ of revolutionary power. *Apart from this the Soviets are a meaningless plaything* that can only produce apathy, indifference and disillusion among the masses.... [Italics added]

The Soviets' 'Decorative' Function

From the theoretical point of view, the Soviets were conceived as an alternative to the 'bourgeois' system of separation of powers. They were to be endowed with both legislative and executive power.[26] On the one hand, the move was intended to be an embodiment of the democrats' opium, namely, the idea of direct popular rule.[27] On the other hand, however, it could not help paralysing the governmental hierarchy. Since every Soviet was instituted as an agency of direct authority and was thus supposed to possess what bourgeois political science would have called 'sovereignty', it was bound to find itself in conflict with every other Soviet that had nominal jurisdiction over the same territory, that is, with every higher or lower Soviet.

The only way out of this difficulty would have been to delimit their respective authorities. But, in the first place, this deviation from the principle of the Soviets' sovereignty, and hence from the recognized pattern of legitimation, would have presupposed a drastic change in the mass mentality. In the second place, it would have become necessary to amend accordingly the whole system of the formation of the Soviets, which would have restricted the resources available for political manipulation. That would evidently have been undesirable, from the pragmatic point of view. It is worth noting here that direct elections (if they were indeed elections) were originally practised for lower-level Soviets only; higher-level Soviets and Congresses of Soviets were formed by delegating deputies of lower-level Soviets. This meant multi-stage, indirect elections, which was at odds with the classical conception of democracy (for which the Bolsheviks would not have given a brass farthing anyway) but allowed the outcome to

---

26 Characteristic features of the Soviet system of state power were defined by Lenin as follows: 'Abolition of parliamentarism (as the separation of the legislative from executive activity); union of legislative and executive state activity. Fusion of administration with legislation' ('Ten Theses on Soviet Power' in Lenin 1965e, p.154). That in practice this would amount to eliminating all distinctions between an ordinary resolution and a bill of law, to raising any decision of any Soviet on any question, no matter how trivial, to the rank of law and hence to devaluing the very notion of law, as light-heartedly repealed as it was adopted, Lenin never seemed to understand.

27 'The socialist character of Soviet, that is *proletarian*, democracy...', Lenin wrote, 'lies in the fact that all bureaucratic formalities and restrictions of elections are abolished; the people themselves determine the order and time of elections...' (Lenin 1965b, p.272). We shall discuss below the devastating effect of this 'abolition of bureaucratic formalities' on the fate of representative institutions.

be controlled. From the standpoints of both abstract law and common sense, this system, once adopted, would limit the authority of the Congresses of Soviets to whatever authority the lower-level Soviets that formed the Congresses cared to delegate to them. In case an issue was brought up that called for wider powers, the powers of the lower institutions had to be usurped. It is hardly necessary to explain how often issues would arise that transcended local matters and how ineffective the whole system would prove to be as a result. It is not surprising that it proved so short-lived, for all the slogans, symbols and official titles.[28] Had it not been for the Civil War that started soon after the October coup, the disintegration of the Russian state would have ensued from the first attempt to implement the coup's slogan of 'All Power to the Soviets!'

The result would not have been surprising, of course: in principle, direct (that is non-representative) democracy can hardly be realized in political formations larger in size than ancient *poleis* or Swiss cantons. Any attempt to introduce the system into a larger territory would inevitably result in disintegration, while rejection of representative democracy would leave no alternative to separatism except despotic central power. If only for self-preservation, the state power would have to be shifted elsewhere, as in the Soviet case it soon was.

But, as mentioned above, there are good reasons to believe that the idea of the sovereignty of the Soviets was never meant to be implemented. The authors of the slogan themselves viewed Soviet power not as a system of actually functioning government institutions that was for some reason to be preferred to alternative systems, but as a convenient cover (perhaps the most convenient in the circumstances) for the strong, despotic power they called 'the dictatorship of the proletariat'. Hence, it was not long before the only function left to the Soviets was to dress the windows. If Rabinowitch is right in his assertion that the Bolsheviks owed their victory mainly to the Petrograd workers, whose support for the Bolshevik cause was due to their fascination with the idea of Soviets as 'genuinely democratic insti-

28 Striking evidence of the esteem the Bolsheviks really felt for the celebrated 'sovereignty' of the Soviets is provided by numerous telegrams dispatched by Lenin during the Civil War. To cite but one example: on 15 April 1920 Lenin ordered the Cheka (political police) in Saratov 'to arrest for three days the Chairman of the Kamyshin *Uyezd* Executive Committee for intolerable interference in the food supply' (Lenin *PSS* 51, p.179).

tutions of popular self-rule', they were deceived by those in whom they placed their confidence.[29]

This evolution of the Soviets into a purely decorative frame for the rule of the Communist Party began, indeed, almost at once. The Soviet model of state power could exist and operate only as long as it had a kind of 'backbone' in it – inasmuch as there existed and operated behind the scenes an entirely different political hierarchy which was totally independent of the Soviets and could undertake to solve the problems and conflicts that proved beyond the capacity of the amorphous Soviet system. The paean sung to the Soviets by Lenin in *The State and Revolution* turned out to be an introduction to quite a different opera.

The transition was facilitated by the factors discussed in the preceding sections. It proved possible to draw on the national political tradition to justify this usurpation of state power by a political party. It will be remembered that within the Russian political culture 'right' would be realistically interpreted as 'objectively true' and 'wrong' as 'objectively false'. The people's somewhat mystic ability to distinguish between right and wrong, true and false – the belief in which had once been *confession de foi* of the revolutionary elite of the 1870s and the 1880s – yielded to the winds of time and was replaced with the omnipotence of 'the only true scientific theory of society', all the more easily as the holder of that singular knowledge professed itself the champion of the people and the defender of the oppressed.

The party, on the other hand, was prepared for the role. Theoretically, the way was paved by *What Is To Be Done?* The purpose of the pamphlet was to ensure the party's leadership in the revolutionary movement of the time. Lenin's argument was based on the assumption that society and history are governed by objective laws and whoever knows these laws is likely to have his way. It took little effort to infer from this that 'scientific' understanding of society entitled one to rule over it. Although not easily swallowed by the sceptically-minded intellectual elite, the idea appealed to the masses who had come to worship all-powerful science, both natural and social, as they had worshipped the omnipotent and omniscient God only a generation earlier.

Thus trends of different origins converged to give birth to the

29 Rabinowitch 1976, pp.xvii, xxvi.

political phenomenon which is known today as 'Soviet power'. This was a singularly misleading name, for it was not the councils of workers' deputies that ruled the state, but the party that operated within those councils and dominated them as, for that matter, it did everything else in the country. It was the party hierarchy, acting over the head of the Soviets, that ensured the coordination of local and national interests, or rather the subordination of local authorities to central power, without which the country could not be preserved as a single whole.[30]

Whether the party's monopoly of power was the natural outcome of the Soviets' failure to deal with the problems of a modern state, or whether it was the Bolsheviks' long-term goal from the very beginning, is indeed not particularly important. What matters is the fact that the Soviets offered no or little visible resistance. Slogans like 'Soviets without Communists' enjoyed but limited support and their proponents' concern was to remove the Bolsheviks from power rather than to secure the Soviets' constitutional priority. If the Kronstadt insurrection or some other anti-Bolshevik rebellion had succeeded, the Soviet system would have been doomed. But victory over the rebels was for the Soviets a purely nominal victory. The Soviets were to yield power to the party because the principle on which they were based was flimsy. That sort of system would be ineffectual anywhere, if it were to function in earnest rather than for show. But if, on the contrary, it were merely for show, it might look more than impressive. The Soviets could always boast about their appearance: they used to have exactly the number of party and non-party men and women, Komsomol members, writers, steel-makers, war veterans, Russians, Ukrainians, Chechens, Yakuts, Jews and so on and so forth that was *required*. And all this in spite of the fact that neither women, nor veterans, steel-makers, Yakuts, nor even party members were ever allowed a real choice. Elections were fictitious, the deputies were

---

30 In his speech at the Moscow City Conference of the RCP.(b) (Bolshevik Party) on 18 January 1919 Lenin condemned 'purely local interests ... that have given rise to the opposition to centralism, which, nevertheless, is the only way out of our present predicament' (Lenin 1965g, p.405: 'Speech at the Moscow City Conference of the RCP(b) on 18 January 1919' in *Collected Works*, vol.28). 'The Conference resolutely condemned attempts to belittle the Party's authority over the Communist groups in the Soviets', the editors add (ibid., p.525).

carefully selected under strict party control, and this manipulable system would easily assume any predetermined shape.

Since, in retrospect, this development appears more or less inevitable, or at least natural, its institutional consequences must have been unavoidable, too. We shall point out but three. In the first place, party rule soon acquired all the legitimacy the party might have wanted. The process was over by the mid-1920s. In due time the party's authority would be recognized abroad, too: while Nikita Khrushchev's episodic claims to be treated as was due to a head of state and the diplomatic efforts made to support them were not particularly successful, by Leonid Brezhnev's time the General Secretary of the party's Central Committee came to be considered a counterpart to presidents and monarchs, whether he held the appropriate state office or not.

In the second place, the Communist Party itself lost (or transcended) its status of a political party and evolved into a purely administrative hierarchy. It soon became, in theory, as well as in practice, 'the political system's pivotal element' and the real instrument of state control. This in turn made the introduction of the one-party system inevitable: the ban on activities of all other parties was a logical consequence of the ever-diminishing field of legitimate party strife, so that ever since that time in order to seize the state power a potential rival had to establish his control over the ruling party, that is to stage a *coup de parti*, to coin a phrase. And to complete the sequence, the remnants of what little had been left of intra-party democracy from before the revolution had to go, for there was, of course, no place for an institutionalized opposition within the state hierarchy. The latter task proved easy: in spite of its name, the underground organization had had little use for democratic procedures. It is, however, noteworthy – paradoxical though it may seem – that when the first steps towards political pluralism were made many years later, they were to be found nowhere other than in party organizations. It was only there that the democratic procedures, still preserved, albeit formally (all officials were theoretically to be elected and held accountable to the rank and file), could be set off against behind-the-scenes decision-making: they themselves were supposed to be those behind-the-scenes decision-makers.

Finally, as a *conditio sine qua non* for the survival of this party-state leviathan, the notorious system of *nomenklatura* developed: it was only through close and unwearying party control over both nomination and promotion to any influential position within any sphere of activity that the uninterrupted operation of this peculiar mechanism could be ensured.[31]

It may be wondered, however, why this system of Soviet power based on the principles of election and representation,[32] although defective in practice, did not evolve, if not into genuine representative democracy then at least into some kind of moderate pluralism. Granted, it proved ineffective; granted it could not help being ineffective in the circumstances; nevertheless why did there turn out to be no alternative to its serving as a cloak for party rule? To answer this question we must return to that pseudo-democratic model of *sobornost'* discussed in the preceding chapter. As is clear by now, it was this model, somewhat modified, that formed the basis of the Soviet system.

The notorious triune formula of imperial Russia, 'Autocracy, Orthodoxy, Nationality [*narodnost'* - which may also be translated as 'populism']', had often been subject to criticism and ridicule. Not all critics seemed to realize, however, how internally congruous it was, or to feel the intrinsic agreement of its constituent elements. *Narodnost'* may be interpreted in different ways, of course, and so indeed it was. There were conservative populists in Russia, even reactionary populists, and there were revolutionary populists. Some populists would defend autocracy, some would conspire against it. Some of them were religious, others were indifferent, still others were militant atheists. There were even genuine democrats among them, although these would feel somewhat uncomfortable in the company. The idea of populism, we have argued, is not identical with that of democracy. The difference between the two may account, to some extent, for the ordeals suffered by representative democracy under conditions of direct popular rule. As a matter of fact, however, the difference goes even deeper than that. It was not through historic

---

31 See Voslensky 1991.
32 Cf. *The State and Revolution*: 'The way out of parliamentarianism is not, of course, the abolition of representative institutions and the elective principle, but the conversion of the representative institutions from talking shops into "working" bodies' (Lenin 1964h, p.423).

fortune alone that the model of *sobornost'* turned out to be linked with unrestricted autocratic power: in fact, the former may be said to presuppose and generate the latter.

The Slavophiles seemed to sense this at the time, although Khomyakov's apologia for autocracy, for instance, was somewhat artificial.[33] There are no mechanisms or procedures for collective decision-making, still less for collective action, within the unstructured totality of a *Sobor*, and by definition there cannot be. A *Sobor* as a body is able to approve or disapprove of a decision, but it has no means to elaborate it. And it certainly lacks the organs required to implement it. In order to acquire them, it would also have to acquire differentiated structures. Such a development, however, would be manifestly unacceptable since it contradicts the idea and ideal of *sobornost'*. It was not by chance that the majority of Russian thinkers who discussed the notion of *sobornost'* placed it within the spiritual sphere: it was certainly ill-adapted to secular affairs. That is why political *sobornost'* – that is, *sobornost'* as a political ideal or rather a distinct type of political culture (and it is this meaning of the word that concerns us here) – cannot be embodied directly in a system of power agencies. It exists and functions as a spiritual background for power that is alienated from the people and opposed to them. The function of power is to act, whereas a *Sobor* is unable to act, for reasons given above. Since no organs of action can be instituted within the *Sobor*, they are instituted outside it. Everybody appears equal *vis-à-vis* this outside agency, and this formal equality helps disguise the existing social differences. The equality is illusory, but the power of the agency that this illusion serves to legitimate is quite real. And it is soon evident that this has been no agency of the *Sobor*'s: rather, the *Sobor* turns out to be an appendage to it.

It was thus not through their bad luck that the Soviets lost real power. They could hardly have retained it, if the political culture

33 A. Khomyakov attributed a unique historic mission to the Russian people, which, however, belonged entirely to the spiritual sphere. That mission would preclude any involvement in politics as intrinsically sinful, although politics would still remain an indispensable element of social life, which otherwise would be impossible. From this contradiction, Khomyakov held, autocracy would be a way out. The tsar would assume all responsibility. He would take the sin of power on himself, and the people would be left in their innocence. Autocracy would still be evil, but it would be a necessary evil, justified by the Russian people's historic destiny.

within which they had evolved were to continue. The Soviet system was created by and for people whose patterns of political mentality would not resist the development of power structures outside and above the Soviets, but would, on the contrary, presuppose them.

Towards the end of the Civil War disappointment at the Soviet system spread to include even its makers. It would be interesting to trace the evolution of Lenin's views on the nature of Soviet power from *The State and Revolution* to his last writings, sometimes called his 'political testament'. His attitude underwent a major change: while the emotional impact of his earlier work had been given by his apologias for the Soviets in terms that revolved around the idea of *sobornost'*, the later writings were full of criticism that bordered on anti-Sovietism. On the one hand, Soviet power was branded as bureaucratic;[34] on the other hand, the author seemed fully to realize

34 Lenin was not 'disillusioned' at once. The process can be divided into three stages. The first covers the period before Soviet power was established and a few months after that. Whatever was written at that time on the subject was full of exalted praise for Soviet power and confidence in the near and final victory over bureaucratism: see his speech at the First All-Russia Congress of the Navy on 22 November (5 December) 1917 (Lenin 1964f) and 'Ten Theses on Soviet Power', cited above (Lenin 1965e).

   A year later Lenin was less optimistic. In his speech at a Joint Session of the All-Russia Central Executive Committee, the Moscow Soviet and the All-Russia Trade Union Congress on 17 January 1919 he reckoned bureaucrats and profiteers among the most dangerous enemies of the Soviet power (Lenin 1965f, p.394 'Speech at a Joint Session of the All-Russia Central Executive Committee, the Moscow Soviet and the All-Russia Trade Union Congress on 17 January 1919' in *Collected Works*, vol.28). But he still blamed their very existence on the old regime ('The Basic Tasks of the Dictatorship of the Proletariat in Russia' in Lenin 1965a, p.109):

   Those strongholds of the bureaucracy which everywhere, both under monarchies and in the most democratic bourgeois republics, have always kept the state bound to the interests of the landowners and capitalists, have been destroyed in present-day Russia. The struggle against the bureaucracy, however, is certainly not over in our country. The bureaucracy is trying to regain some of its positions and is taking advantage, on the one hand, of the unsatisfactory cultural level of the masses of the people and, on the other, of the tremendous, almost superhuman war efforts of the most developed section of the urban workers.

   Old bureaucrats whom the revolution had thrown out would disguise themselves as communists, he maintained, and 'creep' into positions of power (*Collected Works* 29, pp.32–3, 182–3). How they managed to do this, and why the celebrated election of deputies by industrial workers failed to stop this penetration of *old* bureaucrats into new government bodies, Lenin never cared to explain.

   The third stage started towards the end of the Civil War and lasted until Lenin's death. He openly held the Soviets up to shame for their bureaucratism. In his 'Notes on the Immediate Tasks of the Party', written on 19 October 1920, Lenin proclaimed that the party had grown absolutely unchallengeable. As a remedy for 'Communist swagger' Lenin proposed to create Rabkrin (the Workers' and Peasants' Inspection) and to enlarge the Central Committee by a great number of workers. But he still failed to understand the decisive role of procedures: Lenin continued to think in terms of personnel – hence his naive hope that a struggle for power between party leaders might be prevented by a few dozen workers who were to constitute the numerical majority. Lenin seemed sincere in his lack of understanding that the presence of those 'decorative' or 'buffer' members could, at best, change the circumstances of the struggle, most probably in favour of the strongest: it would increase the number of their potential supporters and help them square accounts with the weakest. What is most surprising is that the persistence of his belief in any cook's ability to rule the state matched the clarity of his understanding that an 'unsatisfactory cultural level' would result in every 'single' cook becoming a bureaucrat. The cook's rule would do no good: everything would be ruined; still, success would be ensured if one hundred cooks could get together![35] Here we seem to have

'struggle against bureaucratism and red tape of Soviet institutions' as one of 'the main questions upon ending the war with Wrangel' (Lenin *PSS* **42**, p.11), while in his speech at the Moscow *Guberniya* (province) Conference of the RCP(b) delivered on 21 November 1920 he stated in plain words: '*There has been a revival of bureaucratic methods*, against which a systematic struggle has to be waged' (Lenin 1966, p.421 'Our Foreign and Domestic Position and the Tasks of the Party' in *Collected Works*, vol.31; italics added). Moreover,

> The bureaucratic methods that have reappeared in Soviet institutions were bound to have a pernicious effect even on Party organisations, since *the upper ranks of the Party are at the same time the upper ranks of the* [*state*] *apparatus*; they are one and the same thing [ibid., p.421–2; italics added].

Lenin seemed to regret his rashness in declaring the end of bureaucratism, and tried to adopt a more realistic position and, at the same time, to shift responsibility for the preservation or 'revival' of bureaucratism from his Party elsewhere. It is noteworthy that the source of the 'pernicious influence' that affected the Party organizations is seen in 'Soviet institutions' where 'bureaucratic methods have reappeared'. And at the Eighth All-Russia Congress of Soviets (22 December 1920) Lenin finally declared: 'I realize the gravity of bureaucratism, but *we have not had its extermination in the Party programme*. This is not a question for the Congress, this is a question for a whole epoch' (Lenin *PSS* **42**, p.165; italics added).

35 Cf. Lenin: 'We are no utopians. We know that an unskilled labourer or a cook cannot immediately get on with the job of state administration' (Lenin 1964a, p.113). Nevertheless: 'For the administration of the state in *this* [*revolutionary*] spirit we can *at once set in motion a state* apparatus consisting of ten if not twenty million people' (ibid., p.114; original emphasis).

identified a deep-rooted ontological belief, against which all argument and evidence would be powerless.

It was, by contrast, Stalin's strong point that he managed to understand or simply guess what Lenin had failed to understand, namely, the decisive role of institutional mechanisms in creating and maintaining structures of power. That may account for the fact that Lenin lost the last set of his political game (and had to spend his last year in honorary confinement). Unlike Lenin, Stalin deliberately sought to create *controlled* mechanisms of power, although he would preserve intact the full scope of the Soviet and socialist rhetoric. Retention of the Soviets as symbols of 'socialist choice' serving to legitimate the actions of party leaders would answer the purpose, but behind (or rather above) the Soviets, the shadowy power of the party hovered.[36] The success of this castling manoeuvre in the echelons of power was ensured not only by the feebleness of the Soviets, but by the efficacy of the rhetoric used to disguise it. The efficacy, in turn, was mainly due to the fact that the rhetoric fit the ontological belief patterns of mass consciousness, from which Lenin finally failed to free himself.

Were it not for these belief patterns, Stalin's rhetoric would have been powerless. Nevertheless, it worked, and Stalin managed to solve, albeit by barbarous means, the problem of creating a system of political control for a given social environment – the task that Lenin, in our best judgement, had failed to cope with. If the political and social reforms introduced by Lenin in 1921 (the so-called 'New Economic Policy' or NEP) essentially amounted to the renunciation of total party control over every aspect of social life and every social group of the country, the abolition of NEP by Stalin a few years later may be regarded as a repeated, and this time successful, attempt to establish that control. Stalin solved the conundrum. The totalitarian monster was born and the idea of *sobornost'* was implemented in

---

36 In this respect Stalin's 'Contribution to Questions of Leninism' (January 1926) is
   singularly illuminating: the conventional lip-service paid to Soviet power is suddenly
   superseded by a discussion of 'drives' and 'levers' of the dictatorship of the proletariat,
   from which we are to learn that the Soviets' proper place is between trade unions and
   cooperative societies. The Party is the last on the list, it is true, but by no means the
   least: it is 'the main directing force in the system of dictatorship of the proletariat whose
   mission is to guide all these *mass organizations*' (see Stalin 1941, pp.120–21; italics
   added). No more, no less: one would have thought the Soviets to be a government
   agency, but they turned out to be but a 'mass organization'.

reality. That reality turned out to be a nightmare, with concentration camps, mass repressions, ravaging of the country and so on, but what else could one expect if Utopia was to be made real? Communist Utopia, at least, has always been accompanied by mass repressions, which makes one wonder whether the GULag really was a creation of the bloodthirsty tyrant and not a phenomenon determined on the level of the system. To put it otherwise, if you resort to socialist (communist) rhetoric and want it to be effective, you need to enclose your country with barbed wire.

The Soviets as a Symbol of Unity

It would be a mistake, however, to believe that the decorative façade of the Soviets was intended for outward effect only, whether domestic or abroad. References to presumably democratic representative institutions might, of course, be used to beat off accusations of lack of genuine democracy. But it was scarcely possible that anyone would sincerely expect such arguments to be convincing. But the invariable and unfailing demonstration of unity in elections could not help influencing the mentality and behaviour of the deputies themselves.

It is hard to believe that in all the years of its history the USSR Supreme Soviet never had among its members a single individual who would have reason or whim to vote just once against the majority. Such situations must have arisen, all the more so as the corps of deputies was by no means composed of mere puppets or extras admitted for the sake of observing the proprieties. There were influential persons among the deputies, truly influential: government officials, generals, top-rank party functionaries, well-known representatives of free professions – in short, the national elite. They could not always have been of the same opinion: that would have been ridiculous. But since there were different interests involved and different views held, there had to be some effort to achieve a consensus. But if anything was done to arrive at mutually acceptable decisions, that would take place outside the Supreme Soviet. If its deputies argued and quarrelled among themselves, that was always elsewhere. Within the Soviet, pathetic accord would invariably be displayed: the deputies seemed to be imbued with a desire to demonstrate their unity to the whole outside world, or perhaps to themselves. Even those who were *contra* would unfailingly vote *pro*. The Supreme Soviet was thus able to perform its basic function successfully, a task far more important, indeed, than any overseas propaganda might have ever been: to maintain the myth of monolithic unity of the Soviet people rallied around the Communist Party in the struggle for their common cause.

This unity, of the kind that would have been worthy of the ideal of *sobornost'*, was the embodiment of the deep-rooted understanding of what constituted the people and representation of the people. The word *sobornost'*, as has been pointed out, was never heard: it sounded 'pre-revolutionary' enough to be suspected of being 'counter-revolutionary'. But its functional substitute, the idea of a classless society, was considered Soviet society's official goal. Marxism proved opportune again. From the standpoint of social theory, the Marxist paradigm stresses class contradictions. But it was not the theory but the *myth* of Marxism that was the foundation of the Soviet political mentality: the myth of the proletariat that had nothing to lose but its fetters, and that in pursuing its specific class interest would abolish itself as a class of the have-nots, and with it class differentiation as such. When class contradictions disappeared following the elimination of class distinctions, the ideal of popular unity would be realized and political institutions that embodied it would be legitimated.

Within the operational experience acquired in these institutions, disagreement with the majority is not regarded as a natural, although unfortunate, manifestation of divergent interests or beliefs, but precisely and fundamentally an intentional demonstration of dissent and disunity. Such behaviour is inadmissible, for it threatens to undermine the sustaining myth of the political culture.[37] The deputy must realize that if he votes *contra*, he opposes not those who vote *pro*, but the whole people. In this, he exposes himself to be a secret 'Enemy of the People' and a traitor. The myth demands the renegade be cast out. The ostracism might assume different forms and have different consequences for the outcast, but the depth of the roots the myth had put down was attested by the fact that it took 35 years after

---

37 The notion of a political culture's sustaining myth was advanced by Robert Tucker (see Tucker 1987, p.22).

the bloody repressions of the Stalin era had ceased before the Soviet parliament had occasion to witness a deputy who dared to break the rules of the game and express his disagreement by openly voting *contra*: the picture of Academician Sagdeyev, his hand raised in a vote 'against', became the sensation of the day.

The idea of a representative institution that formed the basis of the Soviet model was thus radically different from the parliamentary idea. A Supreme Soviet deputy was certainly a 'representative', but not inasmuch as he or she 'represented' his or her voters or, terrible to think, his or her party (this was altogether inconceivable since there was only one party, and it did not need to be 'represented'): the deputy was a 'representative', because he or she was a member of a body that 'represented' the people as a whole, and was the people's deputy in direct intercourse with the authorities. In this capacity, the Supreme Soviet, for one thing, could claim no authority for itself. Secondly, it could not and ought not to be considered an arena in which particular interests were defended or reconciled and conflicts were settled or solved: it was the Supreme Soviet's task to presume that there were no conflicts within the people and within the society.

It was to this presumed lack of conflict between various groups of Soviet society that the Soviet political system owed its peculiar institution of *nakaz* (electors' mandate; plural *nakazy*). A *nakaz* is a commission a deputy-to-be is charged with by a group of electors, which in theory may not be declined. A deputy's refusal to accept this commission on the grounds, for instance, that it contradicts his or her own beliefs is as inconceivable ('against the rules') as his or her voting *contra* at a session is impossible. Presumably, a *nakaz* cannot contradict a deputy's beliefs because there may be no contradictions between the people and their representatives. If there are such contradictions, a deputy has simply no right to 'represent' the people. But what kind of 'deputy' is he or she then? Similarly, commissions cannot contradict each other, since the interests of all groups of the population are basically identical. As this identity of interests is indeed a myth, the procedure itself is pure ritual - pure, but not empty. This is a legitimation ritual: its function is not to find out and help meet the voter's needs, but to demonstrate and establish the link between the people and their deputy. To be sure, *nakazy* would sometimes be fulfilled, which however does not affect our argument that to maintain the myth, *nakazy* had to be obligatory; whether they were feasible or not was of no importance. The 'obligation' was quite mythical, too, but then a myth would demand nothing else.

It is noteworthy that there is an analogy to this aspect of Soviet political life in the presumably different political system of post-Reform Russia:[38] like the Soviets later, *zemstvos* were not regarded as representing the various social groups, but the civil society as a whole in its intercourse with the state. In relations between the civil society and the state viewed from this perspective, the latter is no longer regarded as an agency for the society or some part or class within it. It should be kept in mind, however, that society becomes aware of this opposition ('civil society versus the state'), if and when the power of the state becomes alienated from its social support and develops into an agency of violence that pursues no interests but its own, that is, the interests of bureaucracy. That bureaucracy will behave in precisely this way is already suggested implicitly by the idea of the opposition: 'society versus the state', and the idea is then interpreted after Djilas. In the light of that interpretation, social homogeneity symbolized in *Sobor*-like representative institutions turns out to be to some extent a prerequisite, but mainly a natural outcome of this enslavement of the society by the new class of state bureaucrats. A mind that is permeated with the idea of social homogeneity and is at the same time critical of the political status quo faces a choice between two alternatives: it must either follow Djilas in his analysis of the class structure of socialist society, or else discard altogether the communist (Marxist) conceptual approach with its emphasis on social class antagonisms. The latter course has proved much easier in present circumstances.

At any rate, the rhetoric that is characteristic of this type of political mentality differs radically from the communist rhetoric. Since, however, rhetoric implies social ontology, transformation of pre-understanding patterns turns out to be a necessary precondition for new rhetoric. However, new anti-bureaucracy rhetoric cannot be based on Marxism, hence Marxist *Weltanschauung* destroys itself if *sobornost'* is chosen as a model for state-building, as it was in the case of the Soviets.

---

38 In Russian history the term 'post-Reform' refers to the period between the Reform of 1861 (which abolished serfdom) and the Revolution of 1917.

THE SOURCES OF CRISIS

By the late 1920s the development of the system described in the preceding section was by and large complete. Since that time it functioned without major breakdowns, despite a number of severe crises both inside and outside the country, such as the agrarian crisis of the late 1920s and early 1930s, the political calamities of the Great Terror, the military catastrophe of 1941, and so forth. This does not mean that the Soviet political system was a faultless machine, free of structural defects. On the contrary, the crisis it was afflicted with by the early 1980s was a natural outcome of its own evolution.

Analysing the causes of this crisis, two groups of factors may be identified that account for the eventual collapse of the Soviet political system. First among them are immanent sources of crisis: the system's structural flaws that would cause recurrent failures and demand regular effort to maintain it in operating condition. Secondly, there are features and circumstances that are not related to the initial model but to its subsequent evolution, and that have developed under a variety of influences, both internal and external.

The Partocrats–Technocrats Conflict

The immanent sources of crisis of the Soviet social system were mainly due to the peculiar model of economic life the system supported. Lenin's project to model the national economy as a single factory under centralized control[39] was carried out through nationalization of industry and transport and virtual nationalization of agriculture. The administration of the national economy that appeared in consequence of the '"Red Guard" attack on Capital'[40] and the subsequent collectivization was an agglomeration of monopolistic departments – bureaucratic hierarchies within the state apparatus – each practically sovereign within its particular sphere of competence. Given the size of the country and the scale of the processes that were to be controlled from a single centre, the system could hardly have been any different from what it actually was. However, since these bureaucracies were

39 Elaborated mainly in *The Immediate Tasks of the Soviet Government* (Lenin 1965).
40 Lenin's expression from ibid., pp.247ff.

not subordinated to each other, the inter-department conflicts differed substantially from those that were responsible for the political impotence and disorganization of the system of Soviet power. In their everyday activities the departments tended to 'disengage' themselves from the 'national' interests, that is the interests of the top party leadership. This would inevitably result in incessant bickering between the hierarchies of the departments and the party hierarchy, with personal relationships between the former and the latter to complicate the picture further.

From this standpoint, even the Terror may be regarded as one of the most dramatic episodes of this struggle. In 1937 the most severe repressions befell the ever stronger army apparatus and the apparatus of the People's Commissariats who were responsible for the economy. As time went by, the forms of this struggle grew 'milder' and the Terror became history, but relations between the two parallel power structures – the party and the 'government' (economic) hierarchies – were invariably strained. One of the basic motives that would prompt the state (that is the party) leadership to take the field repeatedly against 'technocrats' was clear enough, given that from the economic point of view the system was functioning unsatisfactorily. On the other hand, however, the nature of the conflict would determine the 'field' on which the 'battle' was to be waged: on this field economic bosses would feel both more experienced and more secure. Moreover, if we take into account the priority (not to say 'exalted') status which the economy enjoyed in the eyes of a party leadership brought up in the spirit of economic materialism, the eventual victory of the managerial hierarchy can hardly appear surprising. By the early 1970s, that is, soon after Khrushchev was removed from his combined post as head of both the party and the government, the struggle between the two power structures practically ceased: the 'departments' were close to establishing almost total control over the party apparatus.

The party might still remain dominant in other spheres of social life, but it could no longer be relied on as a counterbalance to the influence of the 'departments'. Moreover, thanks to personal union with the party leadership, the managerial apparatus was able to lay its hands on those levers of state power that had hitherto been the party's monopoly. After that the departments' activities were subject to no outside control, all restrictions were removed, and it took these monopolistic hierarchies a decade and a half to drive the country to the verge of economic, ecological and social disaster.

In these circumstances individuals were bound to appear among the party leadership who would feel a kind of nostalgia for the times when the party was able to oppose, more or less successfully, the departments' expansionism. There was no need for these people to be Stalinists. Khrushchev was an energetic fighter against the claims of the 'departments', and the economic growth of the late 1950s and early 1960s may have been due, in part, to his anti-departmental reforms: Khrushchev at that time disbanded or reined in many 'departments', including the army and the KGB (the Committee for State Security). *Perestroika*, too, may be conceived in its early stages as a struggle of the party against the economic hierarchies. At any rate, the reformers' first attack was against local-level party and administrative clans and their bosses, and the main weapons were charges of corruption. And the local party and administration elites would immediately manifest the familiar symptoms and retort with counter-charges of planning mass repressions on the scale of 1937.

The resistance offered by the 'departments' proved so strong that the leaders of *perestroika*, who seemed to rely initially on the traditional party–state levers, were forced to look for new allies. They found them soon among that section of the intelligentsia that had long been in opposition to the regime and welcomed the reforms enthusiastically. In order to enable it to join the battle against the 'corruptionists', *glasnost'* was introduced – to the great surprise of the intelligentsia, which could hardly believe its luck.

The Opposition of the Intellectuals

The intelligentsia's almost unanimous conversion to opposition was another major source of crisis in the Soviet social and political system. The intellectuals' relations with Soviet power had never been easy. A considerable number of them had been forced to emigrate during and after the Civil War. They had suffered severe losses in the years of the Great Terror. On the other hand, a significant portion of the intelligentsia, particularly people engaged in technology and engineering, had remained loyal to the regime until the mid-1960s. This loyalty had been stimulated by the comparatively privileged

economic conditions the authorities had cared to provide for those
strata, at least, that they had relied on to ensure the desired level of
technological development and the country's defence potential.

The situation began changing rapidly in the years that later came to
be labelled 'stagnation'. As to their well-being, a growing number of
intellectuals were gradually reduced to the level of the average-paid
and then the low-paid groups of the population. From the psychological point of view, the situation was aggravated by the fact that this
downward social mobility took place against the background of a
revolution in technology and information science that was unfolding
in the leading Western countries and was favourably affecting the
social status of brain-workers there. The intellectuals' conditions in
the USSR would, by contrast, be characterized by narrowing social
horizons, which could only contribute to their natural resentment at
the totalitarian order. The result of this development was that the
ideals of political freedom and a law-based state would spread far
beyond the comparatively narrow circle of persons who were ready
for immediate action and were known as dissidents. In a way, almost
the whole of the intelligentsia that was not directly associated with
the authorities identified themselves with the dissidents. In the years
of 'stagnation' a joke circulated about all people being divided into
two basic categories: 'ante-sidents' [*do-sidenty*] and 'post-sidents'
[*ot-sidenty*], alluding to *sidet'* – 'to sit' (a verb that is used in the
Russian idiom to mean 'serve terms of imprisonment').

This change in the intelligentsia's political attitudes determined the
outcome of *glasnost'* that seems to have been unforeseen by the party
leadership (or was at any rate undesired): total criticism initially of
the regime's past crimes, then of the regime itself, and eventually of
the communist ideology in general.

Part II

The USSR Supreme Rally

Back hath come the spring of beneficent being, and streams of radiantly flowing life stretch around, for the light hath shone of our long-awaited hope, the great God. And, by His grace, from one end of the Russian land to her other end men of orthodoxy, humble and great, rich and beggars, young and old, enriched were with rich reason by Him who giveth life to all and illumed with the light of benevolent consent, and though of different places, spake with one mouth, and though in no agreement were, separated by great distances, were as of one council, in unity and equality.

— The Other Narration.

4 Constitutional Reform

> *But good men in the world are few and*
> *bad men are many, so in fact the sage*
> *brings little benefit to the world, but*
> *much harm.*
> — Chuang Tzu

THE PARADOXES OF *GLASNOST'*

The Prerequisites of *Glasnost'*

The changes that began after Gorbachev came to power and were slow at first gradually picked up speed, and they finally started to affect institutions of power. In the new circumstances representative institutions that had long been content with a role more symbolic than authoritative, were acquiring new functions and becoming the focal point of the country's political life. The short history of the Congresses of the USSR People's Deputies – our chief concern in the following chapters – will not be particularly intelligible unless preceded by the story of their birth.

The Nineteenth All-Union Conference of the Communist Party of the Soviet Union held in the summer of 1988 signalled the beginning of an unprecedented constitutional reform. The first legislative steps were taken the following autumn, but these dramatic changes were preceded by what turned out to be the initial stage of political innovations of which *glasnost'* constituted the most conspicuous single element.

Glasnost' was in itself an unprecedented novelty on the Soviet political scene. The Bolsheviks had no sooner seized power than they gave up their old demands for freedom of speech and of the press and banned first whatever organs belonged to their immediate political opponents, labelled as 'counter-revolutionaries', and in due time all other newspapers and magazines whether they were controlled by political parties, including those that had once been considered 'revolutionary', or by some absolutely non-political groups.

Throughout the seven decades of Soviet power, monopoly over the mass media was one of the main features of the Soviet political culture and the regime's major political resource. That was, of course, the natural outcome of the total control the Communist Party had long exercised over the press, radio and television, or, for that matter, over almost every other sphere of social life. But no sooner had that control been relaxed than a number of mass media organs that belonged to the state and the party were miraculously transformed into organs of political opposition.

The mystery was easy to unravel, however: by the mid-1980s the dissident attitudes, which had already been building up for some decades, increased sharply and spread out to include the bulk of the intelligentsia. Apart from the general causes discussed in the preceding chapter, of major importance was the crisis of the power structures that befell Soviet society in the last years of Brezhnev's rule and was developing at an increasing rate after his death, while his short-lived successors were rapidly replacing each other. The regime's prestige was growing ever lower; discontent was spreading to practically all strata of the population. Even the power elite was no exception: a considerable part of it proved susceptible to opposition sentiments. Therefore, when intellectuals – who, it goes without saying, formed the bulk of mass media personnel – felt themselves relatively free from party surveillance and attempted to use their publications to express the prevailing opposition attitudes, they found appreciable support in the corridors of power. Without that support *glasnost'* would have scarcely been possible, at least in the beginning. That was clear to everyone: to leaders of *glasnost'*, the most popular figures in the country in the early years of *perestroika*, and to their opponents, who would refer sarcastically to the 'newly acquired courage' of the 'clerks' and 'pioneers' of *perestroika*, to their notorious 'capacity to *reorient* themselves' ('reorientation' is one of a number of possible translations of *'perestroika'*), and – not to waste gunpowder – to the 'freedom within limits set from above' in general.

Still, the result was obvious: the opposition press was born and started its 'triumphal advance'[1] rapidly gaining in popularity and support. The irony of this dawn of *glasnost'* was that the organs of the press that had converted to opposition continued to enjoy their status of official government agencies and were consequently able to benefit from the monopoly within their particular domains which they possessed by virtue of that status. In that way opposition or simply captious newspapers and magazines were able to enjoy unprecedented, giddy circulation (one again the Soviet Union appeared to have won the world record), and with it unprecedented influence on the public. Complaints, on the part of the conservatives, that 'all the press has become yellow' were, though unjust, not without ground. If not in the number of publications (the majority would for a long time yet remain duly obedient and conformist), then in the number of readers and subscribers, the press labelled 'yellow' by the conservatives was beyond reach.[2]

That could hardly have been the case if the spokesmen for the opposition had been obliged to establish their own newspapers and magazines, instead of just finding themselves one fine day in control of a number of government and party publications 'ready for use'. The monopoly of the press which the party had laboured to impose backfired: a few intellectuals who enjoyed (or were allowed) access to the opposition press and were engaged in writing on political topics (or topics that passed as political at the time) were brought to the forefront of national political life and soon discovered that they were among the most influential figures in the country. The regime's ideological enemies availed themselves of the opportunity unintentionally afforded them by the regime and were laying the foundations of their future political careers.

The Triumph of the Intelligentsia

The press monopoly inherited from the past thus made the intelligentsia the dominant opposition force: all other social strata and political groups that might join the opposition had practically no access to the mass media and remained politically mute. As for the

1 See Chapter 3, Note 19. The quoted term is from Lenin, 'Report on Ratification of the Peace Treaty', delivered at the Extraordinary Fourth All-Russia Congress of Soviets, 14 March 1918 (Lenin 1965d, p.175).
2 For details see Kliger 1989.

intellectuals, they first used the opportunity to satisfy their own spiritual needs and those of the people as they understood them. The spirit and themes of the time were best expressed by two titles: those of Tengiz Abuladze's film, *Repentance*,[3] and A. Orlov's memoirs, *The Secret History of Stalin's Crimes*.[4] Historians and journalists set off enthusiastically to fill the gaps in the country's post-revolutionary history. Hitherto banned writings – *samizdat* and *tamizdat*[5] – filled the magazines pushing aside the more recent works and bringing upon the editors the somewhat putrid accusation of 'necrophilia'. Historians were attacked, too: for 'blackening the past', for 'violating the sanctity of national symbols' and for 'spiritual masochism'.

The conservatives' protesting voices were lost, however, in the exultant chorus of opposition. From the sociological point of view, all this ideological onslaught, carried out under the slogans of 'returning to the common values of mankind' (which implied rejecting 'class values') and 'debunking of the Stalinist model of socialism', was none other than dissemination of the values and ideals of pluralist democracy espoused by the preceding generation of dissident-minded intellectuals. The implantation of elements of the Western political culture that had begun in the 1950s and 1960s picked up speed in these circumstances, but, as is often the case, the deeper layers of mass political consciousness were affected by these dramatic changes to a much lesser degree than one would have judged by appearances.

The situation in the mass media as it appeared in the summer of 1988 did not reflect the actual alignment of social and political forces in the country. In the press the left-wing, opposition-minded intelligentsia was apparently the master. It did not exercise complete sway: a considerable number of newspapers and magazines were still controlled by the Communist Party, to say nothing of radio and television. But as far as popularity was concerned, the pro-party and pro-government media were no rivals to the opposition. This newly acquired independence of the press appeared shaky, however, and the ruling party still retained powerful means to influence the recalcitrants. The party's non-interference with the press depended largely

3 Released in 1986.
4 See Orlov 1989; in book form, Orlov 1991.
5 These two neologisms are modelled on commonly used abbreviations for publishing houses and can be translated as 'Self Publishers' and 'There Publishers', respectively, 'there' standing for 'abroad'.

on the reform-minded group within the party leadership – if, indeed, that patronage could be considered non-interference. Moreover, the question remained open of how long the reformers' dominance would be preserved. The conservative *coup de parti* (which implied a *coup d'état*) was a real threat. It was not surprising then that the intelligentsia perceived no opponents at first, apart from the party conservatives. The only exception made was for right-wing Russian nationalism. (As for the 'left-wing' nationalists, especially from the Baltic republics, they were considered a 'progressive' force and relied on as potential allies of democracy.)

Political forces that were not related either to the left-wing intelligentsia or to the party *nomenklatura* were initially not represented in the mass media at all. Their voice was yet to sound, but it remained rather indistinct at first. However, it was not necessary to be a prophet to foresee their entrance to the political scene before long.

These ostentatious changes in political consciousness, stimulated and attested by the press in the new conditions of *glasnost'*, affected mainly its most superficial, ideological level: discredited were, first and foremost, the communist slogans and ideals (and, naturally, the Communist Party itself). But these victories were easy. As regards the socio-ontological models that constitute the basis of mass political consciousness, the situation was more complicated. Political forces that patterned their behaviour on the old political culture would for a long time yet be able to draw on this resource – all the more so since the communist ideology itself had been superimposed on the traditional patterns of the national political mentality after the revolution, and the collapse of communist rule and the bankruptcy of communist ideology, therefore, did not necessarily invalidate the original patterns themselves.

As a result of these conflicting influences, an outside observer was presented with a picture of political reality that was a gross distortion. The political culture of intellectuals was in the foreground, but intellectuals were not the whole nation. The change in political mentality was not as fundamental as it appeared, and the rupture, however radical, with the communist ideals did not mean rupture with the communist political culture.

When the democratic opposition came to power a few years later, first locally and then on the national level, the democrats would have an opportunity to discover that their social support was not as extensive as the circulation of democratic press in the Golden Age of *glasnost'* might have implied. But the legacy of the pre-*perestroika* political culture was to be felt much earlier.

ONE STEP FORWARD, THREE STEPS BACK

The Preconditions of Political Reform

The 1988 constitutional reform paved the way for a radical transformation (*perestroika*) of the country's political system. If one were to ask oneself today how the leaders of a party that was not merely ruling but had a *constitutional monopoly* of power conceded a political reform that was bound to limit that party's influence and, moreover, threatened (as was soon discerned but was doubtless easy to guess in advance) the very existence of both the party and the regime that it headed, one would have to admit that the motives must have originated *inside* the party.

This does not mean that *outside* the top echelons of power all was peace and quiet. (We have already dealt with the crisis of the regime and its causes in the previous chapter.) But to admit that there was a social and political crisis does not amount to explaining – however grave the crisis was and however acute, therefore, was the need for reforms – why the impulse to reform was to come from, of all places, the leadership of the party that was mainly responsible (and could not help feeling responsible) for that crisis. The reforms were inescapable, indeed, but it would have been far more usual to expect the opposition to initiate them, rather than the establishment.

One might object, of course, that the totalitarian regime had reduced the opposition's political opportunities to almost nothing. Leaders of the opposition might have believed the reforms to be advisable or urgent, but it would not have been easy for them even to inform the people of their opinion, and even less to engage in practical activities. But the only conclusion to be drawn from the above argument was that the reforms were to be postponed 'indefinitely', that is until the regime crashed down, once and for all, under the burden of those problems it continued to create but had no longer the means to solve. Despite the fact that there was no other political force in the country able to initiate the reforms, it did not follow that, for want of something better, the party itself would do it. For this to occur, at least some of the party leaders had to realize that the regime was about to collapse anyway and that reforms could no longer be delayed.

But for this realization to be psychologically possible, it was not enough to perceive and recognize the general symptoms of the crisis. Politicians about to take such a hard and, if we are allowed the expression, unnatural decision must have had far more immediate reasons than the calculations of economists and the forecasts of political scientists. Before the owner of a house will cut the beams, the house must be ablaze – distant thunder will hardly make him raise the axe. Soviet decision-makers, too, must have viewed the crisis as a problem that was directly relevant to their everyday activities and everyday cares, and they brooked no delay. For the professional politicians who ruled the party – and through it the entire country – there was only one such problem: power.

The Crisis of Power

Only a crisis in the top echelons of the party leadership such as could not be managed in a traditional, familiar way could force a part of that leadership to enter upon dangerous political reforms. At the present moment we do not possess enough information to venture a systematic account of what was going on, so the following is but a hypothesis. Still, something must have been going on, and it must have been going on at the very top of the party hierarchy, otherwise the actions of the Politburo reformers would be incomprehensible. It must have had something to do with the traditional means of power consolidation: the mechanism of party rule that, it will be recalled, was the backbone of the Soviet political system proved to be failing. In the circumstances the decision to embark on the reforms must initially have been simply a move in the party's game of power. It proved something immensely more momentous only because the real crisis that afflicted Soviet society was not limited to the narrow circle of party functionaries and their professional problems, but spread out to affect almost every vital sphere of social life.

This latter circumstance, of course, was contributing to the crisis at the 'top'. It may also help explain the way it unfolded: it would be hard, indeed, to deny that the crisis of leadership was directly relevant to the more general crisis of the Soviet system and its social basis. The disunity within the party leadership, which would be absolutely inadmissible from the orthodox point of view (suffice it to mention the Tenth Congress's resolution 'On Party Unity'[6]), and would formerly have been suppressed by all available means, including repression, cannot be explained away by a mere statement to the effect that the party found itself at a crossroads. After all, it was not the first and only instance of this. In this case the situation was peculiar inasmuch as there appeared to be no alternative that the party, and particularly its leadership, could accept without reservation. The party leadership, therefore, must have felt itself not so much at a crossroads as at a dead end, for there were no groups inside it capable of exercising over the party apparatus the type of control that would have been tight enough to secure the unity demanded by the official doctrine and sanctified by long-standing tradition. Meanwhile, the Soviet political system was arranged in such a way that no state administration was possible unless this control was secured and this unity maintained.

The legitimacy of the communist regime, it should be recalled, rested on three bases: first, the doctrine of the revolutionary vanguard – a party of a new type, equipped with the best social theory available and able, therefore, to ensure scientific management of social affairs and optimal solutions of social problems; second, its claim to express and represent the interests of the true life-makers, the workers; third, the totalitarian patterns of mass political consciousness, rooted in the traditional political culture and, in the course of 'building socialism', adapted to fit the new socio-political circumstances. Of these three supports, two were shaken, if not destroyed. The ever growing economic difficulties and the social contradictions they were bound to aggravate, coupled with the authorities' obvious failure to find an acceptable way out of the difficulties, undermined the belief not only in the wisdom of the party leadership, but even in its genuine fidelity to 'the interests of the working people'. The notorious claim that 'the

6 'On Party Unity: Resolution of the Tenth Congress of the RCP(b), 8–16 March 1921', in *CPSU in Resolutions* (1983) 2, pp.334–7.

Party is the wisdom, honour and conscience of our era' elicited only mockery and irritation. The mass consciousness considered the authorities' alienation from the people an established fact, which would substantially diminish the authorites' manipulative power.

In Marxist jargon the situation could only be described as 'the eve of revolution'. Strange as it may seem, the regime, the revolution's most likely and most immediate victim, seemed to be almost relaxing. Whether those who headed the regime relied on its descent into revolution, or whether they believed in all seriousness that no revolution was possible unless prepared and guided by their 'new type' of party and, hence, by them personally: for whatever reason, the word 'revolution' did not frighten them – rather the opposite. Perhaps they were simply inspired by the approaching anniversary of the revolution, the seventieth. Or perhaps, they tried to be clever and counted on killing two birds with one stone: on the one hand, justifying the reforms they contemplated to their potential opponents among the party conservatives by presenting them as the final attainment of the yet unachieved or only partly achieved goals of the Great October; and, on the other hand, releasing the revolution, to which they traced their legitimacy, after all, from the stigma that had been left by decades of totalitarianism by dressing up the new and promising reforms in seventy-year-old slogans. Whatever the reason, they would indulge in revolutionary rhetoric again. 'The revolution continues,' Gorbachev suddenly asserted in his television address on New Year's Eve. 'The revolutionary spirit of the *perestroika* we have embarked on is the live breath of October.'[7] 'The party of the revolution is the party of *perestroika*,' he told Leningrad communists a few months later,[8] and his traditional report at the jubilee meeting on the convenient occasion of the revolution's seventieth anniversary linked the two again.[9] Nevertheless, on the eve of these jubilee celebrations the most impatient of the revolutionaries, Boris Yeltsin, was dismissed from his influential post of the First Secretary of the capital city's party committee, just to make sure.

7 Gorbachev 1987, p.275.
8 Gorbachev 1988b.
9 Gorbachev 1988a.

The Ideology of the Reform: Back to Lenin

To complete the sequence, when a year later the draft law on the constitutional reform promised by the Nineteenth Party Conference was at last made public, the reform appeared thoroughly 'disguised' as a restoration of the Soviet institutions of the revolutionary years. At any rate, the newly conceived institutions of power were to be endowed with attributes that were frankly modelled after patterns of October. It should not be supposed, of course, that the principal motive for these innovations (or should we rather say 'inveterations', since they were far from new) was nostalgia for the glorious past: there were more immediate and more practical considerations, and these will be discussed below. Still, it would be a mistake to ignore the pressing, critical need for a renewed legitimation of their power which the Gorbachev leadership doubtless felt. Whatever legitimacy the communist regime had acquired in the Stalin years was lost, and the new leaders themselves had had a hand in it. Any attempt to regain it on the old basis was impossible, of course, unless the entire policy was reconsidered, which implied rejection of the reforms in favour of a restoration of the old order. (It is hardly necessary to emphasize that in the circumstances, that is, taking into account the role the reformers had played in the process of 'de-Stalinization', this change of policy would also automatically imply a change of leadership.) But it was equally impossible for the General Secretary of the Communist Party Central Committee to make a complete break with the communist past. The only way out of the dilemma was to search that past for institutions and elements of the political system that, because they were not directly related to the notorious figure of Stalin, were not stigmatized by his regime. On these assumptions, the appeal to the pre-Stalinist period of Soviet history appeared natural.

Besides, the rhetoric of the revolutionary epoch proved singularly consonant with the attitudes that prevailed in the late 1980s, while slogans like 'Power to the Soviets, land to the peasants!' would make perfect sense when applied to the social and political realities of *perestroika*.

From the institutional standpoint, the principal innovation envisaged by the reform was the reorganization of the USSR Supreme Soviet into a bicameral representative body permanently in session.

The old Supreme Soviet used to meet only at regular intervals for short sessions to ratify without any undue logomachy - that is without going into the matter at all - decisions already taken elsewhere or elaborated without its participation. In between the sessions the Presidium of the Supreme Soviet was supposed to act as its substitute. It was invested with legislative powers and was even formally regarded as a collective head of state, although in the hierarchy of the central institutions of Soviet power it invariably occupied the last place: after the Party Central Committee and the Council of Ministers (the government). Many normative decisions would be issued in precisely this way, by 'the CPSU Central Committee, the USSR Council of Ministers and the Presidium of the USSR Supreme Soviet'. Its chairman was likewise the least influential person in the hierarchy, unless he was also the General Secretary, as was often the case in recent years. The new Supreme Soviet was to be convened twice a year, in spring and in autumn, to sessions three to four months long[10] - in other words, to be practically permanently in session. This was perceived as signalling the birth of 'Soviet parliamentarianism' to be awaited in the immediate future.[11] To Lenin, obsessed with the idea of a difference in principle between the Soviet and the parliamentary systems, the very expression would have sounded self-contradictory.

No less, and from the standpoint of a student of political culture perhaps even more radical, were the changes envisaged in the electoral procedure. The main innovation here was renunciation of the total control that the joint party-state apparatus was accustomed to exercising over every stage of the election campaign: from nominating candidates to tallying votes and framing the resolutions of the electoral or credentials commissions. Although sensational, this was an understandable decision: if an election was required to renew the legitimacy of the regime, it was indeed to be an election, not the usual 'festival of socialist democracy'. On the other hand however, a completely free election was fraught with the threat of the reformers' immediate loss of power: Gorbachev and his colleagues were subject to numerous attacks from various quarters. Free elections would give their opponents a perfect chance to rally around an anti-government

---

10 'Law of the Union of the Soviet Socialist Republics on Amendments and Supplements to the Constitution (Fundamental Law) of the USSR' (quoted from *Twelfth Session* 1988, p.195).

11 See Burlatsky 1988.

platform all those who felt discontented with the authorities, for whatever reason. This spontaneous coalition could unite those who opposed the reforms as a matter of principle with those who simply feared their unfavourable effects, and might even be reinforced by those who thought the reforms were either not radical enough, or not fast enough, or both.

Restoration of Traditions or Political Modernization?

In the circumstances the party leadership headed by Gorbachev was naturally tempted to retain at least a part of the manipulatory facilities allowed to the old regime, and this inevitably made the constitutional reform somewhat ambivalent. Having made a *leap forward* towards democracy, the reformers immediately countered it with *three steps back.*[12] The constitutional amendments, presented for public discussion in October 1988 and, notwithstanding a squall of protests, adopted a month later without substantial amendment by an extraordinary session of the Supreme Soviet, would restrict the citizens' electoral rights on three major points.

In the first place, the elections were to take place in at least two stages: the citizens were to elect directly the People's Deputies (2,250 in number) who would constitute the Congress of the People's Deputies to be convened once a year; the Congress would in its turn elect a bicameral Supreme Soviet (271 deputies in each chamber) – 'the permanent legislative, distributive and controlling organ of state power'.

In the second place, one-third (750) of the deputies were to be elected not in territorial constituencies but by 'public organizations': the Communist Party, the Young Communists' League (Komsomol), trade unions, organizations of women and of war and labour veterans, unions of creative workers, and the like. The distribution of seats among the various 'public organizations' was subject to Article 18 of the Law on Elections of the USSR People's Deputies, passed by the Supreme Soviet at the same session. One hundred mandates were to be reserved for the CPSU, 100 for trade unions and for cooperative societies; the Komsomol, the women's councils and organizations of war and labour veterans received 75 mandates each; the rest were to

12 The allusion is to Lenin's anti-Menshevik pamphlet *One Step Forward, Two Steps Back: The Crisis in Our Party* (Lenin 1965c).

be distributed between unions of 'scientific workers', unions of 'creative workers' and 'other' (unspecified) public organizations (75 mandates for each category; the Law did not specify the distribution of mandates within these categories, or criteria by which particular organizations were to be allocated to particular categories, or for that matter, whether they were to be allotted or denied deputy mandates at all).[13] Article 95 of the Constitution, as amended, provided for the public organizations to elect their deputies 'at their congresses, conferences or plenary sessions of their All-Union or republican organs'.[14]

Thirdly, Article 100 of the Constitution and, in elaboration thereof, Article 38 of the new statute on elections provided for the holding of *district pre-election meetings* (although this was only a *possibility*, for the regulation did not make the meetings obligatory) 'to discuss the candidates nominated in the district and to make decisions as to the candidates' presentation to the respective election commission for registration'.[15] The meetings were to be convened by the district election commissions, and since the latter were established by the respective Soviets or (as was much more common in real life) by their presidiums,[16] local officials were afforded ample opportunities to manipulate the election campaign: it was easy to stop a potential rival at an early stage, for even duly nominated candidates would not be formally registered and allowed to run in the election unless approved by the district pre-election meetings, whose convocation, membership and procedure depended almost entirely on the district commissions. In cases where the meeting was convened, its approval became a necessary condition for the candidate's registration,[17] although no legal regulation stipulated the permissible grounds for rejection. The law simply stated that the decisions were to be taken by majority vote (by show of hands or by secret ballot),[18] so whether they had a genuine reason or were quite arbitrary did not affect their legal status. The right of appeal was allowed against the meeting's decision to the local or the Central Election Commission, but concerning what the Commission's judgements were to be based on, the Law had nothing

13 *Law on Elections* 1988, pp.10–11 (Article 18).
14 *Constitution* 1988, p.32 (Article 95).
15 *Constitution* 1988, p.34 (Article 100); *Law on Elections* 1988, pp.27–8 (Article 38).
16 *Law on Elections* 1988, p.16 (Article 24).
17 *Law on Elections* 1988, p.30 (Article 40).
18 *Law on Elections* 1988, p.28 (Article 38).

to say, so that their decisions would be no less arbitrary.[19]

Equally confused were the legal requirements and legal consequences of another procedure mentioned by the Law on Elections: refusal to affirm a decision on nomination. A nomination could be revoked 'at any time before the election', and 'the respective election commission' was to be notified.[20] The Law, however, failed to specify what the election commission's actions were to be in such a case. This refusal to confirm a nomination might be thought to provide legal grounds for cancelling the registration, if that had already taken place, but there was no hint of that in the text. Arbitrary attitudes on the part of the Soviet officials were further encouraged by the fact that the legal status of institutions entrusted with nominating the candidates was far from clear. The right belonged to meetings (conferences) of 'work collectives', district and higher-level organs of public organizations, and meetings of voters at their place of residence and of servicemen. The nomination was valid if it was supported by more than half of the participants in the meeting or by the majority of members of the respective organ.[21] However, the procedural status of a work collective's meeting remained obscure: such meetings did not (and in most cases could not) enjoy steady attendance. This natural circumstance was fraught with almost insoluble identification conflicts. What was the position if members of a work collective were to meet again with some members absent and adopt an entirely different decision?

Such clashes were even more likely to occur if candidates were nominated at the meetings in residential districts. The voters' initiative was not enough for these meetings to be convened: this was the prerogative of 'the respective Soviets of People's Deputies or their Presidiums together with the district election commissions'.[22] Nomination, therefore, depended on whether or not the relevant local authorities were prepared to support the initiative. Meanwhile, their obligations in this respect were more than vague. A meeting was quorate and competent if it was attended by no fewer than 500 voters, but that was the only condition stipulated by the law. It was not clear

19 Ibid. The authority of the Central and district election commissions was subject to Articles 23 and 25 respectively (*Law on Elections* 1988, pp.14-15, 17-18).
20 Ibid., p.31 (Article 41).
21 Ibid., p.26 (Article 37).
22 Ibid,.

whether a separate group of voters was entitled to arrange another such meeting and, if they were, how they were to proceed.[23] Still more confusing was the question of who had the right to revoke the nomination in this case. It would have been totally unrealistic, of course, to expect all those who had been present at the resident voters' first meeting – the one that had nominated a candidate – to attend the second one convened to reconsider the original decision. What would the requirements be for the second meeting to be regarded as an assembly identical to the first one? Or was it possible for a group of voters 500-strong to veto a decision passed by another group of voters? What if the first company were to assemble again to reaffirm the original decision and revoke the revocation? The law-makers apparently never bothered to ask the question.

Was this carelessness (and the resulting confusion) a well-calculated trick of the would-be manipulators? Or are we to consider it a spontaneous outcome of the mentality of *sobornost'*? Although we do not assert that no manipulation was ever intended, we would rather opt for the second explanation. For the mind that dwells on these patterns would seldom care to 'operationalize' the procedures of collective decision-making: it tends to take consensus for granted. The only requirement is to provide for a 'sufficient' number of participants: once they come together, they will not fail to express their will (which, it should be borne in mind, is also the will of the 'people').

Public organizations, likewise, were not guaranteed against such clashes. Although their conferences and plenary sessions differed from the meetings of voters and work collectives inasmuch as there would usually exist some formal procedure by which membership of

23 It is worth recalling that in 1989 an ordinary (territorial) electoral district numbered some 300,000 voters. The number of voters registered in national territorial districts varied considerably, depending on the territory's status (whether its deputies were to represent a Union or an autonomous republic, an autonomous region or district) and its population. Since national territories were to be represented by a fixed number of deputies, the number of electoral districts depended on the territory's status, but not on its population. Therefore, territories that enjoyed no autonomous status would be divided into national electoral districts that were even greater than the ordinary territorial constituencies, especially if they were well populated. The Moscow national territorial district, for instance, had almost nine million inhabitants. Moreover, the entire personnel of Soviet embassies and other overseas institutions was registered in it, irrespective of domicile. Those who care to do so may try to calculate the number of combinations (500 out of 300,000, to say nothing of 7 or 8 million) the organizers of the resident voters' meetings could choose from.

their official organs was defined, and the membership itself tended to remain relatively stable throughout a fixed period of time, this did not mean that it could not be altered. It was quite possible (and in some cases it did happen) that a public organization would nominate a candidate who would, for some reason, prove undesirable and pressure would be brought to bear on the respective organ to revoke its decision. In case its members proved intractable, an attempt might be made to achieve the goal by replacing some of the key figures. This would be a natural and perfectly legitimate procedure in different circumstances, but since election campaigns are limited in time and large and complex organizations are somewhat sluggish, a small group of determined persons could undo the will of the majority. Besides, these electoral functions came out of the blue, and most organizations were not ready to carry them out. Sometimes the situation became ridiculous. There would be public organizations among those referred to by the law that did not qualify for the job at all: with loose membership and functions that had nothing to do with the problems of civil society, they had moreover no organs (and had apparently never been meant to have them) formed in a sufficiently democratic way to justify endowing them with the basic democratic right of electing the country's top legislative body. No such authority was delegated to them by the organizations' rank and file, at any rate, and in many cases there was no reason why it should have been. Their councils and committees were not necessarily elected, and if they could be said to represent the rank and file, that was only in the second sense identified by Birch.[24]

The constitutional reform of 1988 thus tended to restrict those very rights it was supposed to make real. Neither the 'Stalin' (or, as it is sometimes called, 'Bukharin') Constitution of 1936, nor the original version of the 'Brezhnev' Constitution of 1977, then in force, had provided for any such restrictions, for the simple reason this would have been unnecessary. Now Gorbachev and his colleagues were planning to hold – for the first time in Soviet history – a genuine election, instead of staging a phoney one as usual, but at the same time they deemed it necessary to 'insure' themselves against all conceivable risks. As a result, the Constitution and the Law on Elections were to be amended in such a way as to violate all

24 See above, p.8, Note 10.

guarantees of democratic election envisaged by classical democratic theory. The 1989 elections were to be neither direct, nor equal, nor free.

THE 1989 ELECTIONS

The Constitutional Puzzle

The Constitution and the Law on Elections provided for deputies to be elected 'on the basis of universal, equal, and direct suffrage by secret ballot',[25] but the interpretation of this provision might have given George Orwell a striking example of *doublethink*. This is because, although the respective articles of the Constitution (96, 97, 98) and the Law on Elections (2, 3, 4) directly applied the above principles only to elections in territorial constituencies, the provisions for public organizations were part of the same articles and went under the same headings.[26]

Let us begin with the principle 'one citizen - one vote' as a fundamental condition of equal suffrage. That principle was enshrined both in the Constitution (Article 97) and in the Law on Elections (Article 3). Each voter was to have one vote, and all voters were to exercise the franchise on an equal footing: men and women, servicemen and other citizens. But these provisions would make sense only if applied to territorial constituencies. In public organizations the franchise was held by delegates to congresses and conferences or participants in plenary sessions: it was they who had 'one vote' each. It was an Orwellian situation once again: all citizens were equal (in principle), but some would be 'more equal' than others, or, at any rate, would turn out 'equally' more often, according to how many times they would exercise their franchise.[27]

The new version of the Constitution would allow some citizens a good dozen additional votes, besides those they shared with the majority of ordinary voters. They would vote in one territorial and

25 Article 95 of the Constitution and Article 1 of the Law on Elections (see *Constitution* 1988, pp.31-2; *Law on Elections* 1988, p.3).

26 See *Constitution* 1988, pp.32-3; *Law on Elections* 1988, pp.4-5.

27 172,800,000 voters came to elect 750 deputies in territorial and 750 deputies in national territorial districts on 26 March 1989. The average was 230,400 voters per candidate. The 750 seats allocated to public organizations were distributed by 16,200 persons in

one (or two, in the autonomous areas) national territorial polling district, like all the rest. But the luckiest of them might also have a chance to elect deputies: (a) of the Communist Party in his or her capacity as member of the party's Central Committee; (b) of the Young Communist League, in a similar capacity; (c) of the trade unions, in the capacity of member of the Presidium of the All-Union Central Council of Trade Unions; (d) of cooperative societies, as a member of an administration board; (e) of women's councils, as a member of the Committee of Soviet Women; (f) of war and labour veterans, as a member of the All-Union Council of Veterans' Organizations; (g) of the USSR Academy of Sciences, in the capacity of member of the Academy Presidium; (h) of the Union of Scientific and Engineering Societies; (i) of the All-Union Society of Inventors and Rationalizers; (j) of the Union of Architects; (k) of the Union of Designers; (l) of the Union of Journalists; (m) of the Union of Cinematographists; (n) of the Union of Composers; (o) of the Union of Writers; (p) of the Union of Theatre Workers; (q) of the Union of Artists; (r) of the Soviet Peace Committee, and so on and so forth.

It would be not easy to combine all these positions, of course, but we have enumerated more than a dozen (and even then not all of them) and there was no law against this kind of 'pluralism'. It was not particularly plausible, but by no means inconceivable: suffice it to recall Brezhnev's diverse ambitions. Moreover, some of the above positions were not only compatible, but interdependent: top Komsomol leaders or trade union officials would 'naturally' belong to the top party leadership. This was also true of most other organizations, for it was precisely what the system of *nomenklatura* implied. At any rate, at least some citizens did have more votes than the rest.

Even if, for whatever reason, election by public organizations were accepted, to provide for equal suffrage one would have to secure either each citizen's membership of each of these organizations (which is obviously ridiculous), or the even distribution of citizens among them. In that case everyone would have if not one then at least an equal number of votes. Otherwise perfectly improbable clashes would be unavoidable. 'Soviet women', for instance, were allocated

---

total, hence the average was 21.6 voters per candidate (see Boris Gidaspov, 'Report of the Credentials Commission to the First Congress of the USSR People's Deputies', 25 May 1989, in *First Congress* 1989 1, p.42.

75 deputy mandates, while 'Soviet men' were allowed none. The reason was there were *women's councils* in the country, that were 'united' by 'the Committee of Soviet Women' (although they by no means elected it), but no one had ever cared to establish *men's councils* and unite them under the auspices of a 'Committee of Soviet Men'. Meanwhile, Article 3 of the statute on elections provided for equal suffrage for both sexes. Who would manage to explain why stamp collectors had to be represented in the national legislature and coin collectors not? And what if dog-breeders, flower-growers, match-box label collectors and football fans established their 'Union-wide' organizations and demanded suffrage for them?

But the problem was not just that some citizens might have been members of public organizations and some not, or that some organizations might have been granted the right to elect that was denied to others. Violation of equality went deeper. Even *within* organizations endowed with electoral functions, the franchise would not be exercised by all members on an equal basis. It was the prerogative of but a few: of the 'delegates to congresses and conferences, or participants of plenary sessions',[28] that is of those whom Russians would call *nachal'stvo* (which stands for the 'authorities' or the 'leadership' but often sounds subtly ironic).

Besides, in most public organizations, if not all, the election of the central organs was usually a complicated multi-stage process, and the relevant procedures could be called 'democratic' only in a pretty ironic sense. Again, that was natural enough: if one were to be elected a member of the Academy of Sciences, it would be ridiculous to insist on 'universal and equal suffrage', since this is an elite organization *par excellence*. Philatelists, too, are not obliged to be 'democrats' if they do not wish it. Different organizations serve different purposes and have different functions. It is only natural that they should have different structures modelled after different prototypes. The state may also be considered an organization – with specific purposes and functions and not to be modelled after just anything. It was neither the Academy's fault, nor the Philatelic Society's, that their statutes failed to provide for a proper level of internal democracy: professional associations and exclusive clubs should simply not have been entrusted with state functions.

28 Article 96 of the Constitution and Article 2 of the Law on Elections (see *Constitution 1988*, p.32; *Law on Elections 1988*, p.4).

What of the principle of *direct* suffrage? The constitutional amendments provided for a two-step election of the Supreme Soviet. Nevertheless, Article 98 (mirrored by Article 4 of the Law on Elections) defined the elections as direct on the ground that People's Deputies (but *not* members of the Supreme Soviet) were to be elected by citizens 'by direct vote'.[29] It is not surprising in the circumstances that in the constitutional newspeak even public organizations, whose statutes manifestly provided for a succession of elections to their organs at different levels, were said to hold direct election, too, because delegates were to elect their deputies 'by direct ballot'.

Restrictions on Political Freedoms

Last, but not least, the election was not to be *free*. We have already mentioned the restrictions that district pre-election meetings imposed on the franchise. The meetings proved effective at first, and on the whole they may be said to have justified the hopes of those who 'invented' them. In most constituencies the preliminary 'sifting' of undesired candidates proved so successful that the outcome was, for all practical purposes, determined in advance.[30] Of the 9,505 nominees only 5,074 were registered and allowed to run for office, including 2,195 in territorial electoral districts (by 10 March 1989, that is at the end of the election's initial stage, only 1,449), and 1,967 in national territorial districts (1,446 by the close of the initial stage).[31] In some constituencies voters were left with no alternative at all: in 384 districts out of 1,500 there was only one candidate registered (the second phase added 15 more, out of 198, yielding a total of 399 districts).[32] In most districts (953) there were only two competitors, and only in 163 districts were the voters allowed to choose among more than two candidates.[33]

However, public resentment over such a crude manipulation proved so strong that in those districts where elections had to be repeated, district commissions hesitated to stage pre-election meetings a second

29 *Constitution* 1988, p.33 (Article 98); *Law on Elections* 1988, p.5 (Article 4).
30 For details see Troyan 1990.
31 See Gidaspov 1989, p.41; Karpenko 1990b, p.56.
32 See Karpenko 1990b, p.57, and Karpenko 1990a, p.80; Gidaspov 1989, p.41.
33 See Karpenko 1990b, p.57. When the voting was repeated there were, respectively, 13 and 170 such districts out of 190 (see Karpenko 1990a, p.80).

time. As a result, 1,216 candidates competed for the remaining 198 deputies' mandates on 14 May.[34] If on the average, therefore, fewer than two rivals contended for one territorial mandate on 26 March (1,449 candidates in 750 territorial districts, and 1,446 candidates in 750 national territorial districts), seven weeks later there would be more than six. But these districts were not very numerous, for the election was to be repeated only where it had failed to yield a result the first time round – for example, because the voters had boycotted it. By the time the election campaign was resumed in a number of constituencies, the district pre-election meetings had been discredited irrevocably. They turned out to be a disposable *ad hoc* institution. But had that not been the intention from the very beginning?

The resident voters' meetings were not an easy enterprise, either, but as a means of manipulating the election they proved much less effective. That was because voters could resort to alternative nomination procedures, above all through 'work collectives'. Election statistics are revealing: only 282 candidates out of 9,505 were nominated by resident voters' meetings, doubtless because the procedure was both tedious and frustrating.[35] This kind of local politics was a totally unfamiliar phenomenon, and people simply lacked the required operational experience. For decades Soviet public life revolved around the places where people work. Not only had the original Soviet electoral system been based on delegating deputies from industrial factories and military units (a practice that was later abandoned), but these were also the *loci* of all party and hence of all other public activities.

It may have been this tradition that inspired the law-makers when the respective provisions for nomination were introduced, and much evidently depended on the constraints administrations and party committees could impose on their subordinates to secure compliance. However, the control they were able to exercise over the nomination process proved not tight enough in the circumstances, and when the

34 Pre-election meetings were held in only 74 districts out of 198 (37 per cent), compared to 836 districts out of 1500 (56 per cent) at the first stage (ibid.) One should, moreover, take into account the considerable number of districts where the number of nominees had never been more than two: usurpation of voters' rights would have been so blatant in the circumstances that the Law on Elections envisaged no pre-election meetings in such districts.

35 See Gidaspov 1989, p.41.

rear-line barrier of district pre-election meetings fell by the time the election campaign entered its second phase, it turned out that it was possible to nominate practically anyone. (When republican and local elections were held a year later, so many candidates were nominated in almost every constituency that voters found it difficult even to remember all their candidates, to say nothing about distinguishing their programmes. The procedure was appropriate enough within the framework of the old culture, but, like many other elements of its operational experience, was rapidly growing more and more obsolete, not to say irrational. But the ontological beliefs on which it was based remained very much alive and were soon to prompt the idea of endowing the work collectives with the power to elect, not simply to nominate.)

The most abusive restrictions, however, were again related to the notorious elections by public organizations. Those were multi-mandate elections, and that fact gave the officials of the presumably independent bureaucracies a chance to excel in their professional skills and activate the traditional pre-*perestroika* mechanism of *election by list*. In the decades of party rule the procedure had been perfected beyond reproof and was practically faultless. The trick is, indeed, quite simple: advantage is taken of the fact that voters need not choose *between* the candidates. In a single-mandate election a citizen can only give his or her vote once, that is, vote for only one of the candidates: 'Ballot-papers with more than one candidate left on them' are not valid, according to the law.[36] No names need be struck off the multi-mandate ballot paper, however. The candidates that happen to be at the top of the list (within the limit set by the number of mandates) are considered elected, provided they receive more than half of the votes.[37] The result is invariable: 'outsiders' (candidates unknown or almost unknown to voters) become 'favourites', who usually outpoll their better-known rivals for the simple reason that no one is likely to have a grudge against a perfect stranger and hence would care to vote against him or her. By contrast, the more famous a candidate is, the worse are his or her chances.

That the procedure was ridiculous was a point of common affirmation. Nevertheless, it was cherished and preserved as a most

36 *Law on Elections* 1988, p.39 (Article 54).
37 Ibid., pp.41–2 (Article 56).

useful means of securing election for candidates who would stand no chance in fair competition. In most cases, in order to lose such an election, it was necessary to attract more negative than positive votes. However, since voters did not have to cross anyone's name out, that was not likely to happen very often. Under this system the number of candidates who got more than half of the votes was almost invariably equal to the number of names on the ballot paper. In other words, if not everyone could rely on the voters' support, anyone could count on the voters' indifference. Voters might blackball an utterly despicable person, of course, but then it would be hard to invent an election system that could pilot the wretched individual through the reefs of universal hatred. There are limits to everything: if no one likes you, you should make sure you are not nominated. Such cases are, however, always an exception. On the other hand, even if you have a dangerous rival and run the risk of getting fewer votes than him, you retain a fair chance of still getting more favourable than negative votes. And if the number of mandates is fixed and you, in your capacity as political leader, are unpopular enough to fall below the margin, you may seek consolation in the fact that the same will be also true of your adversary (and for the same reason), unless he just happens to be lucky.

But then it would not be fair to treat a candidate who has got more than 50 per cent of the vote as if he had no electoral support. And it seems inappropriate to assume that a leader has lost an election when the majority has voted for him, so that changing the original number of mandates appears a clever way out. Internal regulations would usually provide for the possibility of increasing the quota after the event, so as to make the membership of the elected body match the result of the voting. The voting assembly would be presented with an alternative either to lower the bar and admit as elected all those who have received more than 50 per cent of the vote, or else repeat the whole procedure, beginning with nomination and most probably ending up just as before. No wonder, then, if the weary voters eagerly opted for the first solution. The results of the voting would not be definitive, therefore: they would not only allow, but would indeed presuppose, subsequent manoeuvres and transactions.

If, for some reason, these were impossible after the event, they would have to be conducted in advance. If, for example, the number of mandates was fixed and could not be adjusted after the election, as was the case for People's Deputies, the number of candidates would have to be manipulated. For political leaders desirous of being elected it would be both vital and possible – since they were, by definition, well-known and influential persons – to provide for the number of names to be put on the ballot paper to match the number to be elected, and thus to prevent their own defeat. That would, however, reduce the election to a highly decorous procedure of nomination followed by symbolic casting of votes, with the outcome invariably prepared in advance. The real job was done behind closed doors in the course of secret negotiations between the candidates and the various groups of influentials that stood behind them. As for the voters, their only task is to approve (or, much less likely, to disapprove) the would-be representatives, carefully selected by the bosses. The procedure does not deserve being called an election. It is purely formal and, but for its symbolic function, totally meaningless. But then what else can it be? The system cannot work unless the outcome is predetermined. It is manipulative and plebiscitary from the very beginning.

Still, it was in this fashion that one-third of the deputies were 'elected' in the spring of 1989. When the Communist Party was voting for its deputies at a plenary session of its Central Committee, there were precisely one hundred candidates for the one hundred seats allocated to it. Not a person more, not a person less! But for this prudent arrangement, Gorbachev might well have lost the election, as would a number of other prominent nominees. The published voting data allow no doubt about what the outcome would have been, had the nomination process not been kept duly in check.[38]

38 In this 'election', 641 Central Committee members voted for candidates at the plenary session in question, and all nominees won by overwhelming majorities. The lowest support was recorded for Yegor Ligachev (563 votes against 78). Mikhail Gorbachev received 12 'no' votes to 629 'yes' and, since 14 individuals had more votes than 12 votes against them, Gorbachev 'took' the fifteenth place, as it were (see 'The Results of the Election of the USSR People's Deputies from the Communist Party of the Soviet Union: Information of the Election Commission for Election of USSR People's Deputies from the CPSU, 15 March 1989' in *Materialy Plenuma (1989)*, pp. 18–26). The public organizations had 912 registered candidates for 750 seats (see Gidaspov 1989, p.41), which gives an average of 1.2, compared to 1.9 (in March) and 6.1 (in May) in the territorial constituencies. If, therefore, the ratio of candidates to seats in the Communist Party had been equal even to the average for the public organizations only, there would

Still more unseemly was the compilation of the candidates' list in the Academy of Sciences: out of more than one hundred duly nominated candidates, the enlarged session of the Presidium held on 18 January allowed only 23 to run in the election, despite the fact that the quota of the Academy was 25.[39] We would call that overdoing it!

However, the procedure could be used to blackball an undesired candidate just as well, his or her standing being instrumental in the defeat. When the Russian Federation later nominated twelve candidates to run for the eleven seats allocated to it in the Soviet of Nationalities (at the First Congress of the USSR People's Deputies), the one 'extra' name on the roll proved enough for Boris Yeltsin, of all the contestants, to lose the election, even though he got the required 50 per cent of the vote: 1,195 against 964.[40] The resulting scandal had to be settled by means that were, constitutionally, more than questionable.[41]

The Purpose of the Reform

Viewing the constitutional reform from the standpoint of political culture, it must be admitted that its results were pretty ambivalent. It

---

have been 20 candidates who would have lost. The voting results being what they were, none of those who got more than 8 'no' votes would have been elected. Besides Gorbachev and Nikolai Ryzhkov (10 votes against), these would have been the remaining eight members and candidate members of the Politburo, including all Central Committee's Secretaries, namely, Lev Zaikov, Yegor Ligachev, Vadim Medvedev, Viktor Nikonov, Georgy Razumovsky, Nikolai Slyunkov, Viktor Chebrikov, Aleksandr Yakovlev (59 against, and the second worst result), and the editors-in-chief of *Pravda* and *Izvestiya* Viktor Afanasiev and Ivan Laptev. The results should not be interpreted as indicative of particular opposition attitudes among the Central Committee members: there were casualties on both sides. The potential 'losers' would have included a number of popular figures who remained relatively uninvolved with the party *nomenklatura* and enjoyed the reputation of 'progressives': the writers Chingiz Aitmatov and Daniil Granin, the dramatic actor Mikhail Ulyanov, ophthalmologist S.Fedorov, and some representatives of the scientific elite such as Academicians Leonid Abalkin (an economist), G.Marchuk (President of the Academy of Sciences) and Yevgenii Primakov (political scientist). The voters would have simply heard of them. By contrast, a great number of totally unfamiliar candidates, including those yet to become famous (for example, S.Umalatova), might have claimed unanimous support.

39 See Davydov 1990.
40 See the information of Yuri Osipyan, Chairman of the Electoral Commission, on the results of the election of the Soviet of Nationalities in *First Congress* 1989 1, pp.201, 211-12, 221.
41 See *First Congress* 1989 1, pp.424-33.

could hardly have been the reformers' initial intention to introduce pluralist democracy modelled on Western patterns. They had rather meant to create a system of *controlled democracy*. If it is objected that the expression is a *contradictio in adjecto*, we can only refer to what has been said of the populist interpretation of democracy and the model of representative power defined as *sobornost'* in the preceding chapters. The Congress of People's Deputies was conceived and established as a purely plebiscitary body, and an easily manipulable one at that. It would allow the executive power to pay lip-service to the separation of powers and maintain a representative institution that looked like a parliament, while at the same time having the last word in legislation: the Congress was to be superior to the Supreme Soviet and entitled to overrule the latter's decisions. Whoever mastered the Congress would command its authority.

The constitutional reform, therefore, sought new forms of control over legislative power, rather than a radical *perestroika* of the political system. Hitherto that control had been based on party discipline: all deputies had been subject to it, one way or another. To maintain it, it had been necessary to control the formation of the corps of deputies and, indeed, the entire process of elite recruitment. In a crisis of legitimacy, that had ceased to be either possible or desirable.

The reform, as it had been conceived, was meant to serve a double goal of recovering legitimacy without losing political supremacy. On the one hand, the ruling party elite was to enjoy the privilege of convening and, if necessary, of relying on (or hiding behind) an authoritative elected, rather than selected, legislative assembly. On the other hand, that assembly was not to become genuinely, or at least excessively, independent. What was required was an agency of nation-wide and presumably sincere approval. A Supreme Soviet to be formed on the basis of a two-stage election and a gargantuan, and therefore conveniently helpless, Congress towering above it would answer the purpose perfectly. The Supreme Soviet was to pass for a parliament, while the Congress would act as the pre-*perestroika* Supreme Soviet. Besides, the party *nomenklatura*, forced in the circumstances to give up some of its power and forgo some of its usual privileges, would be decently recompensed with the deputies' mandates and the accompanying set of gentlemanly perquisites – immunity from prosecution, preferences in everyday matters and so on – without having to bear the troublesome burden of real legislative work.

It is difficult to say whether there was more ingenuity in the whole project or more hypocrisy. On the one hand, presented for use by the people were the arguments that would ostensibly appeal to the culture of *sobornost'*: the greater the number of deputies, the closer they stand to the people; and the better (or the more fully) the people's wisdom is represented, the more the nation may depend on it. On the other hand, reserved for private use was the cynical and manipulative attitude towards the would-be legislature that served to promote the ruling elite's particular interests: the more 'populous' the Congress, the less capable it is of self-organization and, hence, the more easily it can be managed by shadowy – that is, party – structures.

And if all this artful construction were to fail in a couple of years, the reason would be the loss of control over significant social forces outside it. But there was nothing to be done about it: the built-in mechanisms of elite control, so laboriously devised for the new representative institutions, proved altogether inadequate for a task on that scale.

In this perspective it would not appear surprising that the long-term effect of the election, despite its ostensibly unsensational and, for the authorities, reasonably successful outcome,[42] proved far more profound and more significant than the formal, albeit exalted, constitutional innovations. It was the election that helped to mobilize strong and ambitious social groups, over which the party elite subsequently had no control. The rest would depend on what mentality the groups in question would bring to the surface of political life.

---

42 Of the 2,249 deputies elected by the opening of the First Congress, 1,957 (87 per cent) were members or candidate (probationary) members of the Communist Party. Of these, 237 (10.5 per cent) were party workers, from local party secretaries to members of the Central Committee and the Politburo. That was one of the largest professional groups represented in the corps of deputies. For comparison, the industrial elite held 6.8 per cent of the seats; the agrarian elite, 8.5 per cent; scientists and educationalists together, 14.1 per cent; medical workers, 4.3 per cent; workers in the fields of culture, art and mass media together, 9.1 per cent; servicemen, 3.6 per cent; ecclesiastics, 0.3 per cent; rank-and-file workers and peasants together, 23.7 per cent (see Gidaspov 1989, pp.44–5).

5 *Sobornost'* versus Parliamentarianism

> *The way out of parliamentarianism is not, of course, the abolition of representative institutions and the elective principle, but the conversion of the representative institutions from talking-shops into 'working' bodies.*
>
> — V.I. Lenin, *The State and Revolution.*
>
> *In statesmanship get the formalities right, never mind about the moralities.*
>
> — Mark Twain, *Pudd'nhead Wilson's New Calendar.*

'IDLE TALK' VERSUS 'REAL WORK'

The Dispute over the Agenda

After the dramatic election campaign of 1989 the country witnessed another equally dramatic event. Even though the democratic opposition had been able to achieve impressive results only in a few big cities, notably Moscow and Leningrad, and could count on no more than two or three hundred votes out of more than two thousand, the opening of the Congress was almost universally expected to boost the democratic reforms. After all, almost all leaders of the democratic opposition had won the election in their respective constituencies and gained access to the parliamentary rostrum. The opposition had managed to succeed even in some 'public organizations', where its positions had been particularly strong, such as the Academy of Sciences and the unions of 'creative workers', dominated naturally by the intelligentsia. Relapse into the old lethargy seemed impossible in the circumstances. The general agitation would be kindled, moreover, by significant historical parallels: it was 1989, the bicentennial of the Great Revolution, and, like *Les États généraux* two centuries ago, the Congress was opening in May.

The country was in an unprecedented state of suspense, glued to television sets. There was even a joke circulating about the Congress provoking the first nation-wide political strike for decades. (At any rate, when the question was later raised of broadcasting the sessions of the Second Congress, Gorbachev referred to a twenty per cent drop in productivity in the days of the First Congress.[1]) The First Congress of the USSR People's Deputies turned out to have little in common with an ordinary parliamentary session. It would rather resemble a mass rally, made nation-wide thanks to the direct television broadcast. After years of imposed silence the opportunities appeared fantastic: the deputies were pushing their way to the microphones, eager to deliver their speeches with programmes to save the country.

However, it is not our intention to chronicle the event here. What we are concerned with is presenting a socio-cultural portrait of the Congress, assembled from those psycho-ideological elements that an inquiry into the deputies' political behaviour, and particularly into their political rhetoric, promises to reveal.

In our analysis of the political culture, as it manifested itself at the Congress, we have found it expedient to follow the general approach outlined in our Introduction. We shall ask questions that refer to all three of its basic elements, namely, the operational experience, the values and the social ontology. For this we shall review the parliamentary debates in terms of: (1) the nature and purpose of parliamentary activity; (2) the basic values of parliamentary culture; (3) the patterns of deputies' self-identification, as indicative of their socio-ontological beliefs. We shall then attempt: (4) to draw conclusions that might help us understand the internal logic of the subsequent development.

Let us consider first the question of procedure. It was on an issue of this kind, incidentally, that the first skirmish was to occur at the

1 See *Second Congress* 1990 1, p.184.

Congress. The agenda, prepared the day before by an assembly of representatives of territorial groups and presented by Nursultan Nazarbayev, then Chairman of Kazakhstan's Council of Ministers, provided for the election of the Chairman of the Supreme Soviet, and of his First Deputy and of the Supreme Soviet itself (items 2-4), before Mikhail Gorbachev, the obvious candidate for the office, made his report 'On the principal orientations of the USSR domestic and foreign policy' (Item 5). The proposal evoked objections on the part of Academician Andrei Sakharov, who saw in it 'a violation of the natural order'. 'First discussion and presentation of the candidates' platforms and then elections,' he said.[2] He was supported by Gavriil Popov, who characterized the proposed election of deputies to the Supreme Soviet without discussing their political standpoints first as 'a departure from such democratic principles as genuine secret ballot and choice between alternative candidates'.[3] The procedure was consistent with the Constitution, he admitted, and was in that sense 'natural', but that only meant that the Constitution itself had to be amended.

Their general message was that accepting the proposed agenda would make the Congress an assembly of electors. Incidentally, those were precisely the words that Sakharov used. His concern was about the powers and status of the Congress. One of his opponents chose to view it from the practical standpoint. Why deliver and discuss the report before the election, if there was but one candidate, supported, moreover, by the Moscow deputies themselves? 'To listen to the future Chairman of the Supreme Soviet, we must first invest him with authority. ... For we cannot listen to idle promises here, we must know what will be backed by deeds.'[4] Here the account of the proceedings registers 'applause'.

Difference in the Deputies' Operational Experience

That was the first occurrence of the two crucial words that the deputies were to hear repeated many times. Opposing 'deeds' to 'words', or 'real work' to 'idle talk', soon became a figure of speech most popular with the deputies. This rhetorical stance might have

2 Sakharov's speech at the first sitting (25 May) (*First Congress* 1989 **1**, p.10).
3 Popov's speech at the first sitting (25 May) (*First Congress* 1989 **1**, p.12).
4 Deputy Meshalkin's speech at the first sitting (25 May) (*First Congress* 1989 **1**, p.14).

served some pragmatic goals, of course, but this does not mean it was a mere pose. On the contrary, it was rooted in and was, in turn, intended to invoke the existing patterns of the political mentality. Its particular occurrence may have been motivated by purely tactical considerations; it may even have been instigated by interested persons, but the fact was that it appealed to both the audience inside the Kremlin and the public outside it. At any rate, a call to 'stop the chatter' and 'start working' would invariably be met with applause.

A few more examples. No sooner had Deputy Obolensky (a geophysicist from the northern town of Apatity and later one of the founders of the Russian Social Democratic Party) put himself up for the chairmanship of the Supreme Soviet – the only one, indeed, to challenge Gorbachev – than he was accused of wasting time: his own and that of the people. 'The country is on an edge, and we begin to indulge in empty talk.'[5]

A day later a proposal was discussed to suspend the regulations that restricted the freedom of assembly for the period of the Congress. A deputy interrupted the debate with the following statement:

> I am a driver. Daily during my shift I drive great numbers of people of different nationalities, different origins and different professions. And from everybody's lips I hear that our people face so many problems to be solved today. And we indulge in demagogy here. We have come here to work, after all, not to engage in demagogy. Comrades, come to your senses, what are you doing? Our precious time is being wasted absolutely uselessly. After all, we must do what is to be done, work we must, comrades! [*Applause.*][6]

The next day a deputy raised the question again, this time on behalf of his 'numerous electors': 'We are sick of the twaddle, they say. When will you turn to concrete matters?'[7]

One more example:

> It seems to me, there is a lack of understanding here that we have engaged in the wrong business. My electors – and I have been elected by an All-Union

5 Deputy Korshunov's speech at the second sitting (25 May) (*First Congress* 1989 1, p.96).
6 Deputy Akbarov's speech at the third sitting (26 May) (*First Congress* 1989 1, p.117). It is interesting to observe that this speech and the one cited in the preceding paragraph belonged to members of the same deputation (territorial group): both speakers were from Tashkent. However, even if there was someone to 'encourage' them, their speeches sounded sincere enough.
7 Deputy Sazonov's speech at the fourth sitting (27 May) (*First Congress* 1989 1, pp.277-8).

organization - have sent me here to solve basic questions. That is, to form our government bodies and to solve immediately the following question at least: to feed and to provide with elementary living facilities those who have endured industrialization, collectivization, the repressions, the Great Patriotic War and the rehabilitation of the national economy. ... To work! We must work! Really - and all of us![8]

Note a curious detail: the same speaker, and in that very speech, suddenly called on them 'immediately to set about elaborating an approach to the education of Man in socialist society', because 'since the times of Peter I [*sic*] no one would attend to the education of Man in this country'.[9]

On second thoughts, however, a digression is not so surprising: a desire to 'educate' and resentment about 'idle talk' appear to arise from the common set of beliefs.[10] It was not long before 'twaddle' acquired 'democratic' as its regular epithet.[11]

What kind of 'work' was it to which the deputies were entreated to devote themselves, and what would be called 'idle talk'? Let us begin with the second question. If we compare the contexts of the above-quoted or similar statements, we discover that the expression would be applied without fail to any attempt to bring up a general political or procedural issue: the former if it was not directly on the agenda but emerged in the course of debate, the latter almost invariably. Besides, it would become a routine rhetorical device to accuse (or pretend to suspect) an opponent of raising a particular question with the exclusive intention of 'wrecking the Congress', 'hampering its work' or 'leading it astray'. The first to resort to it was none other than Gorbachev himself, and the first to be accused was Yuri Boldyrev, a Leningrad engineer, who suggested registering the votes on all issues except personal matters in order to give the voters information about their deputies' stands.[12] Gorbachev chose to view it as 'one of the attempts to draw us into something the Congress must not be drawn

8 Deputy Obraz's speech at the fourth sitting (27 May) (*First Congress* 1989 1, pp.284, 286).
9 Ibid., p.285.
10 See Chapter 2, Note 33.
11 Deputy Samsonov's speech at the fourth sitting (27 May) (*First Congress* 1989 1, p.305).
12 Yuri Boldyrev's speech at the first sitting (25 May) (*First Congress* 1989 1, p.17).

into'.[13] It might have been this remark of his that induced someone to send a note to the presidium:

> Certain deputies' attempts to lead the Congress into a discussion of procedural questions are very harmful. This will not earn our Congress prestige with the voters, even with those voters who elected Comrades Sakharov, Boldyrev and others. The people are waiting to see how the Congress is going to solve the basic problems of life; Congress must therefore be asked whether those who actively contribute to the disorganization of the Congress's work are to be given the floor for the third or the fourth time.[14]

These charges soon became a regular feature[15] and would sometimes assume a very dramatic form. Since elections of the Chairman of the Supreme Soviet had been delayed (presumably through the fault of those democratic chatterboxes), one of the deputies argued, the country had been left without a Head of State for a full thirteen hours. Just imagine what might have happened![16]

One might be puzzled, indeed, by the apparent contradiction. Since you insist on doing a 'real job', why object to it being done thoroughly? Did those who wanted to listen to and discuss what the candidates for both the chairmanship and the membership of the Supreme Soviet had to say before casting their votes aim at wrecking the elections? Would not serious consideration of parliamentary procedures eventually facilitate and expedite the work of them all? Would not imperfect procedures lead to the very waste of time the champions of 'deeds' sought to prevent? A deputy later interjected, with reference to the election of the Chairman: 'The situation now is a little bit ridiculous, indeed. We are discussing the report Mikhail Sergeyevich [Gorbachev] hasn't yet delivered. [*Applause.*] You see, events have forced us to have a discussion on the substance first. Let it be a lesson to us.'[17]

Still, not everyone would accept that conclusion or notice the above contradiction. To recognize it, one had to proceed from different assumptions, to have a different understanding of parliamentarians'

13 Ibid.

14 The note was sent by Deputies Gorinov and Karpochev, from the Mari Republic (see *First Congress* 1989 1, p.27).

15 See, for example, speeches by Deputies Mamedov and Kravchenko at the fourth sitting (27 May) (*First Congress* 1989 1, pp.238, 289–90).

16 Deputy Meshalkin's speech at the fourth sitting (27 May) (*First Congress* 1989 1, p.237).

17 Deputy Palm's speech at the fourth sitting (27 May) (*First Congress* 1989 1, p.302).

tasks and to attach a different meaning to parliamentary 'work'. Those were the differences that accounted for the mutual misunderstanding and the vehement polemics that resulted from it. The majority firmly believed that whatever might be worth being called 'real work' was by no means being done right there at the Congress: it could only be done elsewhere. They had no objections to becoming 'a congress of electors', a prospect Sakharov might abhor. They had come to the Kremlin to do what should be done there, since that had, for some reason, turned out to be necessary, but to do it as quickly as possible. And then they would leave and attend to 'real matters'.[18] Parliamentary work itself was of no interest to them: they would hardly concede calling it 'work' at all. Their vision of a representative assembly was still that of a 'talking shop', not a 'working body'. They would not be convinced by Anatoly Sobchak's argument that it was not just solving minor procedural issues they were engaged in, but laying the foundation of a new political order.[19]

One should not have been surprised in the circumstances to hear a manager of a Moscow plant (already referred to above) retort to Yuri Afanasyev and Gavriil Popov's expressed disappointment at the results of the election to the Supreme Soviet, just then made public, with a proposal that the latter take a job at his plant and organize there what he was 'preaching' instead of 'nattering away at the matter in hand with democratic twaddle'.[20] Some deputies doubted whether it made sense to have a parliament at all. An objection was even raised to having an election to the Supreme Soviet: 'What do we want to create? Two Supreme Soviets virtually – the Congress and the Soviet – or a really working agency of the People's Deputies? There ought to be a Presidium of the Congress of People's Deputies and no Supreme [Soviet], and two sessions of the Congress.'[21]

The model of representative institution these speakers had in mind was not that of a parliament, but of a People's *Sobor*.

18 A particularly striking example of that attitude is to be found in the proceedings for 29 May (incidentally, only the fifth day of the Congress): 'Comrade male deputies [*sic*], if we are going to work at this pace – Vacations are beginning in the schools; we women must be at our homes; so let us work in a businesslike way. [*Applause*.]' – Deputy Amangeldinova's speech (*First Congress* 1989 1, p.378).

19 Anatoly Sobchak's speech at the fourth sitting (27 May) (*First Congress* 1989 1, p.261).

20 See above Note 11.

21 Deputy Klokov's note read at the third sitting (26 May) (*First Congress* 1989 1, p.141).

JUSTICE VERSUS LIBERTY

We have demonstrated substantial differences in the deputies' operational experience. What about their values? To answer this question, one has to find out what values dominated the debates at the Congress, what hierarchy they displayed and how different their intrinsic structures were.

The prevalent value categories were 'justice' and 'equality': they are encountered in more than a third of the deputies' speeches. 'Rule of law' and 'discipline' fall a little bit behind, in slightly less than a third of the speeches. 'Alternative choice' is referred to in one out of six speeches, 'liberty' (or 'freedom' - translated by the same word in Russian) in one out of ten.[22]

Alternative Choice versus Freedom

It is easy to see that 'alternative choice' is a substitute for 'freedom'. This is a revealing substitute: a significant number of deputies would avoid speaking of 'freedom' - the word was unseemly. They would prefer a euphemism instead.

As far as values were concerned, therefore, the debates focused on the basic contradiction of 'justice' versus 'liberty' ('freedom'). The first of these was indisputably taken as positive; the second was so negative that even when one could not do without it (the deputies' right to free choice had to be protected, after all), a Soviet newspeak substitute was used instead.

This euphemism, however, is not as harmless as it looks. A semantic analysis of the value notion of 'freedom' would presuppose that there exist: (1) someone who is, or may be, free; (2) his or her inner world; and (3) his or her external world. 'Freedom' is a capacity to create objects in both the inner and the external worlds, and to change the former's status within the latter. 'Choice' is a change of status. If we choose a book to be read, for instance, we change the object's status in our outer world and create a new object (the book's contents) in our inner world. If we choose to buy something, we change the chosen object's social (property) status. If we make a decision, that is, choose between alternatives, we change the inner

22 The figures are borrowed in part from Sergeyev and Baranov 1990.

status of some knowledge (about the situation); and if the result of the choice is our vote, we change the social status of that knowledge – inasmuch as the number of 'yes' votes is a measure of social status.

'Alternative choice' is a reduced or, rather, bureaucratic variant of 'freedom'.[23] In the first place, the expression itself is a tautology, like calling oil 'oily'. A 'choice' would presume there are alternatives. To speak of 'alternative choice' is possible only in a society that has newspeak for a language, where the word 'election' is deprived of its natural meaning and stands for some ritual act with a predetermined outcome or, at best, for a plebiscite.[24] The latter allows one to vote against, of course, so one is, therefore, free to choose; but this is always a choice of the negative. 'Alternative choice' differs from the newspeak for 'election' only inasmuch as it presumes there is a 'positive' variant as well – two candidates, for example.

'Freedom of choice' is different from 'alternative choice' inasmuch as it presupposes that the chooser is capable not only of *choosing* between, but also of *creating* objects of choice within both his or her inner world and external world (the inner and outer freedom). The difference is crucial, for 'alternative choice' presumes the chooser is to choose between alternatives that are created by someone else.

23 The word 'alternative' was widely used when discussing the candidates and the election procedure itself. The following are a few examples. Deputy Obolensky's speech at the second sitting, when he proposed himself as candidate for the chairmanship of the Supreme Soviet: 'I want a precedent of election to be set in our history, in our practice. Even if this is not a truly alternative base, this is still an election' (*First Congress* 1989 1, p.96). Deputy Belozertsev's speech at the same sitting (25 May): 'As to the alternative candidate, we have been sent here to hold a democratic election, to lay a future foundation of democratic procedure' (*First Congress* 1989 1, p.98). Boris Yeltsin's speech: 'I have abstained there from voting, because I think that some alternative candidates still ought to be proposed, even if only as an example, even if only to educate our young' (*First Congress* 1989 1, p.104). A most conspicuous example is provided by Deputy Karganov's speech at the third sitting (26 May): 'I am for alternative election, and even more for deputies' self-nomination' (*First Congress* 1989 1, p.150).

24 We cannot help quoting an anecdote to illustrate the point. Brezhnev comes across a man who is holding a water-melon. 'Is it for sale?', Leonid Ilyich asks, 'What's the price?' 'Choose!', answers the other, 'What do you mean, choose?', Brezhnev says, 'You've only got one!' 'Ha!', answers the water-melon man, 'You are also one, but we are to elect you every now and again!' (Russian has one verb for 'choose' and 'elect'.)

Sovereignty versus Freedom

In this respect, one is reminded of another euphemism for 'freedom', acquired by the Soviet newspeak in the present transition from totalitarianism to chaos. We refer to 'political pluralism', which is to 'freedom of political activity' precisely as 'alternative choice' is to 'freedom of choice'. 'Political pluralism' no more implies that you are free to create political organizations than 'alternative choice' implies that you are free to create your own alternatives.

This analysis of the newspeak of *perestroika* is a major premise for understanding the process of democratization in Russia. The intrinsic structure of the two basic values of the political discourse of *perestroika* considered above - 'alternative choice' and 'political pluralism' - would attest to the fact that the claims of even the radical wing of the reformers remained lamentably narrow; we shall comment below on the deputies' indignant reaction to an attempt at establishing a 'faction'. To sum up, the basic values of political democracy proved totally incompatible with the political culture of the majority of the Congress. Even if some fragments of those values were required in order to justify the existence of the Congress itself, as a new political institution befitting the period of reforms and the *perestroika* (restructuring) of society, astonishing schemes were devised to eliminate, unmistakably if only intuitively, the undesired elements of the meaning.

We can see that the participants in the Congress were speaking their own language and, hence, shared a political culture of their own. It was to the deficiency of this culture, which proved inadequate to the tasks it was faced with, that the Congress owed its fate - as, for that matter, did the entire country.

This reminds us of another substitute for 'freedom' that was also born of the polemics at the Congress, the much-celebrated word 'sovereignty'.[25] Examination of distinctions between the notions of

---

25 Vytautas Landsbergis, the future Chairman of the Lithuanian Supreme Soviet, seems to have been the first to use the word 'sovereignty' at the Congress. That was in the ultimatum he made on behalf of the Lithuanian deputies, threatening to boycott the election of the Supreme Soviet unless the procedure were changed:

We think we have no right to meddle, say, in Tajikistan's affairs when it elects its deputies. This is an internal matter that affects the sovereignty of the republic, we

'republican sovereignty', 'national freedom and self-determination' and 'independence of the state' may help us better understand the background of the process that was soon to bring about the disintegration of the Soviet Union.

Why did this particular acquisition of the *perestroika* newspeak, 'the sovereignty of the republics', rather than freedom and self-determination of peoples or state independence, become an integral factor in the political debate of the time and a substantial constituent of the political culture of *perestroika* in general? In order to answer this question, let us compare 'freedom' and 'sovereignty'.

Analysis of the intrinsic structure of 'sovereignty', a notion incorporated by the political vocabulary of Europe in the seventeenth and eighteenth centuries, reveals the following: 'sovereignty' is basically unrestricted freedom within some ontological sphere; this is usually a sphere of social life, of course. It was this interpretation to which Hobbes would have subscribed, for instance. What is most important is *absolute freedom within a defined field*. Hobbes's Leviathan is absolutely free in the sphere of social life, but not in the sphere of natural existence.[26] A sovereign may pass whatever social decrees he likes, but he cannot interfere with the laws of nature. Sovereignty within the world of nature is nonsense; the Creator of the world alone could enjoy such sovereignty.

According to international law, a state is sovereign as far as its internal affairs are concerned, but not when it comes to its relations with other states: in this field its freedom is limited by obligations

---

have no moral right to that. Nor do we infringe the sovereignty of Moscow in the persons of its group of deputies.

(Speech at the third sitting, 26 May: see *First Congress* 1989 1, p.167.)

The theme would sound ever louder, until it became a dominant one by the time the Soviet Union was about to fall apart. It is interesting to observe the immediate response to Landsbergis's statement:

We are not to hold an election of the Supreme Soviet of Lithuania, we are to hold an election of the Supreme Soviet of the Union of the Soviet Socialist Republics. And I fail to understand at all what the Lithuanian spokesman meant [by saying]: 'we shall not interfere with the sovereignty of Moscow City.' Moscow has no sovereignty ...

(Roy Medvedev's speech: see *First Congress* 1989 1, p.169.)

If Roy Medvedev only knew what a Pandora's box Landsbergis was opening at that moment!

26 See Hobbes 1980, pp.228–39, 395–408.

arising from international treaties, as well as by the assumed obligation to observe international law as such. If certain aspects of domestic life are the subject-matter of an international treaty, restrictions on sovereignty apply to them, too. That is why the clash of 'international obligations' and 'sovereignty' was the pivotal point of the controversy over human rights.[27] It is beyond doubt that if a state signs an international agreement on human rights and assents to the establishment of mechanisms of checking and control, it restricts its sovereignty in favour of the international community, but it is bound by its obligations only in so far as it recognizes them.

The first feature of sovereignty is, therefore, that it is a kind of freedom in the social sphere, and that this freedom is absolute. That is why it is theoretically permissible to speak of sovereignty in respect of states, which may be regarded as sovereign (if they are not parts of empires), at least before international organizations like the Holy Alliance, the League of Nations and the UN are established. But it would be odd to speak of a citizen's sovereignty, for what absolute freedom may be enjoyed within the sphere of social life that is already governed by the state and the law of the state?

The other feature of sovereignty is that basically it is *not a freedom to choose*. It is not easy to deny freedom of choice to anyone as far as political life is concerned. In totalitarian societies the price to be paid for the elimination of that kind of freedom was abolition of citizenship as a social status that presumed (and entitled individuals to engage in) political activity. Sovereignty is a *freedom to create*. Above all, it is freedom to create rules that govern social life: it is unlimited freedom to enact laws.

It was no mere coincidence that the notion of sovereignty came to play such a substantial role in European culture in the seventeenth and eighteenth centuries, that is after the rise of absolute monarchies. *'L'état, c'est moi'* - that was the most complete embodiment of the idea of royal sovereignty. It had not been possible hitherto because God and the Church set limits to secular (state) power. 'Sovereigniza-

---

27 In the controversy over the 'basic principles' of the Helsinki Concluding Document Soviet delegations invariably referred to the principle of sovereignty to counterbalance the principle of human rights. Demands to bring national law and national legal practice into full conformity with the international regulation of human rights would be routinely declined as an infringement of national sovereignty.

tion' of royal power in the age of absolutism meant basically its emancipation from the authority of the Church. Later, by the time of the Great Revolution, it was supplanted by the notion of popular sovereignty,[28] with similar features but (a significant difference) a sovereign defined far more vaguely.

There is a striking affiliation between 'sovereignty' and 'alternative choice', in so far as analysis of the contexts in which the two notions recur is able to reveal their intrinsic structures: within the framework of a wider notion of 'freedom' they tend to complement each other. Whereas 'alternative choice' is 'freedom' for citizens who have no right to enact laws and institute political organizations, 'sovereignty' is the state's absolute freedom to do precisely what is denied to its subjects. In short, this triad of 'freedom', 'alternative choice' and 'sovereignty' is a fine model of the political system of *perestroika*.

It is, therefore, easy to see the source of the whole problem of 'republican sovereignty'. As the Soviet government would have appealed to state sovereignty in its former controversy with the West to justify violation of human rights and freedoms by reference to 'national laws and customs', so republican elites would appeal to republican sovereignty to protect their right to maintain a political order different from what was about to emerge on the all-Union level.

The republican leadership's political stance was of no particular importance. There used to be republics that were more radical than 'the Centre'. There were also republics that were less radical. The conflict over sovereignty was *institutional*, not ideological. In the

28 Compare Robespierre:

> Assert first of all the following incontestable maxim: that the people is good, and that its delegates are corruptible; that it is in the virtue and in the sovereignty of the people that one must seek protection against the vices and the despotism of the government' ['Posez d'abord cette maxime incontestable: que le peuple est bon, et que ses délégués sont corruptibles; que c'est dans la vertu et dans la souveraineté du peuple qu'il faut chercher un préservatif contre les vices et le despotisme du gouvernement'. (Robespierre 1957, pp.145-6).]

The following statement, which refers to Louis XVI's trial, attests to the way this sovereignty was to operate:

> In the very nature of things, the court would be the nation itself if it could all come together. Since this is impossible, the court must be an institution or an assembly that presents the most perfect image of national representation. The National Convention is of this kind. Regarding the scope of its authority, I ascertain that the nation has invested it with unlimited authority. [Robespierre 1965, pp.82-3].

circumstances, to safeguard sovereignty would mean to secure the right of a social elite, located in a particular institutional milieu, to exercise unchallenged control over the social and political life within its domain. That was why the conservatives in the Russian Supreme Soviet would vote for sovereignty as unanimously as would the democrats.[29] That was why the Uzbekistan party elite would make common cause with Russian or Moldavian democrats, as far as sovereignty was concerned. And that is why the conflict over the sovereignty of the autonomous units in Russia is now following precisely the scenario that culminated in the collapse of the Soviet Union.

Thus, the conceptual system that evolved within the Soviet political culture during the *perestroika* period had the idea of civic political liberty replaced by two mutually complementing surrogates: 'alternative choice', that is reduced, defective freedom, and 'republican sovereignty', that is regional political elites' absolute power to play off national feelings against 'the communist Centre' or else 'the Centre that has betrayed the ideals of social justice and of communism'. In both cases the result would be identical: 'sovereignization'. The problem was that this kind of sovereignty would preclude political freedom for citizens. They would only be allowed to support their respective elites. Whether these were new (democratic) or old (communist) elites would be of no particular importance: the pattern would be the same. That is why the situation in the new states that have emerged from the ruins of the Soviet Union is hardly better, as far as human rights and political freedoms are concerned, than under the *ancien régime* - indeed, sometimes much worse.

Recent political developments in the USSR have shown, as the European Helsinki process did earlier, that the principle of sovereignty may be a means to suppress political liberty and human rights. In this respect, there is, indeed, little difference between 'democratic' Latvia and 'conservative' Uzbekistan. In the former it is the 'national democratic' elite that is jealous of its own 'sovereignty'; in the latter, the 'national communist' elite. In both cases the social groups (and, naturally, the individuals they consist of) that present, or are expected to present, a threat to the local elites are pushed back: in

29 See *First Congress* 1990 (39–41), 11–12 June.

the first case, the 'Russian migrants'; in the second, the Islamic 'democratic' intelligentsia.

Thus, liberty as a political value tended to be supplanted in the Congress debate by two different values, depending on the context: 'alternative choice' and 'sovereignty'. Let us now consider the values of justice and equality.

Equality as the Principle of Decentralized Distribution

In our Introduction we discussed the intrinsic structure of 'justice'. The notion presupposes the existence of a 'resource' to be distributed, a 'distributor' to perform the task, a number of 'recipients' to 'benefit' from it, and, finally, a 'principle' of distribution. 'Equality' is easily derived from this structure by establishing the principle of distribution: 'into equal parts'. It might be interesting to observe that debate at the Congress yielded what may be a euphemism for 'equality', too, namely 'social justice'. The contexts testify to the fact that, whenever 'social justice' was mentioned, 'equality' was implied.

The euphemism appears natural, given the above transformation of one value into another. The levelling principle enters the structure of 'justice' with the word 'social'. This may have its semantic reason, too: we are all humans, we are equal inasmuch as we are human, and hence we must all get equal portions of whatever is to be given out.

This interpretation of justice is in poor agreement with the 'basic principle of socialism': 'from each according to his ability, to each according to his work'. However, the history of 'real socialism' attests to the fact that 'the basic principle' belonged to the same stock of commitments as 'working-class power' (whether it is preferred to view them as wishful thinking or as hypocrisy).

It would be worth inquiring what were the resources that were regarded as subject to 'egalitarian' distribution. Paramount would be resources connected with the deputies' activities: the right of access to the rostrum, a time limit on speeches, access to the mass media, and so on. Negative resources were also of importance: incompetence, mistakes, responsibility. In this last case, 'egalitarianism' in a form such as, 'I've made mistakes, so have others' or 'I am responsible for this, but I share responsibility with others' would be a convenient rhetorical means to plead not guilty – by distributing the fault equally among all, which would eventually amount to presenting the undesired consequences of a political action as a natural calamity, rather than a human blunder. And a most curious example of 'equality in inequality' was presented by Gorbachev's attempt to justify privileges of the party *nomenklatura*: since miners, pilots and the like enjoyed privileges, party workers were likewise entitled to them.[30]

Especially significant was the almost total lack of any indication of the identity of the distributor when 'justice' or 'equality' was mentioned. As a rule, it would remain uncertain who it was that was to dispense justice: the Congress, or its Presidium, or the Government? The recipients, however, would be often designated as 'we'.[31]

This 'egalitarian' interpretation of 'justice' (with the identity of the distributor left uncertain) would fit in perfectly with the mentality of *sobornost'*. It is 'we', who have assembled here, that are to decide everything; for it is 'we', as a *Sobor*, or a *Veche* (popular assembly in medieval Russia), or a *mir* (in the traditional sense of a village community), that is taken together and acting as a single body, that is the distributor. The picture was singularly unconvincing, but the spokesmen for the 'we' seemed to be perfectly unaware of (or, at least, did not seem to be concerned about) that fact. However, social distribution is always procedural, always an outcome of a specific decision-making process, unless it is a result of spontaneous and disorderly pilferage of social property. The setting seems to suggest that it was precisely this kind of 'distribution' that the deputies (subconsciously, of course) had in mind. At least, this would be the only way to reconcile the idea of distribution with the absence of a suitable procedure, for it would be difficult to imagine any other situation when distribution could take place without a distributor. In that case, only the principle of distribution would have to be 'egalitarian'. It would allow the maintenance of at least a semblance of 'order' in this disorderly process: let everyone watch everyone to

---

30 Compare Mikhail Gorbachev's speech at the second sitting (25 May):

> The top leadership (this is a limited circle of people) ought, nevertheless, to be allowed state *dachas* for the period of their office. ... But this is a problem, indeed. I would put it this way: there are privileges everywhere. Heroes have them, miners have them, Northerners have them, academicians have them, trade union members have them, enterprises grant their own privileges. [*First Congress* 1989 1, p.91.]

31 The use of the pronoun is discussed in detail below.

ensure that all get equal shares. Or, to put it otherwise, 'steal, but not more than others do'.

This may be viewed as an example of how the patterns of pre-understanding operate. It is not through a conscious process of logical reasoning that the conclusion is achieved. Indeed, one might abhor the outcome if one stopped to ponder the whole process. However, it is not likely that this would be allowed to happen frequently, and one is likely to remain logical enough to block out any assumptions that obviously contradict basic attitudes. In the long run, intrinsic cohesiveness tends to prove more important than overt dictums.

Many bizarre features of Russian national culture might appear intelligible, indeed, if a village community's routine behaviour, for instance, were viewed in this perspective, that is as a collective consumption of natural resources. In the first place, prosperity would turn out to depend on intensive exploitation of the resource, rather than on efficient labour. Secondly, it would be easier to understand the tendency towards egalitarian distribution, and the regular re-allotment of land, and the hostility towards *kulaks* and *miroeds* (blood-suckers). The latter, for example, would not be viewed as harder workers, but as less scrupulous exploiters of nature. Should they be allowed, still less encouraged, to steal more than the others?

A similar attitude toward natural resources and their social function could be derived from the Congress debate. The reasoning was simple: it is not mainly on work that people live, rather they live on nature, hence natural resources are to belong to all the people, so land (as a primary natural resource) must not become private property, and so on. Hence the ingrained belief in equality: given the above *Weltanschauung*, egalitarianism appears to be the only reasonable way to distribute resources.

In Chapter 3 we inquired into the origins of the nihilistic attitude towards intellectual activity, so characteristic of the Soviet mass consciousness. Consideration of its egalitarian tendencies might allow us to probe into the source of nihilistic attitude towards work as such. The 'ecological thinking' of the modern 'village writers' can, it seems, be traced to similar roots. If a peasant's work is consumption (of natural resources), rather than creation, a 'true' man (and a 'true' man is a peasant, of course) ought to have a feeling of guilt towards nature and towards his 'native land'. But if, moreover, even traditional manual work is an evil, albeit a necessary one, industrial technologies are a greater evil by far – unpardonable indeed – while all the efforts of human reason to develop science and technology are ruses of a thief anxious to grab even more.

The 'organismic' vision of nature, society and their intercourse, therefore, is likely to give rise to egalitarianism, on the one hand, and to a nihilistic attitude towards intellectual work and even work in general, on the other. The conflict between a 'tough master' and a 'village lumpen' is essentially a clash between the mentality of a farmer (a grower and a breeder) and that of a harvester or a hunter. The latter's subsistence would, indeed, depend on sheer consumption and exploitation of natural resources. In this respect, the victory of the egalitarian-minded lumpen at the times of collectivization may be viewed as a victory of a harvester's mentality over the mentality of a farmer, and hence a step back towards the pre-neolithic way of life and primitive communism.

This psychology of 'exploitation of nature' permeated all structures of Soviet society. The country has long lived on natural resources, owing its very existence to their extensive development. Ideologues have not been idle, either: suffice it to recall the common interpretation of the much-celebrated maxim 'We cannot wait for Nature's favours', which has come to be equated now, from the standpoint of abstract moral and aesthetic ecologism, with the somewhat different 'Nature is no temple, it is a workshop'.[32] However, the difference between 'communist industrialism' and 'native soil ecologism' appears secondary, since both take exploitation of nature to be the only source of human existence, and their argument boils down to discussion of which means of exploiting it are permissible and reasonable and which are not.

To turn to more recent issues, even industrial factories would be commonly regarded as artificial 'mines', destined to supply whatever resources they possess to those employed by them. The phenomenon would become colloquially known as *tashchilovka* (which may be approximately rendered as 'universal pinching' or 'universal filching'), and may be instrumental, indeed, in spreading the alleged

---

32 The former maxim is attributed to selection geneticist Michurin; the latter comes from Yevgeny Bazarov, the principal character in Turgenev's novel *Fathers and Sons*.

aversion to the idea of privatization, that is, to turning what is seen as a common resource to private use. By contrast, to turn this social property to the collective use of employees would be considered the consummation of social justice.

Thus, the socio-ontological patterns ingrained in the traditional political culture and inherited by that of the Soviet Union, and the values associated with them, emerged from the depths of mass consciousness as soon as the situation was changed sufficiently to allow for their open display.

'WE' AND THE PEOPLE

The Deputies and the Electorate

The above inquiry into the values of the discourse of *perestroika* has brought us to the political culture's third and deepest element: the social ontology. Since the prevalent understanding of the nature of society and of the purpose of social intercourse is likely to affect the character and contents of political rhetoric, examination of the latter may, inversely, be used to reconstruct the models of social reality shared by the participants in the political discourse.

The first feature to attract our attention here is the return of the rhetoric of popular rule, so typical of the Russian political discourse before and after the revolution. One is struck, indeed, by the persistence with which the majority of deputies would repeatedly emphasize their status as representatives of the people. That applied even to those who had been elected from public organizations and who would have been well advised not to touch upon that sensitive point at all, the legitimacy of their status being questionable enough as it was. They would, nevertheless (or rather, moreover), seldom hesitate to introduce themselves as representing the wide social strata which formed, if only in name, the mass basis of their particular 'organizations'. The following are a number of the most typical examples:

> I am addressing you in my capacity as deputy of the women's councils. I am addressing you on behalf of the women, of those whose voices often remain

unheard. Meanwhile, the issues we raise are among the most acute and the most painful issues of our social life. They affect the interests of half of the population of our country, of half of those employed in our national economy.[33]

I and my comrades, 75 people's deputies, represent more than 50 million [*sic*] pensioners, veterans of war and labour, of the Party and the Armed Forces. This social group has not been taken heed of as a political force before. Unfortunately, the inertia of this thinking is still visible today.[34]

I am a representative of an apparatus, an apparatus whose numbers are 140 million: that of the Soviet trade unions. I am one of the representatives of the more than 20-million-strong army of Soviet communists.[35]

Statements such as 'After several days of work representatives of the youth have at last been given the floor',[36] or 'My mandate at the Congress is that of the peasantry',[37] or 'My voters, and I have been elected by an All-Union organization, have sent me here to solve basic questions'[38] would intermingle with complaints against alleged discrimination of deputies 'from public organizations': 'I don't think my voters [!] would like to hear me called an appointed deputy'.[39] More often than not these references to the voters were encountered in a context that unambiguously alluded to territorial constituencies and their electorate, irrespective of which particular group was represented by the deputy in question. A deputy who represented the Communist Party and had been elected, as envisaged by the latest constitutional amendments, at the plenary session of his party's Central Committee, would speak of his voters as if they were ordinary folk from the district he lived in and in which he was secretary of the district party committee, rather than some three to four hundred

33 Deputy Pukhova's speech at the seventh sitting (31 May) (*First Congress* 1989 2, p.40). Pukhova chaired the Committee of Soviet Women and was elected to represent 'the women's councils as united by the Committee of Soviet Women'.

34 Kirill Mazurov's speech at the eighth sitting (1 June) (*First Congress* 1989 2, pp.179-80). Mazurov, formerly First Secretary of the Central Committee of the Communist Party of Belorussia and Politburo member, was at that time Chairman of the All-Union Council of War and Labour Veterans; he was elected by the All-Union organization of war and labour veterans.

35 Deputy Korshunov's speech at the eighth sitting (1 June) (*First Congress* 1989 2, p.210).

36 Deputy Chervonopisky's speech at the ninth sitting (2 June) (*First Congress* 1989 2, p.340).

37 Text of Deputy Mukhametzyanov's undelivered address (*First Congress* 1989 5, p.373).

38 Deputy Obraz's speech at the fourth sitting (27 May) (*First Congress* 1989 1, p.284).

39 Deputy Kalish's speech at the eighth sitting (1 June) (*First Congress* 1989 2, p.175).

members of the power elite. His voters, he said, were worried about
the effectiveness of the agrarian policy and lack of work discipline,
and they insisted on continuing the anti-alcohol campaign.[40] It could
hardly be doubted that those were, indeed, matters of concern for
quite a number of Central Committee members. But it is difficult to
believe that, as members of the ruling party's topmost body, they
lacked any other means of bringing that concern to the notice of the
Congress, except via a secretary of an obscure district party committee. The speaker could hardly have meant Gorbachev and his like
when he referred to 'his electors'.

It is also not easy to imagine members of the Central Committee
turning to a Kirgiz shepherd when they feel the need to have the
government's attention drawn to an issue, whatever the issue might
be. After all, if not they, who were the government of that country?
And yet the shepherd, elected again by the CPSU Central Committee,
refers to her 'numerous meetings' with her electors and colleagues in
the course of her election campaign, and the commission she got from
them to bring up the question of prices for meat and wool at the
government level.[41] Were they indeed Central Committee members
whom she met? To judge by their requests, one would rather expect
them to be shepherds. But the shepherds were not her electors, and
her meetings with them could hardly be considered part of her
election campaign. Meetings with her proper electors would have
been more appropriately held at the Central Committee headquarters,
not in the Kirgiz mountains.

What are we to make of these passages? Ought we to dismiss them
as slips of the tongue, or should we rather expose them as sheer
demagogy? Whereas an inexperienced speaker might well make a slip
of the tongue when addressing a large and distinguished audience, it
would be surprising, indeed, for such a slip to occur in a written text,
never delivered from the rostrum but submitted on paper to be
enclosed with the proceedings.[42] And when, moreover, these slips of
the tongue become habitual and if demagogy seldom fails, it may be

40 Deputy Nazarov's speech at the twelfth sitting (8 June) (*First Congress* 1989 **3**, p.63).
41 Deputy Beishekeyeva's speech at the thirteenth sitting (9 June) (*First Congress* 1989 **3**,
    p.208).
42 See, for example, the text of Deputy Iovlev's undelivered address (*First Congress* 1989
    5, p.39); Iovlev also was a deputy of the Communist Party.

wondered, indeed, if it is not a political culture of a peculiar kind that one is dealing with. The type of political culture the quoted passages display is by no means unfamiliar to us. If deputies who were elected, as the popular expression went, 'from amongst themselves' and held mandates issued on the basis of a few dozen or a few hundred votes cast in their favour still found it appropriate to speak on behalf of '50 million veterans', or '140 million trade union members', or even 'half of the population of our country', would this not be sufficient evidence to demonstrate that the myth of 'the monolithic unity of the Soviet people', even though, perhaps, it no longer 'rallied round the Party of Lenin', was still alive? Would not that myth alone account for the conceit of those who presumed to call themselves legitimate representatives of the people in matters of the utmost importance, even though the people had never commissioned them to act in that capacity, and did so simply on the ground that no commission was needed where there was an innate affinity between the deputies and the people at large? Whether we consider this presumption justified or not is irrelevant to our argument, for it is not the observer's judgements that create cultural facts.

It might be objected, of course, that these claims were groundless and insincere. It would be difficult to deny the first charge, at least insofar as legal grounds are implied; however, the second would be libellous, unless supported by some positive proof. But even if it were admitted that some deputies were too cunning, this would hardly affect our argument. For, as a matter of fact, speakers who apparently had no reason to be insincere displayed essentially the same attitude and the same understanding of representation.

Let us consider, for example, the tendency of deputies who chose to speak 'on behalf of' their particular 'regions' to identify themselves with the population of those regions. The procedure was still routine at the First Congress. Much of its activity would still revolve around the so-called *deputations*, that is groups of deputies united on a regional basis, whereas lack of established organizational forms would not allow for other genuine interests to be adequately expressed. Evident in the rhetoric of these 'regional speakers' was the vision of a territorial unit as an organic whole, whose population was properly represented by whoever came from it. All this despite the fact, that 'the population of a region' is the kind of community whose political consolidation is not easily brought about, unless it is artificially provoked from outside or facilitated by ethnic unity, or both. There are matters of common concern in each particular region, of course, that are specific for that region and may provide a basis for such consolidation. But matters that separate and alienate those living together are no less numerous. This latter circumstance seems to justify our disposition to view the preference spontaneously given to problems that tend to consolidate not as evidence of their genuine priority (this is the exception, rather that the rule[43]), but as indicative of the mentality of *sobornost'*.

A striking example of that attitude is provided by an Altai physician who informed her audience that 'our Altai delegation and the delegation of Belorussia wish us to ensure that our society had more respect for bread'.[44] What are we to make of this? Was it a hint that the two groups of deputies had formed a coalition? Or are we to understand that respect for bread was a point of particular concern in their constituencies? Both seem unlikely. But then why would it be said at all? If the speaker wanted to express her anxiety about the matter, why refer to the Altai delegation or to that of Belorussia? Why bring them together on such a peculiar occasion? One wonders whether the statement was not born exclusively of some unconscious tendency to construct a social unity wherever possible. This does not mean the 'consolidating' problems are invented *ad hoc*: there are always enough genuine problems not to bother about inventing artificial ones. But this 'regionalization' of problems of national, if not universal, concern would create no genuine unity on the regional level, of course. It is but a figure of speech, indicative, however, of the implicit intentions set by the speaker's political culture.

Is it necessary in these circumstances to quote from the deputies elected in territorial constituencies? They were sure to be justified in their claims to be recognized as elected representatives of the people. (Let us lay aside suspicions about manipulating the election: this is not our concern at the moment.) Their references to the voters' will would be natural and therefore not particularly informative. However, strange statements can sometimes be encountered, such as the

43 Like nuclear contamination resulting from the Chernobyl disaster for Belorussian deputies or the ecological catastrophe of the Aral Sea for deputies from Central Asia.
44 Deputy Yegorova's speech at the twelfth sitting (8 June) (*First Congress* 1989 **3**, p.70).

following: 'When the peoples saw me off to the Congress, they used to say...'[45] This sounds odd enough, even if the peoples in question are small in numbers, as was the case,[46] thus allowing for the deputy to communicate with a whole people at once.

But sometimes they would drop remarks that might be identified as formulas of *sobornost'*. Consider, for instance, the following ardent assertion of the infallibility of the people's will; the speaker was protesting against deputies suspecting each other of incompetence:

And I suppose the statements some of the speakers have allowed themselves to make about the deputies' incompetence and inability to solve problems in the Supreme Soviet are not justified. *We are all elected by the people, and the people cannot be mistaken about their deputies.*[47]

Another deputy referred to 'the people's unerring intuition' in order to substantiate his point.[48] Indeed, the image of the people waiting outside the Kremlin walls, but watching their representatives intently, knowing and understanding everything and judging them all according to their deserts was remarkably popular with the deputies.

For all the praises sung to the people, however, and all the curtsies made to them, the deputies would seldom fail to praise themselves. The infallibility of the people in the above quotation, as may have been noted, would incidentally imply the infallibility of the deputies.

Divergent Models of Political Representation

We shall finally turn to the main and most straightforward means of self-identification, namely, the use of pronouns 'we' and 'our'. Examination of usage and clarification of the meanings attached to these pronouns in a particular text or a group of texts may be regarded as one of the most promising means of exposing the models of social reality that underlie the political discourse. 'We' is not only

45 Deputy Gayer's speech at the twelfth sitting (8 June) (*First Congress* 1989 **3**, p.85).
46 Gayer was an ethnographer from the Far East and would think of herself as voicing the concerns of the small ethnic communities of the region (to one of which she herself belonged by birth).
47 Deputy Shevlyuga's speech at the third sitting (26 May) (*First Congress* 1989 **1**, p.141; italics added).
48 Text of Deputy Mironenko's undelivered address (*First Congress* 1989 **5**, p.349).

a conventional form of social and political self-identification and thus the obvious, immediate object of inquiry. It is also a most effective rhetorical or sophistical device that allows an author or a speaker, by varying the meanings of the word or substituting one of the meanings for another, to bring to the audience's notice or even impose on it an idea that does not need to be stated explicitly and hence is not likely to be subjected to rational analysis and criticism. This is not to imply that all who do all this always engage in conscious manipulation of their audience; on the contrary, conscious manipulation is a marginal practice. More often than not, these rhetorical tricks are quite spontaneous. The resulting substitution of meanings occurs as a 'natural' manifestation of the pre-understanding patterns, not consciously held, but no less real for that. This 'natural' substitution may be due to a shift of emphasis or a change of subject, or it may be brought about by a need to appeal to a different person and so on, but it will be no less effective in spite of that. On the contrary, the more spontaneous the substitution, the more favourable the conditions for the display of the implicit socio-ontological models and the easier their transfer from the speaker to the audience. On the other hand, it is only when the participants in the discourse share models that are sufficiently congruent that the substitution may appear unforced and hence be functional.

Our analysis cannot be exhaustive. It would be tedious to cite all our examples in detail. We shall confine ourselves to but a few that we find most illuminating, and conclude the commentary with a brief survey of the results.

Comrade Deputies! The sharp and controversial character of the discussion to spread at **our** Congress is quite understandable. **We** are discussing the most urgent, most vital problems that relate to the bases of development of **our** multi-national state in the fields of economy, politics and inter-state relations. And no one of **us** is entitled to claim the truth in the final instance, entitled to assert that [his] own standpoint alone is correct. Only collective reason based on the social practice and realities of **our** life and on scientific foresight can serve as a guarantee against serious blunders that neither contemporaries nor descendants will forgive **us**.

The question today is: either **we** shall give in to emotions, to group interests, to personal ambitions and lead the Congress away from solving the most acute problems in the political, economic and moral-spiritual spheres, or else, proceeding from the real conditions, from objective analysis, shall elaborate a programme of helping the country out of the crisis, map out concrete ways to realize it in practice. We must remember that the electors, all the Soviet people expect no resounding speeches, no promises, no lightweight slogans from us, but weighted, well-considered, constructive decisions.[49]

In the Russian version, the personal pronoun 'we' (in various forms) and the possessive pronoun 'our' appear in the quoted passage nine times. In seven cases they refer to participants in the Congress; in two cases ('our multinational state' and 'the realities of our life') 'the people' ('the nation') is implied. It is noteworthy that the second of the two meanings occurs in the sentences in which 'we' and 'our' have already been used in the first sense, meaning 'the deputies'. The resulting 'interference' creates prerequisites for an involuntary identification of the two meanings and, hence, of the deputy corps and the masses of people, despite the fact that the sentence concluding the quotation clearly counterposes the former and the latter.

In the remaining part of the text in question[50] the word 'we' and its derivatives are encountered 21 times; in addition to that, on one occasion the pronoun has been omitted, apparently for stylistic reasons, as the Russian grammar allows (in the relevant extract – (18) – this is shown in brackets and emphasized). The various meanings are distributed as follows (the numbers in parentheses refer to the fragment's position in the sequence given below):

(1) In three cases 'we' indicates the deputy corps or the Congress: 'Among the top priority [problems] that the voters particularly expect us to solve, ... is the provision of pensions to war and labour veterans, to collective farmers...' (15); 'Many letters and telegrams are arriving addressed to our Congress... ' (23); 'Let [us] be equal to the crucial tasks, let [us] justify the expectations and the confidence the people have in us' (31; unemphasized pronouns enclosed in square brackets highlight their absence from the respective Russian expression; however, the verb is in the form that indicates the same person as in English).

(2) 'The people' ('the nation', 'the society', 'the country') are implied on seven occasions: 'The radical *perestroika* of all sides of

---

49 Text of Deputy Mesyats's undelivered address (*First Congress* 1989 **5**, pp.316-17; emphasis added). Mesyats was First Secretary of the Moscow Provincial Party Committee.
50 Ibid., *First Congress* 1989 **5**, pp.317-22 (emphasis added).

our life has literally revolutionized the situation in the country' (10); 'In recent years radical transformations have appeared in **our** political system' (11); 'The situation **we** are in is complicated, sometimes critical' (12); 'The problems that face **us** now are very many' (14); '[Attacks on the party] are to be considered as attempts to use the rostrum of the Congress for demoralizing, dividing **our** society and the party' (27); 'To deprive the party of its leading role in **our** society, to tear it away from the people is to render the *perestroika* lifeless' (28); 'The present, extremely complicated stage of **our** society's development calls for a tight consolidation of powers of the whole corps of deputies' (30).

(3) In three instances 'we' refers to the party elite (political or administrative or both): 'In **our** opinion, the way suggested will not only prevent [our] solving the food problem, but will, on the contrary, aggravate it' (20; the pronoun in brackets is again absent from the Russian original); 'And **we** do not understand whence come the attempts, here at the Congress, too, to revise, under the pretext of democratization, the role of the Party, which Clause Six of the Constitution of the USSR defines as that of the leading and guiding force of the Soviet society' (26). The instance of the omitted pronoun falls in this category, too: '[**We**] would consider it advisable...' (18; for context, see extract 17 below).

(4) The pronoun is once used to indicate 'the local population': 'In **our** region ... environmental problems are particularly acute and urgent' (21).

(5) Finally, we come across eight instances when 'we' may be interpreted in different ways.

(a) Of these, three instances refer either to 'the people', or to 'the party elite': 'When rural toilers are ensured conditions of work, of private life and of leisure that were not worse, perhaps, even better than those of the urban [workers] – only then shall **we** be able to meet the country's requirements in diverse and high-quality food products,' (19); '**We** need, while strengthening collective and state farms in every possible way, to develop – judiciously, on an economic basis, everywhere – lease relationships in the countryside' (21); '**We** ought to consolidate the discipline of soldiers and officers and enhance their prestige' (25).

(b) Four instances may be interpreted to refer either to 'the party elite', or to 'the deputies': 'Today at the Congress **we** ought to give guidance to the broad working masses, to the effect that economic growth is no palace revolution, it cannot be achieved in an hour' (13); 'If **we** put [the measures suggested] rigorously into effect, the people will accept them with gratitude' (16); 'Lest **our** words and deeds should be at variance, ... [we] would consider it advisable to establish a special commission within the USSR Supreme Soviet for coordination and control' (17, including the subsequent extract 18); 'And **we** must resolutely assert today that these barely masked [literally: 'sewn white'] and vain attempts are doomed to fail completely' (29).

(c) Finally, the pronoun may in one instance be understood to stand either for '(local) party elite', or for 'local population': '**We** think that in Moscow province ... it is no longer possible to allot land for collective gardens and kitchen gardens' (24). For all intents and purposes this might well be included in category (5a). It is also noteworthy that whenever 'we' or 'our' allows for different interpretations, one of the alternative referents is invariably that of 'party elite'.

Arranged in the order in which they appear in the text, the pronouns show the following sequence (the first nine instances have been added to make the picture complete):

$$D = \underline{D = P} = D = \underline{P = D} = D = \underline{D = D} - P - P - P - D/E - P =$$
$$D = D/E - \underline{D/E = [E]} - P/E - E = P/E - L - D = L/E - P/E -$$
$$E - P = P = D/E = P = D,$$

where 'D' stands for 'deputies'; 'E', for 'elite'; 'P', for 'the people'; 'L', for 'local population'; oblique strokes (/) separate various interpretations of the same pronoun; equals signs (=) connect pairs of pronouns that occur in adjacent sentences; underlined are pronouns that occur within the same sentence. These two categories have been highlighted, since they present the most spectacular 'switches' of meaning.

The above investigation allows us to delineate two principal means of meaning-association. One is *alternation* which refers to the consecutive use of pronouns 'we' or 'our' in two or more different senses, thus bringing about a more or less unconscious identification of the meanings and, consequently, of the social entities that the respective notions stand for. The first two paragraphs of the analysed text (quoted in full) are a good illustration of the device. In the subsequent paragraphs 'we' and its derivatives are no longer used in different meanings within the same sentence. The only exception is the sentence containing the phrase with the pronoun omitted (extracts 17 and 18); this indicates 'the party elite' and follows an instance that allows for two different interpretations: 'the deputies' or 'the party elite'. Besides, on four occasions the pronouns occur with different meanings in sentences that immediately follow each other: extracts 14-15-16 (P = D = D/E), 20-21 (E = P/E), 23-24 (D = L/E) and 27-28-29-30-31 (P = P = D/E = P = D).

However, this somewhat diminished pressure is more than recompensed by frequent use of another, no less effective, device. This is *ambiguity* or *ambivalence*, which enables a similar result to be achieved by using the pronouns in a context that would allow for two or more different interpretations of their meaning. The audience is left uncertain as to which particular meaning the speaker has in mind. It is forced to waver between the alternatives, thus involuntarily drawing them nearer and, perhaps, together. The ruse seems to provide for even deeper interdiffusion of meanings and hence closer identification of the respective notions, than alternation.

Another striking feature of the analysed text is the careful avoidance of personal pronouns (or, for that matter, of any names these pronouns might stand for) whenever 'mistakes' or 'failures' of the party leadership are referred to.[51] Use of impersonal pronouns ('this has led to'), passive voice ('many errors have been committed') and reflexive verbs (lost in the English translation: 'development toward pluralism ... has been accompanied by inability', 'aspiration ... has met with powerful resistance ... and in the long run ended in imbalance'), plus monotonous recurrence of abstract verbal nouns ('transformations', 'revival', 'becoming', 'development', 'inability', 'aspiration', 'resistance', 'worsening' – eight instances in only six sentences!), serve to overcome the stylistic problems created and, more important still, to destroy the spontaneous association between the subject, implicated but never indicated ('we' as 'the party elite'), and the displaced predicate ('our' actions and their consequences).

The trick may be interpreted in two ways. It may be seen as an

51 *First Congress* 1989 5, p.318.

attempt to relieve the party leadership of responsibility for the 'failures' and 'mistakes' alluded to, showing the latter as caused by interplay of some spontaneous forces, impersonal, or at least alien, although unnamed. Or it may have been motivated by a desire to distance the speaker from the leadership without declaring open war on them. But why not be open about it? After all, it was in order to condemn their policy that the whole passage was written.

One should take into account, however, that open criticism of the reformers would imply breaking away from them. In that case 'we' could no longer imply 'party leadership'; in the context it would stand for 'opponents of the reforms'. Open conversion of some members of the party elite to opposition to the party's official leadership would have signified collapse of the myth of the intra-party unity. That, in turn, would have challenged the basic myth of the Soviet political culture, namely, the unity of the (infallible) party and the people. After such a drastic step to preserve both myths intact the leaders of *perestroika* would have had to be branded as an anti-party and hence anti-people clique. If the author was not inclined or prepared to go as far as that, the mentality of *sobornost'* would lead him to avoid saying 'we' in a context that hinted at serious discord in the party elite. This 'figure of omission' would allow a passage between Scylla and Charybdis: on the one hand, to condemn the presumably disastrous policy of the leadership and thus register disagreement with it, while on the other hand pretending to preserve perfect confidence in the unity of the party ranks as an integral and most important component of the basic myth about the people and its party.

However, both interpretations of the device in question presuppose, rather than preclude, the other: the party ought to be relieved of the blame anyway, even if by demonstrating the 'anti-party' character of its present-day leadership. Voicing disagreement would then indicate that 'wholesome forces' are still to be found in the party.

It is appropriate to point out that this analysis proceeds from the assumption that it is only natural for a speaker to identify with his audience, such identification providing him with an indispensable rhetorical means of persuasion. Since the object with which he is trying to identify is actually present, and saying 'we' is the easiest way to identify with it, there is hardly a speaker that could dispense with the word. Similar observations will apply to habitual combinations of words and standard expressions like 'our country'. One might therefore conclude that it would be hasty to attempt to make any specific inferences on the basis of such usage. But the more cautious one has to be on these occasions, the more illuminating may attachment of other meanings to these pronouns (and, hence, occurrence of other referents) prove. Not only will combinations like 'our life' or 'our people' be more expressive emotionally in comparison with 'our country', but identification of the self with a social body or social group different from the audience is certainly both more dramatic and more binding than identification with those immediately present.

Taking this into account, it is correct to assume that interpolations of 'we' in the sense of 'those present' ('deputies' in the present case) in a context in which it stands for other objects of identification, too, as well as the specific devices and circumstances of such interpolations, are characteristic of the particular speaker's or author's understanding of the relationship between the two entities. By contrast, systematic use of 'we' or 'our', or both, in only one sense allows us to judge the extent to which the particular person identifies with the given entity (that is on his appraisal of his own social status as belonging to that entity), but is scarcely informative of his understanding of the entity itself. In Deputy Petrushenko's speech (delivered at the fourth sitting) the pronouns 'we' and 'our' are encountered 26 times; of these 20 imply 'deputies' in general, three refer to a particular 'group of deputies', and in two instances the pronoun may be interpreted in either of two ways: as 'deputies' in general, or as 'a group of deputies'. Thus, on 25 occasions out of the 26 (that is, almost invariably) the pronoun represents 'the deputies'; only once is the people (or, rather, the country) implied: 'our multinational Union'.[52]

The undelivered speech of Deputy Sukhov, a driver from Kharkov, yields an entirely different picture.[53] 'We' is used by him in two different senses, distributed almost equally. Out of 34 instances 17 refer to 'deputies'; 12, to 'the people'; two, to 'drivers' (a professional group to which the author belongs and which he is

---

52 *First Congress* 1989 **1**, pp.286-9 (emphasis added); Petrushenko was a political instructor with the rank of lieutenant-colonel from Eastern Kazakhstan, later to become a prominent member of the conservative 'Soyuz' ('Union') faction.

evidently inclined to regard as representative of 'the people' at large); three cases are ambiguous and may be interpreted as meaning either 'deputies' or 'the people'. This pattern in the variation of meanings is indicative of a close relationship that exists – or, if interpreted normatively, ought to exist – between 'the deputies' and 'the people'. There are no hints, however, that a similar relationship exists between 'the people' and 'the political elite'. Nor are there any attempts to identify the deputies, including the speaker himself, with the latter. The author's vision of political representation is thus clearly anti-elitist, which may, incidentally, be regarded as an indirect indication of a negative attitude towards professional parliamentarianism. It would not be surprising to meet the author among the sturdiest opponents of 'idle talk'.

The beliefs the text in question seems to expose conform, on the whole, to the model of representation characteristic of the culture of *sobornost'*. However, statements that suggest a clear perception of acute social tensions might seem to contradict this conclusion, even though the perception is hardly generalized and the tensions are viewed in the light of 'everyday disorders':

> What kind of economic mechanism is this, if some people have two-storey *dachas* built for them, while others cannot get [construction] materials to make their regular homes [a bit more] comfortable? Some have run around for 20 to 25 years trying to have a telephone installed, despite their priority rights; others, who are themselves 20 to 25 years old, enjoy the privilege without complications. Some run from one queue to another like madmen, trying to get the necessities; others follow them with cheeky smiles and enjoy the goods without effort.[54]

But, contradictory though these allegations of social inequality may be to the type of mentality that revolves around the notion of *sobornost'*, they would fit the principle's anti-elitist mode. The apparent resolution of this contradiction would be to discriminate between the 'factual' and the 'proper', between 'is' and 'should'. Hence the following paradoxical demand: 'To my mind, **our** deputy corps must become like a single monolith, but should not turn into unprincipled compromisers.'[55]

53 Text of Deputy Sukhov's undelivered address (*First Congress* 1989 **6**, pp.252–5).
54 *First Congress* 1989 **6**, pp.253–4.
55 *First Congress* 1989 **6**, p.252 (emphasis added).

This anti-elitist stand is not likely to be shared by those who belong – or reckon themselves to belong – to the political elite, of course. It is not surprising then that the text of Deputy Mironenko's undelivered speech reveals a pattern that is significantly different from the one exemplified by the speech of Deputy Sukhov. There are 35 instances of 'we' and 'our' in Mironenko's text, twelve of which refer to 'deputies'; nine to 'the people'; four to 'the elite'; and one to 'the Komsomol deputies'; nine (almost a quarter of the total) allow for different interpretations. 'Elite' is invariably one of the alternatives again: on three occasions it is associated with 'deputies' (besides, each of the two categories can be expanded by adding the 'Komsomol deputies'); on six occasions, with 'the people'. The pattern is essentially the same as in the undelivered speech of Deputy Mesyats. It is also noteworthy that of the four instances that convey the meaning of 'political elite', two refer directly to 'those in power', while the remaining two are apparently more general and imply 'those actively involved in politics'. However, the latter are marginal interpretations, permissible, but not characteristic of the author's pattern of understanding, since the instances do not belong to his own text, but are encountered in a quotation (from Maxim Gorky). A further revealing fact is that in only two out of nine instances where 'the people' is implied is the possessive pronoun 'our' used in 'neutral' (emotionally uncharged) combinations: '**our** new Constitution' and '**our** mass media'. In most cases the author opts for 'we', and the context is usually 'tense': '**We** are being drawn into a vicious circle'; '**We** have suffered from incompetence so much', and so on; or '**Our** economy is literally crying'; '**Our** army must never...'.[56]

If we now compare Deputy Mironenko's address with that of Academician Sakharov, the difference in usage of the pronouns will be apparent. The personal pronoun 'we' and the possessive pronoun 'our' are used by Sakharov 18 times. Of these, twelve refer to 'deputies' in general and one implies 'deputies from Moscow'; one more case ('on this ... **our** position will depend') allows for two interpretations: 'our' may mean 'of the entire deputy corps', or 'of the Moscow group of deputies'. Four instances refer to 'the people' or 'the country'. Characteristic of the speaker's non-populist mentality is

56 *First Congress* 1989 5, pp.344–50 (emphasis added).

the fact that 'the people' is implied only once ('**We** are going through a revolution'), while the three remaining instances presented by the 'neutral' expression 'our country' (the standard Russian equivalent for the English 'this country').[57]

A similar picture is revealed by Gavriil Popov's address. The pronouns 'we' and 'our' occur in it nineteen times. On three occasions they are used to refer to 'the people' ('**our** *perestroika*') or, rather, to 'the country' ('the logic of **our** Constitution', this dispassionate expression encountered twice). By contrast, 'deputies' are meant on 16 occasions, only six of which refer to the deputy corps in general, while nine (almost half of the total number) stand for the Moscow group of deputies, the nucleus of the emerging opposition. The remaining instance refers to the deputies who attended a meeting that had taken place on the previous day. If the least informative meanings are excluded, 'we' appears to stand almost invariably for something close to a political faction. Like identification with a political party, or a social group, or a stratum, this is characteristic of the *pluralist* political culture.

The above analysis of the parliamentary rhetoric has revealed three distinct patterns of deputies' self-identification (and political behaviour), associated with different models of political representation based, in turn, on different visions of social reality. One may be called 'parliamentarianism', if the emphasis is on the models of representation, or 'pluralist democracy', when expressed in terms of political culture. This is based on the 'pluralist' vision of society, as consisting of various social groups, characterized by diverse interests and often in conflict with each other. Identifying with the society as a whole (or with the people taken together) would, as a rule, make little sense for those who think in this way. In their case identification is either purely situational (with those immediately present or directly relevant), or else is with a particular social group or a political party (not in the 'one-party' sense of the word, that has long been customary in the Soviet Union, of course) or faction, inasmuch as the latter are believed to represent the former.

Sobornost' may be seen as a model of political representation alternative to parliamentarianism. Unlike the former, the mentality of

---

57 *First Congress* 1989 **1**, pp.9–11 (emphasis added).

sobornost' facilitates (indeed, requires) identification of self (and, normatively, of the entire corps of deputies) with 'the people'. The rhetoric characteristic of the *populist* version of *sobornost'* resembles that of pluralist democracy, making it sometimes difficult to distinguish between the two types of political culture. Both are likely to appeal to the people's will and declare the rule of, by, and for the people as their ultimate goal. The underlying models of social reality, however, are entirely different.

Communist fundamentalism – as the third style of political behaviour manifest at the Congress might be defined – tends to engage in rhetoric different from that of *populism*, although their patterns of pre-understanding remain basically the same. Both endorse the model of political representation defined here as *sobornost'*. The difference between the *populist* and the *elitist* varieties lies in the extent to which the original traditional pattern and the later Bolshevik additions have become separated in the course of the crisis that afflicted the Soviet regime, undermined the system-building belief in the sagacity of the ruling party, and caused alienation of the political elite from common citizens and deterioration of the established patterns of political interaction.

PLURALISM VERSUS UNITY

Two Models of Representative Institutions

In the preceding chapter we indicated those features of the constitutional reform that laid the foundation of a representative institution which would fit the ontological patterns of *sobornost'*. Let us now see how this type of mentality functioned in the new institutional environment. The difference between the two models of political representation that need to concern us here can be itemized as follows:

(1) The concept that underlies the parliamentary model would depict deputies as basically representing their voters. Although the parliament may be seen as a 'combined' representative of the entire electorate, the idea is functional only in emergency situations, or

when matters of foreign policy (marginal for the institution) come to the fore. However, this is precisely the perception that forms the pivotal point of *sobornost'*: a representative institution is 'representative' only inasmuch as it may be seen to represent the nation (the people) as a whole.

(2) In this perspective, a *Sobor* is to be viewed as a single whole, too. All kinds of political disunity (conflicts of interests, disagreements over principles and approaches or about particular steps and persons) are lamentable and must be eliminated. The model of *sobornost'* is incompatible with pluralism. The parliamentary model, by contrast, is based on the assumption that the existence of groups or factions that express and defend particular interests in a representative institution is not only natural but is its sole justification.

Hence, (3) the parliament's principal function is to reconcile diverse interests and work out mutually acceptable decisions. Debates and negotiations are members' basic occupations. The *Sobor*, however, is to represent the people in its intercourse with the authorities; its function is to confirm (or deny) the latter's legitimacy. It is, therefore, convened only when this legitimacy has, for some reason, been lost and is to be re-established. In this capacity it is expected to say either 'yes' or 'no', thereby assuming a markedly plebiscitary character.

We have already referred to some deputies' staunch reluctance to hold lengthy debates about the issues put to a vote: such debates would be habitually censured as a waste of time, while speedy voting would be considered the proper way to deal with the matter. The plebiscitary tendency was perfectly evident.

The Bogey of Factionalism

Still more revealing was the Congress's response to the motion of some Moscow deputies elected by scientific organizations and creative unions to form an independent group, later to be known as the 'Inter-Regional Deputies' Group'. The intent was made public by Gavriil Popov[58] who was immediately accused of factionalism; in this connection Gorbachev mentioned a 'splitting of the Congress'.[59]

After the interval (and, presumably, the proper 'encouragement') accusations became sweeping:

I think our Moscow colleagues are somewhat carried away. Carried away also are those who, voluntarily or not, call upon us to enter confrontation. What is the Congress to do to prevent further development of our Congress's 'infantile disorder' of democracy? I would like to call on the deputies to think my proposal over and reject the harmful, politically erroneous idea of confronting the Congress and founding a faction proposed by the honourable Comrades Popov and Afanasyev. *The voters won't understand a deputy who would desert his deputy post with his delegation now and go over to some faction.*[60]

The climax was reached when the floor was taken by Deputy Samsonov:

Now we are talking of factionalism. *We all want to get rid of the thing*, but let us face the truth at last. There are people among us who cannot live without a faction at all. [Some of us] will be ill tomorrow if denied the prospect. [*Applause.*] I think this must be denounced.[61]

To judge by the reaction, the proposal to form an independent deputies' group scandalized the audience. Indignation was somewhat affected, of course, and the protests were obviously a put-up job. But they found a broad response, and it would be misleading to believe they were just due to some backstage manoeuvring. Even potential allies felt obliged to rebuke Popov, however mildly, and join in the warnings:

I think bringing up the issue of faction is, on the whole, unnecessary [said Evgeny Yakovlev, Editor-in-Chief of the popular weekly *Moscow News*]. Of course, a faction is something unusual for us, almost romantic. It reminds me of a man who was brought up in a children's home and who would tell me how he had been reading Dickens all his life and could not understand what a sandwich was. A faction is roughly the same to us. I believe that chances for consolidation are by no means exhausted, that efforts must be spent not on joining a faction, but on seeking consolidation. ... We must consider the possibility of providing a guarantee to the minority on a number of issues. This is what efforts must be spent on, not on factionalism.[62]

---

58 Gavriil Popov's speech at the fourth sitting (27 May) (*First Congress* 1989 **1**, pp.224–8).
59 *First Congress* 1989 **1**, p.229.
60 Deputy Petrushenko's speech at the fourth sitting (27 May) (*First Congress* 1989 **1**, p.288; italics added).
61 *First Congress* 1989 **1**, pp.305–6 (italics added).
62 *First Congress* 1989 **1**, p.283.

And Genghis Aitmatov would ask his fellow-novelist Ales Adamovich:

> Now, tell me, please, if we bring this Congress to such a state that some factions emerge, some groups, some unacceptable relations between us, will that save us, will that help us find the way to cure the society? No, it won't. Factionalism cannot solve our problems now; I don't see any positive element, any energy in this factionalism. If it were like this, if I were sure that if we divided into factions now, and each one stood apart, each one has its own political programme, and that did us any good, I would leave this rostrum, and come to you, and sit down beside you.[63]

Some speeches put the whole matter in a peculiar perspective:

> I want to tell you that I was among those who applauded Yuri Nikolayevich Afanasyev after his speech. I agree with him on many points. But I would like to draw your attention to the fact that Yuri Nikolayevich has not called on the Congress to divide into factions. The appeal has come from no less honourable Gavriil Kharitonovich Popov. What's the difference? The difference is that Yuri Nikolayevich was elected in a territorial constituency, like myself. We both feel our voters breathing behind us: they are watching us intently.[64]

Were we to understand that 'genuine' voters ('the people', as opposed to the 'illegitimate' electorate of public organizations: Popov was a deputy of the Union of Scientific and Engineering Societies) would denounce their elected representatives if the latter chose to defend their interests as members of a faction, rather than of a 'united bloc'? Eventually, Popov himself gave in:

> No one here has any interests, but the interests of *perestroika*. ... I never mentioned the word 'faction' in my speech. I fail to understand why some people should find it necessary to draw a conclusion about striving for a faction from an attempt, on the part of a group of persons, to work a matter out. [*Noise in the assembly hall.*] ... I agree with the considerations of honourable Genghis Aitmatov here. I think that while there remains even the slightest chance for us to work together, we must work together. I am deeply convinced that we do have such a chance. That's why I wish we had no more of this talk about factions. If we are ready to work, let us work. [*Applause.*][65]

The matter was closed. Being accused of 'factionalism' proved so

63 *First Congress* 1989 **1** pp.299–300.
64 Deputy Kirillov's speech (*First Congress* 1989 **1**, pp.291–2).
65 Gavriil Popov's speech (*First Congress* 1989 **1**, pp.309–10).

frightening that even leaders of opposition would waver, although they had no objections to factions in principle. They used to think it went without saying that parliaments must have factions. In the course of the election and later, when the deputies-elect had been preparing for the Congress, the prospects of forming a faction of democratic opposition had been discussed in the open and had never seemed to embarrass anybody. Americans had even managed to 'calculate it in advance', as Leonid Kravchenko, TASS General Director, later said with affected indignation.[66] Still, no one dared to defend 'factionalism' right there at the Congress.

It was only in Yuri Afanasyev's undelivered speech (published many months after the Congress) that the factionalists' principal attitude was stated:

> Deputy Popov has announced the establishment of an independent group of deputies. No, not of Moscow deputies, but from all over the country, that, avoiding having to sit according to the geographical principle, could unite round common platforms: economic, political, social. This independent minority group could propose its own means to work for [the benefit of] the country. This simple idea, that even the Tenth Party Congress had found natural[67] - the right to propose a platform and to elect the ruling bodies on the platform basis: this idea has caused alarm. Some began to say that was a call to split the Congress. But any TV viewer can see that the Congress is already split. And this is normal. The only thing that is required is for groups of deputies who hold different views about ways out of the crisis [and about] the content of *perestroika* to be able to unite openly, to work out means of parliamentary struggle for their views. They say, with their eyes on stalks out of fear [literally: with eyes round with fear]: 'But this is a faction!' Why, that's a normal party and parliamentary word! It means that, while being a part of the Congress as a whole, a group of deputies finds it necessary to form itself in the face of the people as a special part, in view of the fact that many of their notions and proposals differ from the standpoint of the majority that, it must be said, follows another faction, already existing and well built. ...[68]

These words reached the public much later. Why were they, or their like, not heard in the conference hall? Was it, perhaps, the general atmosphere, the pressure of the audience, that prevented opposition leaders from saying what they thought? And though the Inter-Regional Deputies' Group was established, it was only half a

66 *First Congress* 1989 1, p.289.
67 See Chapter 4, Note 6, above.
68 Text of Yuri Afanasyev's undelivered address (*First Congress* 1989 4, pp.113-14).

year later that it formally declared itself an opposition, after the next - Second - Congress of People's Deputies had rejected all its proposals for political reforms.

The Congress debates demonstrated the majority's confidence that pluralism was something inadmissible, or at least unwelcome - despite all the hymns sung in its priase. The bogey of factionalism, which had long dominated the minds and life of the Bolsheviks and was instrumental in suppressing all sorts of opposition within the party in Stalin's time, was still very much alive. The majority of the deputies still seemed to model their vision of the state's supreme legislative body on the familiar pattern of a Party Congress, whose 'discussion' was limited to reports 'from the provinces'. A similar trend to offer local information on the subject as a substitute for a substantial discussion of the issue in question, albeit somewhat amended to suit the new 'critical' frame of mind, is clearly discernible in the proceedings. One wonders if that was not the original intent of those who chose the name for the new institution.

Part III

A New Behemoth, or
The Not Very Long Parliament

> *As to the time of attempting the change of government from monarchical to democratical, we must distinguish.*
>
> — Hobbes, *Behemoth, or The Long Parliament.*

6 The Crisis

Yeltsin, Korotich, Popov, Sakharov,
Garin, Zaslavsky,
Vlasov, Stankevich, Dikul, Drutse,
Sobchak, Gorbachev.
Mazurov, Grossu, Belov, Gvozdev,
Masol, Rodionov,
Chervonopissky, Paton, Kalish, Kasyan,
Gorbachev.
The system of one-party rule does
presumably have some advantage,
But of its nature, alas, mortals are
knowledge denied.

— I. Irtenyev, *Imitation of the Ancients.*

THE SECOND CONGRESS

The Issue of Article 6

We shall not try to examine the subsequent four Congresses as closely as we have done the first. Our purpose in the preceding chapter was to probe for features of political mentality and political behaviour that would be relevant to our task of providing a meaningful description of the political culture of both the corps of deputies and the society it was supposed to represent. We have been able to establish that the break with the totalitarian culture was not as radical as might be inferred from the curses hurled at the old regime. The following will be an attempt to understand the post-totalitarian phase of social development. It was the fate of the Congress that its consecutive sessions would turn out to be milestones of that development.

When the Second Congress of the USSR People's Deputies opened in Moscow on 12 December 1989, it was no mere six months that separated it from the previous one. Much had changed on the national political scene. The Supreme Soviet, elected by the First Congress, had already held two sessions and had enjoyed an unprecedented degree of publicity (*glasnost'*), by Soviet standards at least, and of pluralism. The latter would gain a foothold despite the fact that the 1977 Constitution still guaranteed the Communist Party its monopoly of power. By the time the Congress was convened, Article 6 of the Constitution, which proclaimed the Communist Party of the Soviet Union 'the leading and guiding force of Soviet society and the nucleus of its political system, of all state organizations and public organizations',[1] had become the focal point of public concern and subject of bitter controversy. On the eve of the Congress a number of leading members of the Inter-Regional Group, perhaps inspired by the successful 'velvet' revolutions in Czechoslovakia and East Germany and the resulting collapse of communist regimes in those two countries, had called for a general political strike in support of their demand to repeal Article 6 and legalize the multi-party system. The Supreme Soviet itself had voted 198 to 173 that the issue be put on the agenda of the Second Congress; however, the votes had not been enough to pass the resolution.[2]

The issue was brought up again at the Congress. Speakers took the floor and argued that Article 6 was obsolete and 'posed an obstacle to rapid changes',[3] that the problem was crucial for 'the prestige of *perestroika*'[4] and that public opinion definitely favoured its abrogation.[5] Objections were made to the effect that the Congress was not prepared to discuss the question. 'Everything must take its normal course,' said a party official from Riga. 'We must approach this, but not specially, not in such a way that we have today to tear a piece out of our Constitution and replace it.'[6] He was supported by a

1 *Constitution* 1985, p.16.
2 See *Second Congress* 1990 1, p.39.
3 Deputy Lauristin's speech at the first sitting (12 December 1989) (*Second Congress* 1990 1, p.23).
4 Yevgeny Yevtushenko's speech at the first sitting (12 December 1989) (ibid., p.24).
5 Deputy Sulakshin's and Deputy Shchelkanov's speeches at the first sitting (12 December 1989) (*Second Congress* 1990 1, pp.28 and 38); see also Andrei Sakharov's encounter with Gorbachev (*Second Congress* 1990 1, p.32).
6 Deputy Klautzen's speech at the first sitting (12 December 1989) (ibid., p.26).

fellow-secretary from Nikolayev: 'To rip out Article 6 alone or consider questions that the Supreme Soviet has not gone into seems unethical to me.'[7] That the Congress was not ready to discuss the issue, the other side argued, was because the second session of the Supreme Soviet had failed to fulfil the commission imposed on it by the First Congress and the relevant decision of its own first session. That commission had been to prepare constitutional amendments concerning the electoral system and other vital problems for the next Congress. It would be appropriate, therefore, the argument ran, 'to return to the formula recorded in the Resolution of the first Congress and to take a vote just on it'.[8] The Congress voted 1,194 to 868, with 58 abstentions, against putting the issue of Article 6 on the agenda.[9]

It was a scandalous decision in the circumstances. To reaffirm the ruling party's monopoly over state power was to make all declarations about democracy and pluralism pure fiction. Public opinion – and it was this opinion that was behind the decision that the Supreme Soviet had nearly passed – would unequivocally blame the present predicament on the Communist Party and insist on constitutional guarantees of free political activity and on legalization of a multi-party system. The continuing delay was becoming simply disgraceful, and the Congress's blunt refusal to reckon with public demands dealt a severe blow to its prestige.

The Congruence of Legislation and the Sovereignty of the Republics

There were two more interrelated items on the Congress's agenda that promised bitter controversy: the USSR Law on Constitutional Supervision and the election of the appropriate committee. The bill was vehemently opposed by deputies from the Baltic republics, supported by a number of leading Russian democrats. The Baltic representatives were worried that the new committee might repeal the laws already passed or about to be passed by their legislatures as contradicting the Constitution of the Soviet Union. That they did contradict the Union

---

7 Deputy Sharayev's speech at the first sitting (12 December 1989) (ibid., p.27).
8 Deputy Lopatin's speech at the first sitting (12 December 1989) (ibid., pp.29-30).
9 The division figures were checked by a special commission (ibid, pp.40-63; **2**, pp.277-9).

Constitution was impossible to deny: the deviations were visible to the naked eye. Such collisions usually turn on some key point. This time it was Article 74 of the Constitution. The article ruled that in the event of discrepancy between a republican and an all-Union law, the law of the USSR was to prevail.[10] This would automatically invalidate whatever law was passed by the republics that contradicted the Constitution of the Union. The republican parliaments, however, ruled that priority was theirs and that union legislature was subject to their ratification. They would refer to Article 76 of the Union Constitution that proclaimed Union republics 'sovereign states'.[11] 'Imagine a sovereign state, whose supreme representative body has no right to enact laws, because they may be declared invalid any time,' said a professor of Riga University.[12]

He was backed by colleagues, from both Baltic and other republics, including Russia. It was argued that the Committee for Constitutional Supervision might prove an obstacle to constitutional reforms: the Committee would have to determine whether new legislation conformed to the obviously obsolete and undemocratic Constitution. Fyodor Burlatsky thought it was 'juridical nonsense'.[13]

The situation was paradoxical: whereas democrats resisted the institution in the country of a body of established democratic reputation, their opponents from among the party-state *nomenklatura* suddenly began to speak of rule of law,[14] presumption of innocence[15] and human rights.

10 *Constitution* 1985, p.43 (Article 74).
11 Ibid., p.44 (Article 76).
12 Deputy Plotnieks's speech at the second sitting (12 December 1989) (*Second Congress* 1990 1, pp.85–6).
13 Fyodor Burlatsky's speech at the second sitting (12 December 1989) (ibid., p.98).
14 Compare Deputy Dzharimov's speech at the second sitting (12 December 1989) (ibid., p.94):

> We are moving towards the rule of law. Foundations for it are already being laid in the country. The *sine qua non* of success, however, is unconditional observation of enacted laws. They must live and function for the benefit of society. But the practice in our country shows that laws, unfortunately, are often not observed. ... Some people might say that we have lived without a committee for constitutional supervision for 72 years. But does that not account for everything that we are now experiencing, for what we have inherited from the period of lawlessness and the cult of personality?

15 Compare Gennadi Yanayev's speech at the second sitting (12 December 1989) (ibid., p.92):

This unnatural disposition affected both reasoning and voting. Those who opposed the bill on constitutional supervision declared that they supported the measure in principle but found it untimely,[16] and their bid to strike the item off the agenda polled only 438 votes (42 abstained), whereas the opposition was able to collect 868 votes on the issue of Article 6. A number of influential persons who belonged to the democratic wing voted with the majority, including Anatoly Sobchak and Konstantin Lubenchenko, both members of the legal profession. This settled the next question: the election of the Committee for Constitutional Supervision was put on the agenda without voting.

However, the issue was complicated indeed, and the debate exposed the source (as yet only the source) of many a startling detour. To cut a long story short, the controversy indicated discrepancy and even a clash between such motivating factors of political behaviour as interests and values. Those who had already in the new circumstances chanced to be a minority, and those who had experienced the frustration of being rejected by the hostile masses, felt the need to defend the values hitherto regarded aa alien and even 'seditious'. On the other hand, that state of affairs and considerations of expediency put many a declaration to a severe test as regards sincerity.

Among the most pressing issues of the day two were of particular consequence. One was the status of official ('state') languages, on which a number of republics had recently passed controversial new laws. The other was new Baltic legislation on suffrage that tended to restrict substantially the civil rights of the naturalized ('non-indigenous') population and openly sought to exclude it from political life.

The Baltic deputies, whose primary concern was to recover independence for their republics, were regarded by public opinion as a

---

Having as yet not established the Committee for Constitutional Supervision of the USSR, we are already infringing the presumption of innocence, proceeding from the assumption that the Committee must necessarily defend the standpoint of the Centre, rather than the standpoint of a republic.

16 Burlatsky's speech at the second sitting (12 December 1989) (ibid., p.99):

From the political point of view, comrades, this is not the case to break lances. There are cases that are worth fighting, but this is a different case. We shall not be late, if we pass this Law through the Supreme Soviet of the USSR and submit it to the next Congress of People's Deputies.

part of the democratic opposition. Since the right to independence was an axiom of the democratic *Weltanschauung*, the democratic opposition sympathized with the Balts and made no effort to conceal their negative attitude towards the preservation of imperial rule. And since defenders of the old regime would not hear of independence for the Baltic states, a coalition of Russian democrats with national movements seemed natural enough. The Baltic deputies gave their full support to a number of conventional democratic demands, including the opposition's main demand to remove Article 6 of the old Constitution. In this respect, moreover, the Balts set an example: for all intents and purposes multi-party systems were already in force in their republics.

In other respects, however, unflinching fidelity to democratic ideals promised to create problems for the Baltic leaders. Champions of independence in Estonia, Latvia and Lithuania had every reason to doubt that their secession from the Soviet Union would meet with full-fledged support from the Russian and Russian-speaking population, especially after they had enacted their new laws on state languages, so unpopular with those groups. No matter what their reasons had been, the law-makers had complicated their own task: the new laws posed a direct threat of discrimination against the 'non-indigenous' population of the Baltic republics and were bound to deepen ethnic alienation. And if account were taken of the fact that in at least two of the three Baltic republics the proportion of Russian and Russian-speaking population was almost half of the total, the prospects for gaining independence, while strictly abiding by the 'rules of the democratic game', must have appeared doubtful to many. Where painstaking adherence to democratic principles seemed to pose obstacles on the way towards the desired goal, the temptation would be great to forgo them for the sake of the higher purpose. Thus, the national idea would come into conflict with that of democracy.

This circumstance augured substantial shifts in the future, as far as political coalitions were concerned. The conflict of interests might easily pull former ideological allies apart, whereas close or even partly identical interests would not necessarily secure a lasting unity. A temporary coincidence of interests might prove insufficient to overcome the mutual alienation, born of the incompatibility of cultures, and to create a pragmatic alliance, given that values were so different. And this in turn would mean that factors that tended to separate politicians (and the social groups behind them) might soon prevail over factors that tended to unite them.

Procedural Bottlenecks

Let us return to the agenda, however. A discussion of procedures was provided for by Item 4: 'On the Standing Orders of the USSR Congress of People's Deputies and the USSR Supreme Soviet'. Half a year earlier the deputies had displayed perplexity and indignation. The Second Congress witnessed no protests, but there remained enough ambiguity to cause misunderstanding and quarrels more than once.

One such incident occurred at the eleventh sitting (19 December 1989). The deputies had just approved of the economic programme presented by Nikolai Ryzhkov's government and rejected alternative proposals. The next move was to choose one of the draft texts as a basis for the eventual resolution on the matter. The first one to be put to a vote polled 1,106 in favour against 769 against, with 96 abstentions. Now 1,106 was more than a half of the total number of votes (1,971), as well as more than a half of the total number of deputies present (the latter was estimated by the chairman as 2,106); however, it was slightly less than a half of the total number of deputies elected: 2,245 (five seats being vacant at that moment).[17] The chairman (Gorbachev) immediately proposed to consider the decision adopted if more than 50 per cent of deputies registered and present at the sitting voted for it, on the grounds that this had become standard practice in the Supreme Soviet.[18]

However, this *ad hoc* arrangement cast doubt on other votes, some of which were of critical importance. Not a day had passed since the Congress had turned down the constitutional amendment abolishing in the future the election of People's Deputies by public organizations. The motion had polled 1,354 votes, whereas only 509 deputies had voted to preserve the current wording of the respective Article (95); 42 had abstained: the total number of votes had thus been 1,905. Meanwhile, the chairman (Anatoly Lukyanov) had warned that the

17 *Second Congress* 1990 **2**, p.499.
18 Ibid., p.662.

amendment had needed 1,497 votes to be adopted, that is, two-thirds of the total number of deputies elected. It was easy to calculate that the previous day's resolution on Article 95 ought to be revoked if the count was to be made on the basis of those present rather than the total number elected: 1,354 was fewer than two-thirds of 2,245 or 2,106 (which would have been 1,497 and 1,404, respectively), but definitely more than two-thirds of 1,905 (that is, 1,270). Since Article 174 stipulated that the Constitution might be amended by a decision adopted by a majority of not less than two-thirds 'of the total number of the USSR People's Deputies',[19] it was clear that the amendment had been rejected.

However, the relevant Item 4 of the Congress's Provisional Standing Orders also referred to the total number of deputies.[20] The provision might create problems and even lead to a deadlock. It was by no means impossible that the absence of a sufficient number of deputies might bar any decision whatsoever, provided they were counted as voting *contra*. The proposal to proceed on the basis of the number present was, therefore, logical enough, provided a quorum was secured, of course. This, however, required a decision of principle. Adjusting procedures to suit the particular situation would certainly be unacceptable. Besides, the arrangement ought to be consistent. From this standpoint, the idea that 'present' meant 'registered' was not particularly felicitous: instead of counting those immediately available for voting, one was being asked to assume that all those who had registered at the Congress, that is a few days ago, were available to vote. This was an example of the middle point being worse than the extremes: lacking their merits, it combined their weak points. It would not, for instance, preclude deadlocks (when everyone is outvoted) – it would only make them less probable.[21]

We have considered at some length this seemingly insignificant incident in order to demonstrate the kind of procedural jumble in which the supreme body of state power was obliged to function –

19 *Constitution* 1988, p.63 (Article 174).
20 See *First Congress* 1989 **3**, p.337.
21 On several occasions the Congress turned out to be pretty close to such a deadlock. At the fourth sitting (13 December), for example, in the election to the post of Chairman of the Editorial Commission, Vadim Medvedev received 1,072 votes out of 1,843. This was a weighty majority, but it would not have been had the calculations been based on the number of deputies registered (2,106): see *Second Congress* 1990 **1**, pp.341ff.

partly thanks to the deputies' disposition to ignore procedural problems as trifling or even meaningless.[22]

True, in the months that had passed since the First Congress the deputies had had ample opportunity to reconsider their initial attitude. The experience they might have gained in the Supreme Soviet was probably the most important single factor in that. Those who had not valued procedures, and failed to realize the extent to which the efficiency of their combined work depended on them, could see for themselves 'how important it was not to despise procedures and rules'.[23] On 20 December the Congress approved of the Standing Orders for both itself and the Supreme Soviet.

By that time, however, it had become clear that procedural niceties had not been the Congress's sole problem. As early as its first sitting, when the question was debated whether the Law on Constitutional Supervision and the election of the respective committee should be put on the agenda, one of the discussants put forward an argument that might be considered a prophecy, in the sentence: '2,250 persons is not the number of deputies that is required to enact a concrete and very important and serious law'.[24] In the light of this remark, the Congress's prospects did not seem particularly bright. It was not easy to imagine the type of procedural arrangements that had to be worked out in order to make the Congress a working legislature.

If illustration is needed, suffice it to mention the agenda's main item: the Council of Ministers' report 'On Measures for Restoration of the Economy, Stages of Economic Reform, and Principal Approaches to Promulgating the Thirteenth Five-Year Plan'. According to a senior member of the Secretariat, more than 450 applications for the floor were put in by noon of 13 December (the second day of the Congress), including some 300 that referred to the future debate on the government's report. Besides, there were more than 100 applications for the sections that were registered separately from those for plenary sittings. 'It is evident that we are not getting through the business in the time allowed for discussion,' he said.[25]

22 See above, Chapter 5.
23 A remark by an unnamed deputy (most probably, S.Stankevich) at the eleventh sitting (19 December 1989) (*Second Congress* 1990 **2**, pp.663–4).
24 Deputy Levashov's speech at the first sitting (12 December 1989) (*Second Congress* 1990 **1** p.87). His was not an isolated remark: see, for example, Deputy Khmura's speech at the thirteenth sitting (20 December 1989) (ibid. **3**, p.95).
25 Ibid. **1**, p.277.

No serious discussion of Ryzhkov's economic programme was possible at plenary sittings in those circumstances. According to the Provisional Standing Orders then in force, the total duration of sittings was to be six hours a day, whereas participants in the debates on reports and supplementary reports were allowed the floor for not more than 15 minutes each.[26] Four hundred speeches would have taken almost 17 days (with no allowance for intervals) – that is, longer than the whole Congress, with its agenda of nine items, lasted. Even then fewer than one-fifth of the deputies would have had a chance to join in the discussion. And despite the fact that the Congress split into three sections ('Measures for Rehabilitation of Economy', 'Stages of Economic Reform', 'Principal Approaches to the Thirteenth Five-Year Plan') which were in session for the whole day on 14 December, the total number of deputies who took part in the debate was only 162. That was exactly one out of thirteen participants to the Congress and fewer than a half of those who had applied for the floor. Of these, only 50 deputies were allowed to address the plenary sittings; the rest had to content themselves with the sections.[27]

The Failure of the Congress as a Political Institution

When the First Congress was in session, it was natural to think that the new institution's major limitation was its corps of deputies. The mentality and the experience of the majority of deputies belonged, indeed, to the political culture of the *ancien régime*. It was this culture that the deputies elected in spring 1989 (under the circumstances of limited democracy and the law that deviated so obviously from democratic conventions) brought to the Congress. The Congress's first major action – election of the Supreme Soviet (it would be reckless to base any serious assumption on the preceding election of its Chairman, devoid of alternatives and predetermined as it was) – showed what political forces dominated the Congress.

The point, however, was not only that the majority was 'aggressively obedient' or 'Stalinist-Brezhnevist', as Yuri Afanasyev labelled it:[28] a new election would be bound to yield different results,

26 Item 13 of the Provisional Standing Orders for Sittings of the Congress of People's Deputies of the USSR: see *First Congress* 1989 **3**, p.339.
27 See *Second Congress* 1990 **2**, p.352.
28 See *First Congress* 1989 **1**, pp.223–4.

as it did a year later. The point was not even that the mechanism of election to the Supreme Soviet was cumbersome and notoriously illogical: that could be remedied, too. The point was that this cumbersome procedure was not the result of oversight on anyone's part; nor was it caused by anyone's lack of legal experience – no more, indeed, than that had been responsible for the rules of election to the Congress itself. The institution's structural 'flaws' had been frankly aimed at reducing its functions to showy plebiscitary acts, of the kind characteristic of the *Zemskie Sobors* of medieval Muscovy or the Soviets of the revolutionary years. Whatever their intentions, the authors of the constitutional reform of 1988 had managed to set up a political institution which was capable of nothing else.

The Constitution assigned to the Congress the task of attending to the most important problems that life might pose, but it denied it the opportunity to carry out its task: the deputies simply lacked the necessary time. It evoked feelings of shame and unease to watch the Congress vote for 'the line to be drawn against further debate'. Thanks to this procedure, the presidium was always in a position to deny the minority not only the right to influence the decision-making, but even a chance to state its viewpoint. And it was simultaneously amusing and discomforting to hear members of the presidium or the secretariat calculate how many times the floor had been given to representatives of how many Union and autonomous republics on the item in question and how many more would be given a chance to speak. This endless shortage of time made it absurd to hope that the debate could be joined in by all the deputies. It was natural, however, in such circumstances, to ask what the point was in holding this meeting at all. Or what was the point of forming constituencies and staging elections in them, when the right to speak belonged to 'republics' or to 'deputations' that no one had voted for.

Deputies who were denied the floor could not help feeling their rights infringed, of course. They were allowed, as a kind of compensation, to present the texts of their undelivered speeches to the secretariat for inclusion in the proceedings. This compensation, however, was offensively inadequate. True, in 1989, when *glasnost'* had not yet become freedom of the press, many still found this chance 'to appeal to the public' attractive. Perusal of the proceedings of the first two Congresses reveals that such unspoken texts account for no fewer pages (perhaps even more) than the verbatim records of speeches actually delivered from the rostrum. That was not a proper way to handle the problem, of course. It might have been acceptable had it been a symposium of scientists, but for a legislative assembly this 'posthumous' publication of a 'speech' made no sense at all, since any proposals and arguments it contained could no longer influence the audience they had originally been intended for and hence the decisions that the audience had had to make. It was little wonder, then, that the number of these speeches 'in writing' rapidly diminished from the Third Congress,[29] since to include them with the proceedings would have been to counterfeit participation. As for the public, the deputies soon discovered better ways to acquaint it with their ideas.

The model of *sobornost'* was evidently in crisis. Half a year earlier, when the euphoria aroused by the first steps towards democracy had still been present, amid hopes inspired by these moves, the symptoms of this crisis might have passed unnoticed. The First Congress of People's Deputies had in itself been an event unique in Soviet history. For the first time in the past 70 years there had been a legal opposition active within the country's uppermost body of power. Moreover, it had not just been allowed the floor in a legislative assembly: direct television broadcasting had given it a nation-wide audience. In the circumstances the Congress, as a political enterprise, had been doomed to success, no matter what particular decisions it had been inclined to make, or succeeded in making. But the 'honeymoon' could not have lasted for ever. The time came for political routine, for everyday work, and it was soon evident that in the form it had acquired the Congress of People's Deputies was unable to function. Spinoza observed once that 'Academies that are founded at public expense are instituted not so much to cultivate men's natural abilities as to restrain them.'[30] This or something similar

---

29 360 undelivered speeches at the First Congress: see ibid. **4**, pp.3-455; **5**, pp.3-508; **6**, pp.3-509); 345 speeches at the Second Congress (see *Second Congress* 1990 **5**, pp.3-635; **6**, pp.3-622); 39 speeches at the Third Congress (see *Third Congress* 1990 **3**, pp.217-334; it must be noted, however, this was an Extraordinary Congress with a limited agenda that lasted only four days); 131 speeches at the Fourth Congress (see *Fourth Congress* 1991 **4**, pp.3-399). The complete proceedings for the Fifth Congress have not been published at the time of writing.

30 Spinoza 1951, p.369.

was true of the Congress: devised and created by the reform-minded party functionaries, it was intended not so much to promote the political reforms as to restrain them. By virtue of its constitutional prerogative, the Congress was able to revise decisions of the Supreme Soviet, should these prove undesirable, whereas its structure and operating conditions prevented it from doing anything more than that.

The Congress was not willing to acknowledge and legalize this state of affairs formally by introducing appropriate provisions into its Standing Orders, of course, even though proposals were sometimes made to that effect. 'The draft laws presented to the Congress must be put to a vote without discussion,' urged one deputy. 'The draft law is to be either adopted or sent back to the Supreme Soviet, or its commissions or committees, for revision.'[31] Whether we treat such suggestions as loyal attempts to divert the legislative river into a smoother bed, or view them as wicked anti-democratic *démarches* aimed at curbing the constitutional authority of the only body of power elected (albeit only to a two-thirds extent) by direct vote, it is impossible to deny that they had a more or less realistic appraisal of the factual state of affairs to back them.

True, the fact that the Congress was capable of coordinated and purposeful effort only to the extent that the party–state leadership managed to preserve effective control over it hardly added to its prestige. And if the reformers grouped around Gorbachev had ever counted on the Congress to legitimate both their power and their policy, they must have been disappointed: the Congress did not and could not give them what it lacked itself.

The subsequent development and especially the story of the Third Congress of People's Deputies may be viewed as mere illustration of the above analysis.

31 Deputy Naumov's speech at the thirteenth sitting (20 December 1989) *(Second Congress* 1990 **3**, p.101).

THE THIRD CONGRESS

Abolition of Article 6 and Legitimation of Political Pluralism

The Third Congress opened on 12 March 1990, only two and a half months after the conclusion of the Second Congress. It was considered an extraordinary one and was convened, indeed, to make but one decision: to establish the office of President of the USSR. On the previous day, the CPSU Central Committee held its plenary session and decided to exercise its right of legislative initiative and 'to submit ... for consideration of the extraordinary Third Congress of People's Deputies of the USSR a draft Law of the USSR on amendments and supplements to the Constitution (Fundamental Law) of the USSR in respect of political system (Articles 6 and 7 of the Constitution of the USSR)'.[32]

The point was to repeal (or rather, amend) the notorious Article 6 or, as Lukyanov chose to put it in his report to the Congress, 'to define the CPSU's place in a new way'.[33] Henceforth the Communist Party was not to be regarded as 'the leading and guiding force of Soviet society and the nucleus of its political system, of all state organizations and public organizations'. All references to Marxism–Leninism were to be withdrawn from the Fundamental Law: the Constitution was no longer to prescribe to the ruling party the theory with which it was to 'arm' itself. The party's functions were to become less ambitious: instead of 'determining the general perspectives of the development of society and the course of the home and foreign policy of the USSR, directing the great constructive work of the Soviet people, and imparting a planned, systematic and theoretically substantiated character to their struggle for the victory of communism'[34] it was merely 'to take part in elaboration of the policy of the Soviet state and the administration of state and public affairs'. It was to do this, moreover, 'through its representatives elected to Soviets of People's Deputies and in other forms', on a par with 'other political parties, and also trade union, youth and other public

---

32 Quoted from *Izvestiya* 12 March 1990, p.1.
33 Lukyanov's report on constitutional amendments at the first sitting (12 March) (*Third Congress* 1990 1, p.14).
34 *Constitution* 1985, p.16 (Article 6).

organizations and mass movements'.[35] However, a motion to omit all mention of the Communist Party failed to poll the required two-thirds of the deputies' votes and was rejected.[36]

Articles 7 and 51 were amended, too. The latter would henceforth recognize the right of citizens to associate not only in 'public organizations', but in 'political parties', and to 'participate in mass movements' as well.[37] Removed from the former were the list of 'authorized' public organizations ('trade unions, the All-Union Leninist Young Communist League, cooperatives, and others') and reference to their participation 'in managing state and public affairs, and in deciding political, economic, and social and cultural matters'.[38] The new version demanded that 'all political parties, public organizations and mass movements' abide by the Constitution and Soviet law and prohibited 'the establishment and activity of parties, organizations and movements that aim to change the Soviet constitutional order and the integrity of the socialist state by violent means, to undermine its security, or arouse social, national or religious discord.'[39] Following recent legislation concerning property, Articles 10 to 13 of Chapter 2 ('The Economic System') were also amended.[40]

From the purely constitutional standpoint, the reform of 1990 appeared far more radical than its predecessor of 1988. Abolition of the CPSU's privileged constitutional status affected the very core of the Soviet socio-political order.[41] Had this decision been made by the First Congress of People's Deputies in May or June 1989, it would have boosted its prestige enormously. Even in December, when the

---

35 'Law of the Union of Soviet Socialist Republics on the Establishment of the Office of the President of the USSR and Amendments and Supplements to the Constitution (Fundamental Law) of the USSR', *Third Congress* 1990 **3**, p.193.

36 Deputy Akhundov's amendment received 1,067 votes against 906 with 39 abstentions: *Third Congress* 1990 **1**, p.237.

37 See *Constitution* 1985, pp.33–4 (Article 5); 'Law ... on the Establishment of the Office of the President of the USSR ...', *op.cit.*, p.194.

38 *Constitution* 1985, p.16 (Article 7).

39 'Law ... on the Establishment of the Office of the President of the USSR ...', *op.cit.*, p.193.

40 *Third Congress* 1990 **3**, pp.193–4.

41 As Lukyanov correctly pointed out, 'for decades all real power in the country – political, economic, spiritual – was concentrated in the hands of the party, and of its committees at all levels. This position of the CPSU was incorporated into political structures, into the psychology of the leadership and of the apparatus of all levels, and into public consciousness' (*Third Congress* 1990 **1**, p.13).

Second Congress had been in session, it would have evoked a tremendous response. Who knows what consequences this might have had for the Congress itself as a political institution? However, by March 1990 the situation had changed, and the passage of time had nothing to do with it: the matter was not those eleven weeks that separated the closing of the Second Congress and the opening of the Third one. Two or three months earlier or two or three months later: was the difference so important? The country had waited 70 years, so could it not have waited 70 days more? What mattered was not *when*, but *how*.

It was easy to guess that the party was not particularly enthusiastic at having to resign its unique constitutional status and the privileges that went with it, including its monopoly of power. Since the Communist Party could no longer withstand the pressure of the democratic opposition, however, it had better take the initiative – if only to save face. This argument had often been used to urge the party leadership to invalidate Article 6: 'The country is holding its breath, the whole world is holding its breath and waiting for a courageous, considered decision, above all, of the communist deputies. This is no attack on the party, but a fight for its true prestige.'[42]

One wonders, indeed, whether the speaker cared much about the CPSU's prestige and whether that anxiety was the basic motive for this kind of advice. But in any case that advice was reasonable enough: 'voluntary' abdication was more seemly than violent overthrow. Whether the ideal gain of saving face was equal to the thoroughly material loss of monopoly of power was a different question. Theoretically, it was quite plausible that this kind of initiative might have paid a fair political dividend in different circumstances. However, it was hardly realistic to keep counting on this as late as the spring of 1990.

However that may have been, the initiative in December had been that of the opposition, not the party, and the party leadership had done its best to prevent the issue being considered at the Second Congress, even though some of Gorbachev's remarks might have been taken as hints that he, at least, had been ready to have Article 6 repealed:

42 Deputy Sulakshin's speech at the first sitting (12 December 1989) (*Second Congress* 1990 **1**, p.28).

The point, therefore, is that the party's authority, its position, its prestige, does not, indeed - everyone agrees - rest on this article. It is a different matter whether we may put the question so as to create an impression, helter-skelter, to the chime of bells, that if we settle the issue of Article 6 today, everything will be nice, fine and well tomorrow. ... But matters that have matured have to be settled, including Article 6. On this subject, I think, both the Central Committee and the whole party will have their say - and in the course of preparing for the CPSU's Twenty-Eighth Congress, too. We must find a solution that would correspond to the party's position, to its new functions as a political vanguard, that would reflect the process of separation of functions that is going on in the state and that we bear witness to. Therefore, we ought not to be drawn into a conflict.[43]

If we are right in our interpretation of the above passage, in December 1989 Gorbachev was disposed to view the delay as merely an operation to seize back the initiative. To all appearances, his was a wrong appraisal - not because the party's motion was already too late, not even because there was something farcical about it after the obstinate resistance the party had offered before and during the Second Congress. Rather, it was wrong because at stake was no longer the prestige of the party - under the circumstances, probably nothing could have saved it, or what was left of it, anyway - but that of the Congress itself. When the Congress refused to discuss Article 6 in December 1989, it betrayed its political *credo*. When in March 1990 it agreed to consider the matter and then settled it without much ado along the lines of the latest party directives, the Congress did not demonstrate its ability to heed the voice of the people or its capacity for change: it rather made itself look foolish. Consequential here was the very sequence of those incompatible decisions, indicative of the fact that the Congress of People's Deputies was, as Yuri Afanasyev delicately put it, a nominal rather than real legislative counterbalance to the executive.[44] And to put it with no particular consideration for the deputies' self-esteem, by obediently fulfilling the decision of a party plenary session, the Congress only testified to its inability, as well as its unwillingness, to resist manipulation.

---

43 *Second Congress* 1990 1, p.36.
44 Yuri Afanasyev's speech at the first sitting (12 March) (*Third Congress* 1990 1, p.45).

Presidential Election

Meanwhile, whereas the prestige of the newly established presidency did not depend directly on the prestige of the Congress that was to establish it, the prestige of the president did. Since the first president of the USSR was to be elected by the Congress of People's Deputies, the former's authority was to derive from that of the latter. This bond was further strengthened by the fact that the election of the president was, by way of exception, to deviate from the constitutional amendments just ratified. A new Article 127.1 of the Constitution (Section II of the Law on establishment of the presidency) provided for the president to be elected by 'citizens of the USSR on the basis of universal, equal, and direct suffrage',[45] whereas Section III of that very law ruled that 'the first president of the USSR shall be elected by the USSR Congress of People's Deputies'.[46]

The decision was unorthodox, indeed. Principles of democracy and rule of law clashed once again with considerations of political expediency. Advocates of the 'double' decision – to promulgate direct nation-wide election in principle, but to have Gorbachev elected right there at the Congress by deputies' vote alone – would substantiate their position by reference to the complicated political situation in the country which presumably made a presidential election (on the terms provided for by the amended Constitution) impossible at that moment.

The polemic on the issue that surfaced at the Congress's fifth sitting (14 March) was essentially that of like-minded persons. The bulk of the corps of deputies took no part in the debate: the election of the president by the Congress posed no problem to the traditional mentality, as was to be expected, of course. Democrats alone felt uneasy about the procedure. Of thirteen persons who joined in the discussion[47] there was none who had, for example, voted against putting the issue of Article 6 on the agenda of the Second Congress: eleven had supported the motion then and two had been absent (there was, however, little doubt as to their attitude: they were Sergei Zalygin, Editor-in-Chief of *Novy mir*, and Alexander Yakovlev, leader of the reformist wing in the Central Committee).

45 'Law ... on the Establishment of the Office of the President of the USSR ...', *op.cit.*, p.195.
46 *Third Congress* 1990 **3**, p.206.
47 Ibid. **2**, pp.373–87.

The democratic opposition was facing a dilemma akin to the one the communist reformers had faced 18 months earlier (before the constitutional reform of 1988) the kernel of which was best expressed by the proverb 'There is no rose without a thorn'. Supporting democracy and free election in principle, many reformers had realized at that time how likely they had been to lose the election. This time the irony was that leaders of the democratic opposition were not concerned for themselves. They had every reason to believe they would win, and it was not long before their hopes were justified. But they also had every reason to doubt that Gorbachev would win if a presidential election were held outside the Palace of Congresses. Still, they were willing enough to have him as president and were ready to 'compromise the principles' – in the notable expression used by Nikolai Travkin.[48]

No one would say aloud that Gorbachev was most likely to lose the nation-wide election, of course. That would have been tactless both personally and politically: one cannot very well advocate democracy, while electing as president someone known for certain to have no popular support. It is better to speak of a multi-party system not having developed yet and of the resulting absence of 'real conditions for a genuine alternative vote';[49] of 'paralysis of the executive' and 'the state of emergency in a number of regions';[50] of the threat of 'civil war';[51] of months of 'anarchy' the country would have to face;[52] even of the nation-wide election making the Congress useless and ineffective and thus eliminating the counterbalance to the presidency, indispensable for 'our fragile, euphoric ... democracy'.[53] The latter argument – with its allusion to the classical doctrine of 'checks and balances' – was particularly touching in the light of the reputation the Congress had already managed to establish.[54]

Although the forecast behind these arguments was probably right

---

48 Ibid., p.381. The cliché was made famous overnight when *Sovetskaya Rossiya* (13 March 1988) published an article by a hitherto unknown Leningrad chemistry teacher Nina Andreyeva, entitled 'I Cannot Forgo Principles' and attacking Gorbachev's reforms.

49 Deputy Nikolsky's speech: *Third Congress* 1990 **2**, p.375.

50 Anatoly Sobchak's speech: ibid., p.377.

51 Nikolai Travkin's and Dmitri Likhachev's speeches: ibid., pp.381, 385.

52 Sergei Zalygin's speech: ibid., p.383.

53 Alexander Yakovlev's speech: ibid., p.384.

54 Compare, for example, Yuri Afanasyev's appraisal (see above, Note 44).

and Gorbachev stood no chance of winning a nation-wide election, neither were the arguments of the other side altogether devoid of sense. These people would refer to their voters' opinions[55] and question the admissibility of deviating from constitutional norms for the sake of the moment.[56] However, their main and most convincing argument was that no political stability would be secured anyway without participation by the people.[57]

They were right. Election of the president by the Congress, legitimate enough from the standpoint of the national political tradition and quite acceptable under different – more stable and less dramatic – circumstances, could hardly be effective as a means of overcoming the crisis of power. A president with no clear will of the citizenry to rely on would simply never wield authority sufficient to embark on a deep-going and not entirely painless reform. In the eyes of the voters such a president would remain as he had been before: a protégé of the party elite, particularly as another attempt in the Congress to secure the separation of the two leadership posts – those of the ruling party and of the state – failed. What appeared to be distant perspectives were sacrificed again for the sake of more pragmatic considerations: it seemed, and indeed was, dangerous for the reform-minded General Secretary to lose control of the party, most of whose functionaries did not even pretend to favour the reform and were moreover stung by the recent loss of their constitutional monopoly of power. But it was also true that the reform-minded president could gain little by refusing to sever his ties with a political force responsible, in the eyes of the public, for the country's present predicament.

As for Gorbachev himself, his irregular election, involving deviation from constitutional procedures, was doubly hazardous. From the standpoint of legitimacy, his position was already precarious enough: even his status as a deputy was questioned, for, unlike his principal rival, he had not dared to face a constituency campaign and had chosen to be elected by his own Central Committee within the quota set for his own party.

---

55 Speeches by Deputies Shchelkanov, Kryzhkov, Desyatov and Zaslavsky (*Third Congress* 1990 **2**, pp.374, 378, 380, 382).
56 Deputy Zaslavsky's speech: ibid., pp.381-2.
57 Deputy Panov's speech: ibid., p.383.

As a result of all this, the people's deputies, who had been called upon at this Extraordinary Congress to approve of the unavoidable change and to secure the continuity (and stability) of leadership in the changed conditions, voted for a decision that would bring no benefit in the long run. Gorbachev gained the presidency without difficulty: as in May 1989, he was the only candidate and polled 1,329 votes against 495 (of 2,000 ballot papers issued, 122 failed to appear in the box and 54 were declared invalid). However, the executive was not consolidated for long: by autumn the president was forced to ask for extra powers, was given them again – and again in vain.

7 Fiasco

Vouch for no one.

— Thales.

THE FOURTH CONGRESS

The Political Situation on the Eve of the Congress

It was a grave situation that confronted the Fourth Congress of People's Deputies. This was determined by two basic factors: the acute economic crisis brought about by the obvious failure of the hesitant, inconsistent economic reforms of Ryzhkov's government, and the growing tension between the democrats, who occupied influential positions both in Russia and in some other republics after the 1990 elections, on the one hand, and the so-called 'Centre' – the power agencies of the USSR still closely tied to the CPSU, on the other hand. This opposition was accompanied by 'a parade of sovereignties', with republics one after another claiming precedence for their laws over the laws of the Union. This threatened to paralyse the already not particularly successful activity of the Union legislature and plunge the country into a state of legal and political havoc.

However, a compromise was taking shape in the summer of 1990 between Mikhail Gorbachev and Boris Yeltsin, who had by that time become Chairman of the Supreme Soviet of the Russian Federal Republic. The platform for Gorbachev's *rapprochement* with the democrats was the programme of economic reform which later became known as 'the 500-Days Programme' and which offered a quick and, if the authors were to be believed, relatively painless transition to a market economy. In September the Supreme Soviet approved of 'the 500-Days Programme' in principle, but did not adopt it formally.

Towards the end of September the political situation worsened sharply after Gorbachev asked the Supreme Soviet for additional powers and was given them, while Moscow democrats staged a formidable demonstration that called for Ryzhkov's government to resign. Gorbachev's attitude to the democrats changed abruptly. Although Ryzhkov's government was doomed and its resignation was but a matter of time, Gorbachev did not wish to break with the conservatives once and for all. Still, after the 500-Days Programme was eventually rejected in October and replaced by the amorphous 'General Orientations', Gorbachev needed some new impulse for his reforms that would have been less unacceptable to the conservatives than the 500-Days Programme. He found what he sought in the idea of a constitutional reform that would greatly enhance the role of the republics. A substantial element of the reform he had in mind was the establishment of a Council of the Federation. This organ was to consist of the leaders of the republics, but possess rather vague prerogatives. It was not even clear who was to represent the republics in the new Council: the solution was left to the republics themselves, thus adding to the uncertainty.

Gorbachev presented this draft programme to the Supreme Soviet in November 1990 as his preemptive response to the severe criticism he expected to be levelled at him and his policy by the deputies, frightened by the rapidly worsening economic situation.

Another important element of the reform was the establishment of the Cabinet of Ministers directly subordinate to the president, replacing the former Council of Ministers. This *'perestroika'* in the top echelons of power allowed Gorbachev to fire Ryzhkov and his government without too much humiliation by disguising it as a constitutional reform. It also consolidated presidential control over the executive.

The third essential element of the 'new wave' of *perestroika* was to be the Union Treaty. The idea of a new treaty to replace the old one signed in 1922 had long been advocated by the republics controlled by the democratic opposition, but it waned somewhat after 'the parade of sovereignties' reached its peak in the summer.[1]

1 Lithuania was the first to declare independence on 11 March 1990. It was followed by Estonia on 30 March and Latvia on 4 May. The process acquired new impetus after Russia proclaimed its sovereignty (as distinguished from independence) on 12 June. Other republics followed suit: Uzbekistan on 20 June; Moldavia on 24 June; Ukraine on 16 July; Belorussia on 27 July; Armenia and Turkmenia on 23 August; Tajikistan

Gorbachev's New Course: Turning to the Republics

This was the political situation before the Fourth Congress of People's Deputies opened in Moscow on 12 December 1990. The Congress began with a scandal: S. Umalatova, a Communist Party deputy, pounced on her party's leader Gorbachev, blaming him for the collapse of the Soviet Union and demanding his immediate resignation.[2]

Her motion was followed by a long debate on the agenda, which afforded Anatoly Lukyanov, who had replaced Gorbachev as Chairman of the Supreme Soviet, ample opportunity to excel at his manipulative techniques. The chairman would systematically refuse to put amendments to the vote, as if he did not even hear the deputies' proposals. However, the suggestion to put a vote of confidence (or, rather, no confidence) on the agenda of the Congress was voted on, but attracted only 423 votes against 1,292, with 183 abstentions.[3]

The voting was by roll-call and revealed substantial shifts in political dispositions. The familiar distinction of 'democrats' versus 'conservatives' was still valid, but the 'Centre' headed by Gorbachev found it ever more difficult to play the umpire. His policy of incessant manoeuvring and compromising, conciliatory and indecisive as it was, irritated radicals on both sides, so when Umalatova's motion was put to a vote, radical democrats joined with radical conservatives.[4]

---

on 24 August; Kazakhstan on 25 October. Kirgizia was the last of the Union republics to declare its sovereignty and it did so on precisely the day the Fourth Congress opened: 12 December (see Balzer (ed.) 1991, pp.236-8).

2   The first sitting on 12 December 1990: see *Fourth Congress* 1991 1, pp.12-13. Deputy Umalatova first attracted public attention during the Third Congress, when just before the presidential election she challenged Gorbachev to state definitely whom he was 'going to side' with (*Third Congress* 1990 2, p.458).

3   See *Fourth Congress* 1991 1, p.34.

4   The proposal to put the vote of confidence on the agenda was supported by leaders of the 'Soyuz' group: V. Alksnis, Yu. Blokhin, N. Petrushenko, T. Pupkevich, A. Chekhoyev, and by other reputed conservatives such as T. Avaliani, V. Kasyan, A. Makashov, I. Rodionov, L. Sukhov, S. Chervonopisky and, naturally, S. Umalatova herself. On the other hand, leaders of the democratic opposition voted for it, too: S. Belozertsev, G. Burbulis, E. Gayer, T. Gdlyan, I. Zaslavsky, N. Ivanov, O. Kalugin, A. Murashev, S. Sulakshin, A. Yablokov. They were joined by influential republican leaders, such as Yu. Boyars and S. Shushkevich (*Fourth Congress* 1991 1, pp.34-51). Voting to put the confidence vote on the agenda was not equivalent to voting no confidence, of course: some of those who supported Umalatova's motion might have done so because they felt they had no right to avoid considering such an important issue. However, the fact that these irreconcilable enemies voted together was significant.

Nevertheless, the division figures could be considered a success for Gorbachev's policy of balancing between democrats and conservatives, although the substance of this policy had undergone considerable change. Towards the end of 1990 the democrats' main opponents were no longer the conservative wing of the CPSU leadership. The latter's influence had been undermined by the abolition of Article 6 of the Constitution. Their enemies were the 'new conservatives' – a group of conservative activists, more or less emancipated from the central party leadership. They had formed an influential faction they called the '*Soyuz*' ('Union') group of deputies,[5] whose main demand was consolidation of the executive and of the central (Union) agencies of power in general. Compared with this new faction the Inter-Regional Group was too small. Besides, it was seriously weakened by internal conflicts and proved unable to check the growing strength of *Soyuz*. This new balance of power was what prompted Gorbachev to execute the manoeuvre mentioned above: on the eve of the Congress he had suggested considering and signing a new Union Treaty and introducing further constitutional amendments to provide for the establishment of one more body of power, the Council of the Federation. From the structural point of view, this was to be a rather meaningless agency, whose significance was to be revealed later. The Council of the Federation soon became an arena of political compromising between the republics, thus starting the so-called 'Novo-Ogaryovo process', named after a *dacha* settlement near Moscow in which republic leaders met periodically between January and December 1991.

As far as this can be discerned, the manoeuvre was intended as a major tactical change. The new policy was evidently to strike a balance between the Centre and the republics, rather than between the democrats and the party conservatives, as before. Gorbachev's tactical gain in this was obvious: Yeltsin, who was actively supported by the democrats, would be 'dissolved' in the midst of the Council dominated by moderate and conservative republican leaders. Only the leaders of Russia, Armenia and Moldavia could be counted on to support radical reforms at that moment; as for the Baltic leaders, it was doubtful whether they could be persuaded to participate at all.

5 See *Third Congress* 1990 1, pp.133–7.

At the same time the proposed reform meant a substantial strengthening of the executive structures. These had just been remanned by politicians who obviously inclined towards the *Soyuz* group. This allowed the unionist opposition to be neutralized to some extent. In other words, Gorbachev sought to put all his potential rivals into 'safe' positions ('safe' for himself, of course): democratic Yeltsin in the ranks of republican leaders; those close to *Soyuz* in the Cabinet, henceforth under his direct control.

This policy might have succeeded, but only if general political trends had been in its favour: that is, if the various republican political elites, content with more power in the provinces and a greater role in the Union, had supported 'the Centre', and if the *Soyuz* group had recognized Gorbachev's patronage. Within this framework, leaders of major republics, above all Nursultan Nazarbayev of Kazakhstan and Leonid Kravchuk of Ukraine, would have come to the fore, pushing back Gorbachev's old comrades-in-arms Alexander Yakovlev and Eduard Shevardnadze.

The Failure of the New Policy

The reality proved to be much more complicated, in the event. The republican elites, which had formed as far back as the times of 'stagnation', found themselves under growing pressure from democratic and nationalist movements and felt that their only chance of survival lay in 'hi-jacking' the nationalist slogans and promoting 'sovereignization': in independent states they might still hope to retain their power by endeavouring to draw on the conservative political culture of the bulk of the population.

In Russia proper regional political elites, especially those of the former 'autonomous units', faced a similar situation. In the circumstances the 'central' (Union) leadership might be tempted to try to 'dissolve' the Russian Federation in the Union as a whole, reducing the federal Russian authorities to the position they themselves had already experienced. The situation was bound to encourage radicalism on the part of the Russian leaders and to foster their unyielding opposition to Gorbachev's policy. Gorbachev's attempt to force Yeltsin down to the ranks of the republican leaders failed, therefore; moreover, the leaders themselves proved less prone to support the

'Centre' than Gorbachev had hoped. On the other hand, his greater emphasis on the support of the provinces and his association with political figures such as his new Prime Minister Valentin Pavlov, associated with the *Soyuz* group, made Gorbachev a hostage of the pro-imperial party. In such circumstances his old team of reformers, led by Yakovlev and Shevardnadze, could no longer offer Gorbachev their unconditional support.

Gorbachev's alienation from the staunchest champions of *perestroika* was made obvious by the sensational resignation of his Foreign Minister Shevardnadze, whose authoritative warning about the threat of a conservative coup and the impending dictatorship shocked the deputies:

> The democrat comrades in the broadest sense of the word have scattered, the reformers are hiding in the bushes. A dictatorship is coming: I state this with a full sense of responsibility. No one knows what kind of dictatorship it is going to be, what kind of dictator will come and what kind of regime will be established.[6]

It was not easy to read the speaker's implications at that moment, but in retrospect Shevardnadze appears to have had some idea of what the new group of politicians that surrounded the president and had pushed aside his old *perestroika* team intended to do.

One of the Congress's key events was Nazarbayev's speech. This was part of the debate on the political and economic situation in the country that followed Gorbachev's official report, and it gives a clear idea of the role that the republican political elites claimed for themselves. On the one hand, it was intended to express support for Gorbachev and was quite loyal in form; on the other hand, Nazarbayev explicitly stated the terms of that support. The Kazakhstan leader was highly critical of the central bureaucracies:

> Is the tight dictatorial grip of the central apparatus weakened, has the declared sovereignty of the republics shaken the monopoly of the departments? I shall put it directly: they do not give a damn for our sovereignty![7]

The economic policy pursued by Gorbachev and by Ryzhkov's Council of Ministers was not spared either:

6 Eduard Shevardnadze's speech at the seventh sitting (20 December 1990) (*Fourth Congress* 1991 1, p.410).
7 Nursultan Nazarbayev's speech at the second sitting (17 December 1990) (ibid., p.103).

Did we not suffer defeat when we failed to adopt any programme of transition to the market whatever and substituted the non-committal General Orientations for a clear plan? Moreover, the USSR Council of Ministers' latest actions can only be compared to open subversion aimed at splitting up the single economic space of the country.[8]

Gorbachev's policy of 'balancing' also came under attack:

We appreciate our president's diplomatic gift, but it seems as if intensive exploitation of this gift to the detriment of decisive actions has begun to bear bitter fruit. ... Walking political tightropes turns our movement towards a market economy into sheer bluff.[9]

Nazarbayev further suggested that the Union Treaty be signed by the republics alone – without the Centre.[10]

Of interest to the present study was Nazarbayev's appraisal of the Congress, which he compared to a ship in a stormy sea: 'capacious, but too slow and sluggish' and already abandoned by some of its crew, who have taken to life-boats to embark on a voyage of their own (the Congress was not attended by deputies from Armenia and Lithuania).[11] Despite the cheerful call for integration and the establishment of a Union of sovereign states with which Nazarbayev concluded his address, it managed to highlight the principal flaws in the central government's policy that were to bring about the eventual collapse of the Soviet Union.

These were made apparent in the course of the debate that followed the report presented by the Chairman of the Soviet of Nationalities, Rafik Nishanov, on the general conception of the Union Treaty and the procedure for its conclusion.[12] If further proof were needed of the Congress's total incapacity to discuss serious problems, this was it. The diversity of standpoints and the incompatibility of suggestions

8 *Fourth Congress* 1991 1, p.104. Nazarbayev's allusion is to the new taxation and, mainly, to the increase of wholesale purchase prices by the central authorities. Retail prices were left to the discretion of the regional authorities, but, as the retail prices were more often than not lower than the new wholesale prices, this simply meant that the local authorities were allowed to assume responsibility for this unpopular measure. This decentralized price formation would make retail prices differ between regions (while wholesale prices were the same throughout the country), thus adding to the economic chaos.

9 Ibid., p.103.

10 Ibid., p.107.

11 Ibid., p.103.

12 Nishanov's report at the sixth sitting (19 December 1990) (ibid., pp.337–52).

made elaboration of a single comprehensive document a hopeless undertaking. The deputies were not able to agree even on the general outlines of the intended Union: whether it was to be a federation or a confederation or to resemble an international alliance, like the European Community.

The Congress Proves Unable to Cope with the Political Crisis

The chaotic tide of proposals and motions again forced the Congress leadership along the familiar road: the deputies passed a non-committal resolution 'On the General Conception of the Union Treaty and the Procedure for its Conclusion', which described the future formation in a vague and self-contradictory way. The Congress voted for 'transforming our multi-national state into a voluntary union of sovereign republics enjoying equal rights – a democratic federal state'.[13] Such a formulation was quite incongruous: a union of *sovereign* states has to be a confederation, because sovereignty presupposes independence in the domain of internal legislation, at least; if the state was to be *federal*, the republics that were to constitute it could not be considered sovereign. Even the fundamental issue of secession was left uncertain: the right to secede was implicitly suggested by the status of 'sovereignty', but explicitly vetoed by the formula of a 'federal state'.

As a matter of fact, this was one more 'declaration of intent', one more political *plat du jour*: a routine compromise, as meaningless and as hopeless as usual. Thus the Congress had failed in its legislative function once again. Disintegration of the Union was thereafter inevitable: on the one hand, the Union seemed destined to survive, but on the other hand, it still had to be established by the already sovereign republics. The threat was imminent, and Gorbachev suggested a referendum on the future of the Soviet Union in order to enlist mass support and to get a trump card for the game he was playing with the republican leaders.

The idea was again sound enough, provided the referendum was conducted on the republican level and its outcome was legally binding on each individual republic. In that case some of the republics would

13 Resolution of the Congress of the USSR People's Deputies 'On the General Conception of the Union Treaty and the Procedure of Its Conclusion' (ibid., pp.311-12).

have seceded, of course, but where the majority had voted to preserve the Union, the republican political elites would have had to abide by the results, and their freedom of political manoeuvring would have been effectively restricted by the expressed will of the electorate. But to achieve that aim the Union leadership had to present a precise *text* of the Union Treaty, rather than an *idea* of 'a renewed Union' – another 'elastic' formula that allowed for arbitrary interpretation.

Instead of this, the Congress approved (by the overwhelming majority of 1,677 to 32[14]) one more document of doubtful intelligibility: the Supreme Soviet was commissioned to stage a performance whose legal consequences were far from clear. The referendum was conceived as an all-Union venture, but the votes were to be counted for individual republics. The natural question was, therefore, what would happen if in some republics the majority voted against 'the preservation of the renewed Union'? Would it have to be understood as voting against *preservation* or against *renewal* of the Union? This was sheer casuistry, of course, but it added to the emptiness of the undertaking. However, the principal question was whether voting 'against' preservation of the Union was to be considered as voting 'for' secession from the Union. This interpretation was rejected: secession was subject to a special law enacted a few months earlier in the aftermath of Lithuania's declaration of its independence. But in that case why hold a referendum at all? If a 'no' vote was not binding, neither would a 'yes' vote be (as the future was soon to show)! Such a referendum could solve no real problems that the preservation or the transformation of the Union – or both together – might pose, but it was bound to cause widespread irritation by the very intention to impose the will of the Slavic majority on all other nations, for instance on the Baltic peoples.

That the Congress approved of this referendum was further evidence of its incapacity to fulfil its functions. But the protagonists of this enterprise displayed genuine political dexterity: 'the will of the people', expressed in such a dubious way and on such a vague question, allowed for a variety of interpretations – indeed, for any interpretation. However, this dexterity was soon to be paid for, and the price turned out to be unusually high.

14 *Fourth Congress* 1991 **2**, p.232; for the text of the resolution, see *Fourth Congress* 1991 **3**, pp.306–7.

This style of policy-making left no doubt about the Soviet political elite's attitude: by no means and under no circumstances would it consent to restricting its own power, whether by clear legal formulas, or by binding decisions of the citizenry. This 'culture' of referendums – with vague, if not ambiguous or even confusing, questions and uncertain legal consequences – was soon to spread throughout the whole country. The republican elites did not mind fishing in those troubled waters, either: suffice it to mention the 'polls' on independence in the Baltic republics and the formula presented to voters in Tataria.

The Congress ended as it had begun: in a scandal. Its last act was election of the vice-president. Gorbachev nominated Gennady Yanayev[15] – a surprising choice, to put it mildly. The impression made by the candidate on the deputies was of such a kind that his first attempt was foiled: Yanayev failed to collect the required number of votes.[16] Even this submissive assembly, which had just approved of another series of constitutional amendments proposed by the president,[17] while rejecting, with its usual obedience, all the suggestions made by the democratic part of the corps of deputies, refused to vote for this former Komsomol functionary. Gorbachev insisted on a repeat of the voting,[18] and this time the outcome was favourable for Yanayev,[19] although doubts were raised as to possible juggling with the results.

Reviewing the Fourth Congress in the light of subsequent events, one might say that it was then and there that the political knots were tightened which the politicians of the former USSR would have to untie at such a terrible and painful price in the following year.

15 The eighteenth sitting (26 December 1990) (*Fourth Congress* 1991 3, pp.67-8).
16 Yanayev polled 1,089 votes against 583 with an unprecedented number of invalid ballots: 113 (82 were cast uncompleted, 18 had both 'yes' and 'no' crossed out); in addition, of the ballot papers issued 107 were not cast at all. A candidate required 1,120 votes in order to be elected (ibid., p.179).
17 See ibid., pp.313-21.
18 The nineteenth sitting (27 December 1990) (ibid., pp.184-5).
19 This time he polled 1,237 votes against 563 (ibid., p.269).

THE FIFTH CONGRESS

The Soviet Union Begins to Disintegrate

After the Fourth Congress of People's Deputies the political situation changed rapidly. The latest constitutional amendments, the growing political weight of the republics, what seemed to be the president's new course and the *Soyuz* group's virtual advent to power had an adverse combined effect on the psychological climate of the society and increased the political tension. Determined but clumsy and ill-advised economic measures brought in by Pavlov's government stirred up bitter resentment on the part of the entire population. Its peculiar, half-hearted currency reform succeeded only in undermining the rouble, while the officially-imposed price increase, far from returning goods to the shops, merely multiplied the existing problems.

The government's policy towards the republican declarations of 'sovereignty' was inconsistent, also. Amid attempts to intimidate the Baltic republics and conflicts in which the Soviet Army and the Special Militia Forces acted as if independent, leading to human casualties in Vilnius and Riga, the executive was pleading ignorant and officially dissociating itself from these provocations. The effect was the worst possible: men and women were being killed, and hatred towards the Centre and towards Russians in general was growing, and with it the alienation of the Baltic Russians from the local population and the local authorities; nationalist feelings in Russia proper were also developing, and confidence in the Soviet leadership was being shaken both inside the country and abroad. The results were humiliating: having gained nothing in terms of practical return, the president and his government were exposed as either hypocrites or weaklings no longer able to control their army and their security forces.

The 'Novo-Ogaryovo process' was evolving in parallel with these developments. The Centre and the republics were negotiating about the future of the Union, the new Union Treaty and the distribution of authority between the central government and the republics. The republics' claims were growing from day to day, while no definite text of the treaty was likely to be framed in the near future.

The referendum on 'the preservation of the renewed Union' served merely to pour fuel on the flames. The Baltic republics refused to hold it on their territories and conducted their own 'polls' instead. Although, from the legal standpoint, these straw polls were no more binding than the all-Union referendum, their results were interpreted as a popular mandate to secede from the Union.

The fact that in Russia and Ukraine the majority voted 'to preserve the renewed Union' did not substantially affect the official position of these republics: the leaders of both still insisted on downgrading the Centre. Meanwhile, the conflict over Nagorny Karabakh was growing ever more serious, and the Centre's sympathy was obviously with Azerbaijan, rather than Armenia.

In June Prime Minister Pavlov demanded additional powers for his Cabinet. He by-passed the president, and secured the support of the top figures in the army and the law-enforcing agencies. However, to grant him what he requested meant in effect a state of emergency; the Supreme Soviet refused to grant this.

The tension between Novo-Ogaryovo and Pavlov's Cabinet was increasing. Gorbachev, who hardly wished to see Pavlov and the *Soyuz* group still more powerful, swung towards Yeltsin and other republican leaders. In July the text of the Union Treaty, containing numerous, far-reaching concessions to the republics, was finally agreed, and the signing was scheduled for 20 August 1991. Gorbachev took a vacation and left for the Crimea.

The Union Treaty drafted in Novo-Ogaryovo bore no resemblance to a legal document. It was a purely political agreement, and not particularly impressive at that. The leviathan it envisaged was incredible: the old Union was not to be disbanded; state relations between the Centre and the republics that refused to sign the new Treaty were to continue; they would still be subject to the old Treaty of 1922, whereas relations between the others would henceforth be based on the new Treaty. The result would be two totally different states on the same territory at the same time: with different bodies of law and even different boundaries. Whoever devised that plan did not seem to be concerned about the apparent absurdity of the arrangement.

It is difficult to say what the consequences would have been had the Union Treaty been signed on 20 August as intended. History followed a different course. In the early morning of 19 August, one day before the scheduled Treaty-signing ceremony, a state of emergency was imposed. Vice-President Yanayev proclaimed that in connection with Gorbachev's 'inability to carry out his duties of President of the USSR for reasons of ill health' he had assumed all presidential powers. State power was transferred to the newly established State Emergency Committee (SEC). Apart from Gennady Yanayev, the Committee included Prime Minister Valentin Pavlov, KGB Chairman Vladimir Kryuchkov, Minister of Defence Dmitri Yazov, Minister of the Interior Boris Pugo, and representatives of the party, agrarian and industrial elites Oleg Baklanov, Vassily Starodubtsev and Alexander Tizyakov. That very morning the SEC (*GKChP*, in its harsh-sounding Russian abbreviation) issued its 'Appeal to the Soviet People'.[20]

That was a curious document. On the one hand, the authors promised to observe human rights, support business and even 'continue the reforms'. On the other hand, the appeal was permeated with the spirit of enemy-hunting: an obsession with certain dark forces consciously seeking to destroy the country and bring about the downfall of the state. It was probably this ambiguity that accounted for the public's negative response, especially in major Russian cities.

By August 1991 substantial segments of the population, tired of national conflicts and 'parades of sovereignty', economic havoc and inflation, and afraid of new and graver hardships, were likely to support 'law and order' introduced by an 'iron hand', provided they could be reassured that 'order' did not simply stand for the 'old regime'. To judge by the text, the appeal was aimed at securing the support of all those who were no longer willing to tolerate uncertainty and chaos. However, the witch-hunting betrayed the conspirators. Instead of the 'civil peace' that they craved, people were offered greater confrontation: censorship was to be imposed on the press and war was to be declared on the 'profiteers'. Repressions and similar 'delights' of the not so distant past were looming on the horizon.

If Moscow events of 19–21 August are compared with what happened two years earlier in Tiananmen Square, the role of *glasnost'* becomes plainly obvious: if not all the people then at least enough of them were decisively opposed to relapsing obediently into dumb submissiveness.

20 See *Pravda*, 20 August 1991, p.1.

We shall not describe these dramatic events. They are still alive in our memories and have not been ignored by the press. Books have already been published dealing with the August coup, including some in English.[21] Instead, we shall concentrate on the Fifth Congress of People's Deputies. In the spell between the victory of the Russian parliament and Yeltsin over the SEC and the opening of the Extraordinary Fifth Congress a session of the USSR Supreme Soviet was held. Its course and character were evidence of the complete fiasco of the all-Union legislature. The deputies' primary concern was to find an excuse for their own passivity during the coup. Television was broadcasting those distressing scenes to the entire nation, and everyone could witness the humiliation and repentance of the law-makers.

The Congress in Death Agony

By the time the Fifth Congress began its work, the corps of deputies was utterly demoralized. On their way to the Kremlin the deputies were met by an angry crowd shouting 'Shame!'

The Extraordinary Fifth Congress of the USSR People's Deputies opened on 2 September 1991. Deputies were to undergo further humiliation. Instead of discussing the agenda duly prepared by the Supreme Soviet, they were obliged to listen to Nursultan Nazarbayev, President of Kazakhstan, who had been authorized by Gorbachev to announce the 'Joint Declaration of the President of the USSR and of the Leading Officials of the Union Republics'.[22] The Declaration asserted that the existing power institutions had to be abolished; for the transition period, that is until the Union Treaty had been signed and new elections held, they had to be replaced by temporary new structures. Legislative functions and work on the new Constitution of the Union of Sovereign States were to be entrusted to the Council of Representatives of People's Deputies, which was to consist of deputies delegated by the republican Supreme Soviets – twenty deputies from each Union republic. For coordination of home and foreign policy, inasmuch as it affected the republics' mutual interests, a State Council was to be established, comprising the

---

21 See *August* 1991; *Putch* 1991; Sixsmith 1991.
22 See *Izvestiya*, 2 September 1991, p.1.

president of the USSR and the top officials of the Union republics. The national economy was to be managed by a temporary Inter-Republican Economic Committee, formed on the basis of equal representation; that committee was also to coordinate the economic reform.

For all intents and purposes, the Declaration put an end to the existence of the Soviet Union not only as the unitary state it had been right up to the recent 'parade of sovereignty', but even as a federation such as Gorbachev had been speaking of so tirelessly. The republican leaders had effected a revolution and wanted the Congress to legitimate its results. The structure of state power that they suggested was apparently rigged and, taking into account the enormous differences between the republics in size, population and economic potential, certainly unlikely to last for long. The proposal sounded like one to establish a liquidation commission.

The Congress's first sitting began at 10 a.m. on 2 September and lasted for nine minutes: after Nazarbayev had finished reading the Declaration, the deputies were invited to ponder it. The session resumed at 2 p.m. The first to be given the floor was Sergei Alekseyev, Chairman of the Constitutional Supervision Committee. He suggested that a legal examination should be made of the basic provisions of the Declaration. At the same time he pledged support for the president and the republican leaders. Alekseyev's main point was that there was no alternative to the proposals set forth in their declaration:

> Let us speak frankly: our Union has been not on the verge of breakdown, it has been in a state of breakdown. ... And I suppose this decision is the only one possible, if we discard the failed one that the whole people has rejected. There are no two ways about it. Substantial progress has been made. Representatives of Armenia and of Ukraine are sitting at the Presidium table: this is already a great achievement.[23]

The speeches that representatives of different republics made after that were variations on two basic themes: political institutions of the transitional period were 'to prevent uncontrolled disintegration of the country' (Anatoly Sobchak, representing Russia); and 'We must not

23 Deputy Alekseyev's speech at the second sitting (2 September) (*Izvestiya* 3 September 1991, p.4).

be enslaved by any speculative schemes' (Yuri Shcherbak, representing Ukraine).[24] The implication was that observation of the letter of the law was to yield to considerations of political expediency.

After representatives of other republican 'deputations' had uttered something of the same sort, the Chairman (Ivan Laptev, Chairman of the Soviet of the Union) put the agenda, as it had been 'formulated by Comrade Nazarbayev on behalf of the president and the leaders of the republics', to a roll-call vote. The proposal polled 1,350 votes in favour and 107 against, with 137 abstentions; 234 deputies failed to vote.

What the general atmosphere at the sitting was like is clear from the fact that the Supreme Soviet's suggestions for the agenda were not even put to a vote. The fate of both the Congress and the Union was decided, indeed, before the session started. The following remark of Chairman Laptev may be found illuminating:

> I have just held consultations (inasmuch as I was able in the present situation) to clarify the situation and I can say what it looks like to us - for the Congress to understand the realities: there are republics that have adopted declarations of independence, there are republics that have not considered the problem and have not yet established their positions. Whereas we would like only those questions to be presented to this Congress that have been prepared in advance on a mutual basis and agreed upon.[25]

This was a most explicit formula for the function that the Congress, as a *Sobor*-type representative institution, was originally destined to perform and was, indeed, the only one it was able to fulfil: legitimation of decisions already taken elsewhere by someone else. What followed was clear evidence that nothing more was to be expected from the Congress - even in a situation when its own fate was at stake (to say nothing of the fate of the country).

After the agenda was approved, the Congress fixed the time-limits: five minutes for a regular speech and two minutes for a statement from the audience on a procedural matter (and only on an issue of that sort). Thus, by the time its mission was approaching its end, the Congress had fully developed, even from the formal procedural standpoint, into what it seems to have been intended to be from the very beginning: a manipulated crowd.

24 Ibid.
25 *Izvestiya*, 3 September 1991, p.5.

Nevertheless, some attempts were made to save face and to uphold, at least, some remnants of authority: Deputy Lubenchenko suggested that the Supreme Soviet should be preserved if only in name,[26] while unsparing criticism was levelled by Deputy Obolensky at the declaration of the president and the republican leaders. Obolensky stated plainly that what was going on at the Congress undermined legitimacy:

> After the *putsch* was suppressed, the 'wind of democratization' has burst into the uppermost level of the country's executive that has hitherto served as a stronghold of reactionary forces. A genuine opportunity has been created for a breakthrough in the sphere of economic reforms on the basis of a coalition government enjoying popular confidence. And in these circumstance the leadership of the republics that were ready to sign the Union Treaty on 18 August takes steps towards definitive dismantling of the Union authority on 26 August. Does this mean, perhaps, that the dictatorship of the conspirators would suit them better than preservation of the constitutional order? One wouldn't like to believe in that. Isn't it time, perhaps, to stop treating the Constitution like a whore accommodating her for the pleasures of a new courtier? [*Applause.*] We have already managed - by our experiments on it - to bring the country to the verge of collapse. There ought to be some basis of stability, law and order in society! The Constitution determines the degree of the authorities' legitimacy. Outrage against the former deprives the latter of all respect, removes the moral safety device of the society and gives a part of it a moral right to resist by any means.[27]

Obolensky concluded his speech with a proposal to remove Gorbachev from the presidency for 'having failed in his obligation as a guarantor of the rights and freedoms of citizens and having allowed a conspiracy against the constitutional order to mature in his closest circles'.[28] Such calls were already out of place, of course. The deputies were demoralized once and for all and were apparently ready to content themselves with the final consolation: permission to retain their deputy status even after the Congress was dissolved.

However, Obolensky's stand was not without fault, either: before he attacked the Declaration, he talked at length of the activity the Supreme Soviet had displayed in the short interval between the *putsch* and the Congress. Anyone who had witnessed the deputies' pitiful conduct on television would have found this praise excessive, to put it mildly.

26 K. Lubenchenko's speech at the third sitting (2 September 1991) (ibid).
27 A. Obolensky's speech (ibid., p.7).
28 Ibid.

Democrat Obolensky found an unexpected ally in Viktor Alksnis, one of the leaders of the *Soyuz* group of deputies, who also compared the events to the dispersal of the Constituent Assembly in 1918.[29]

That further efforts by the Congress to save face were futile was recognized by Deputy Karyakin, a prominent member of the democratic opposition. His speech sounded like an epitaph for the Congress as a political institution:

> Two years ago this hall (excuse me, most of you) rose with frightening enthusiasm at the catchwords 'The State! The Motherland! Communism!' An ovation followed, and what an ovation it was! And it was only an insignificant group of 'renegades', as they were called then, headed by A.D. Sakharov, that remained sitting, did not rise to their feet. I remember, it was depressing, even somewhat sinister. ... I know, if it had gone otherwise during those three days, this Congress would have voted for the junta. And, therefore, before the people we must now surrender our mandates. This will be the only honest way! [*Applause.*][30]

However, this invective concluded with an odd passage: 'Neither you, nor we, nor myself are to be trusted. The minority is not to be trusted, because it has failed to get the better of the majority'.[31] It is impossible to think of a better proof that the mentality of *sobornost'*

29 From V. Alksnis's speech at the seventh sitting on 4 September 1991 (*Izvestiya*, 6 September 1991, p.4):

> Today, yesterday and the day before yesterday this hall witnessed what had happened in 1918 when the Constituent Assembly was dispersed. I cannot find a different name for it. And if we yield to fear today and renounce our beliefs, I don't think the people will forgive us.

Compare Obolensky (*Izvestiya*, 3 September 1991, pp.6–7):

> The honourable President of Kazakhstan Comrade Nazarbayev in announcing an ultimatum to the Congress has been given the role of that legendary sailor Zheleznyak.
> It was precisely with violence against legitimate authority that all civil wars began, including ours, which began not with the October coup that the public perceived as one provisional authority replacing another, but with the dispersal of the Constituent Assembly.

Zheleznyak was the commander of the unit that had guarded the Tavrichesky Palace, where the Constituent Assembly had been in session; it had been Zheleznyak who had uttered the notorious phrase: 'The guard is tired', implying it was time for the deputies to close the sitting and to disperse.

30 Yu. Karyakin's speech at the fifth sitting (3 September 1991) (*Izvestiya*, 5 September 1991, p.5).

31 *Izvestiya*, 5 September 1991, p.5.

and the consequent understanding of the nature of political representation dominated even the minds of intellectuals in opposition! Let us leave aside the emotional impact of this statement: the idea of repentance. Let us consider its message. To reproach the minority (and a minority it was, indeed!) for failing to check the majority makes sense only if parliamentary activity is viewed as a concerted search for truth, rather than as an expression of political competition. It is impossible to dismiss Karyakin's words as mere rhetoric: it was not the time for rhetoric. But if intellectuals of Karyakin's standing were prone to interpret the meaning and functions of political representation in this way, what was to be expected from the rest? And what was to be expected from a Congress that consisted of such deputies?

The idea of the Union seemed no longer inspiring. Academician Dmitri Likhachev could think of no better reason to preserve the Union than the need to maintain the unity of the museums, libraries and archives,[32] while Academician Yevgeny Velikhov would cite the need to prevent deterioration of the research potential[33] (which, however, did not stop him advocating transformation of the USSR Academy of Sciences into the Russian Academy a few days later). It was hard to believe anyone could have seriously counted on such arguments to convince the republics to stay with the Union.

On its last day the Congress enacted a Declaration of Human Rights and Freedoms. A part of the discussion was a curious exchange on whether a declaration of this kind might contain 'unrealistic' (that is, unqualified) provisions like 'inviolability of the home' or 'privacy of correspondence'.[34] As a result of that exchange,

32 D. Likhachev's speech at the fourth sitting (3 September 1991) (*Izvestiya* 4 September 1991, p.6).
33 Ye. Velikhov's speech at the third sitting (2 September 1991) (*Izvestiya*, 3 September 1991, p.7).
34 As the chairman of the group that was responsible for preparing the draft declaration, Academician Kudryavtsev, put it (*Izvestiya*, 6 September 1991, p.6):

We can follow [either of] two ways: deceive ourselves and the people and discard these reservations, write down that no one, for example, is entitled to conduct a search – at any time, anywhere and under any circumstances, that no bugging of telephone conversations is to be allowed. We can write it down. But it will be a deception. It will be a fiction that cannot be fulfilled.

The honourable Academician Kudryavtsev ought to know, however, of the civilized ways to treat such problems. Why not substitute clear conditions like 'unless on a

'rights' and 'freedoms' were defined in the familiar Soviet way, that is, with reference to 'the legislation currently in effect'. Suffice it to mention the USSR laws that regulated the activities of the KGB (secret police) and of the Ministry of the Interior and reduced inviolability of the home to a mere fiction, in order to realize that formulas of that kind in a declaration intended and proclaimed to be a primary law of direct effect could not be regarded as anything but a mockery of common sense and of the supposed beneficiaries of the declared rights and freedoms.

How 'carefully' the text of the Declaration was prepared is evident from the following excerpt: 'No one may be placed under arrest or taken into unlawful custody except on the basis of a court's ruling or a public prosecutor's sanction'.[35] If the text was to be interpreted literally (it was a legal document after all!), one had to assume that courts and public prosecutors were allowed to order people into 'unlawful custody'. And what about 'lawful custody'? Were we to understand that it required no sanction at all?

The Congress's last deeds were a resolution 'On Measures Ensuing from the Joint Declaration of the President of the USSR and the Leading Officials of the Republics and from the Decisions of the Extraordinary Session of the USSR Supreme Soviet'[36] and a 'Law on Agencies of State Power and Control of the USSR in the Transition Period'. The idea of the Supreme Soviet survived after all, but it was no longer to be formed by the Congress, but by the republican agencies of power.[37]

A more abject humiliation of representative power than that suffered by the Extraordinary Fifth Congress of the USSR People's Deputies is difficult to imagine. Chairmen would interrupt the deputies, and Gorbachev would even threaten to close the Congress and to dissolve it altogether if the deputies refused to affirm the decisions they were expected to. The executive bullied the legislature shamelessly, but it was difficult to deny that the treatment was well

---

court's decision' or, at least, 'unless sanctioned by a public prosecutor' for the foggy reference to an unknown law: 'except in cases and in the order provided for by the law'?

35 Article 15 of the Declaration of Human Rights and Freedoms (*Izvestiya*, 7 September 1991, p.1).

36 See *Izvestiya*, 6 September 1991, p.2.

37 Ibid.

deserved. The fiasco suffered by the Congress was the failure of the model of political representation on which it was based. The model could be traced as far back as the time of pre-Petrine Russia. The Bolsheviks profited by it after they made themselves masters of the country. But it proved singularly inadequate to the tasks set by 'acceleration' and '*perestroika*'.

8 Conclusion: Representative Democracy and Post-Totalitarian Evolution

> *One comes across curious marksmen sometimes: having missed their target, they leave the barrier secretly proud of the fact that their bullet went very far (farther than the target, at any rate) or that, having missed the target, they hit something else.*
>
> — Nietzsche, *Motley Opinions.*

We have witnessed an attempt to establish representative democracy in the Soviet Union, its early triumphs, its crisis and its eventual fiasco, followed by the collapse of the state itself. What are the lessons to be learned from this unsuccessful experiment? Is democracy necessary at all? Or, at least, is it necessary at an early post-totalitarian stage? Or should one rather be content with liberating the economy, or some part of it, from state control?

REFORMING TOTALITARIAN REGIMES: PROBLEMS AND OPTIONS

These are the principal questions potential reformers of totalitarian regimes have to face. If we compare the developments of the late 1980s–early 1990s in the Soviet Union and the People's Republic of China, we shall easily recognize the following differences: China has opted for economic liberalization, particularly in agriculture and

small-scale business, while the Communist Party continues to exercise
strict political control over Chinese society;[1] the USSR has embarked
on political liberalization as exemplified by *glasnost'* and representative democracy, whereas the state preserved almost intact its control
not only over industrial production, but also over agriculture and
trade.

The consequences are self-evident: in China political stability
favours economic growth, even though the country is in a state of
relative isolation due to the human rights problems, while the Soviet
Union has ceased to exist. The comparison seems a strong argument
in favour of authoritarianism as a transitional stage from totalitarianism towards democracy and a market economy. Comprehensive
examination of this problem would require a profound study of
differences in political and civic cultures, including what may be
called the culture of work, between the Chinese and Soviet societies,
and also an exhaustive inquiry into the history of 'real socialism' in
the two countries, which is obviously a major task in its own right.
The following is an attempt to consider the challenge of post-
totalitarian evolution from the remote standpoint of abstract theory.

What is totalitarianism? It is basically a total absorption by the
state bureaucracy of all other social elites: economic, cultural,
scientific. The state seeks to bring all spheres of social life under its
control[2] by making state officials of all those who manage to achieve
some degree of influence in their particular fields, thereby denying
them an opportunity to continue their activities should they resist
becoming obedient instruments of the state. This is the *raison d'être*
of industrial ministries, collective farms, artistic unions and the state-
run Academy of Sciences, as well. The destruction of totalitarianism
means freedom to create other – that is non-state – types of elites,
whose members are relatively independent of the state and pursue
their own careers.

Every independent elite emerging in a society faces the problem of
securing access to a share of state power, for if it fails to gain this
access, its ability to exist and reproduce itself will be questioned.
Farmers want to protect their land property, businessmen are worried
about excessive taxation, writers need funds to help them resist the

1 See, for example, Pleshakov and Furman 1989.
2 See Hayek 1976; Arendt 1958; Popper 1971.

pitiless dictate of the market, journalists wish to secure free exchange of information, scientists expect governments to support fundamental research.

And every potential reformer of a totalitarian society faces a similar, albeit 'mirror' problem: what is the state power to do to secure access to itself for a new independent elite? How it is to manage conflicts that are bound to arise between the various old social elites, formerly created and supported by the state, and the new and independent one? The question is crucial, for it is also a matter of 'taming' the new elite.

It might prove worthwhile to emphasize here that what we have in mind is not only the emergence of entirely new elites of the kind that some totalitarian societies, including the Soviet Union, have never allowed to exist, such as farmers or businessmen, but also changes of 'leadership' in the social groups that already exist. This is the crux of the crisis that afflicts the 'public' organizations of totalitarian societies upon the collapse of totalitarianism: trade and creative unions, associations of women and youth, and the like. Some of these organizations may be seized by 'anti-totalitarian' forces in good time; usually these are artistic and creative unions. We witnessed such a situation in Czechoslovakia in 1968, in Poland in 1980 and in Hungary in 1989. The organization in question is then transformed into a kind of political party, more often than not opposed not only to the 'old regime' but to the reformers as well.

The choice between authoritarianism and representative democracy that faces a would-be reformer of a totalitarian regime may be described as follows. To effect the reform the leader must draw on support from outside the official state structures, for inside them his opponents are bound to prove too strong for him. At the same time, however, to set in moton mechanisms of representative democracy may upset the existing power structures on which the reformer has to rely in order to maintain the minimum social order in his country. The obvious way out seems to be to appeal to corporate structures, that is to the 'public' organizations of various social groups. These organizations must be freed from total state control, of course. The result will be a kind of 'enlightened' authoritarianism, which is believed to secure relative political stability for the period of transition from totalitarianism to representative democracy and help gain the time required to carry out the economic and political reforms successfully on such a grand scale.[3]

THE GLOOMY PROSPECTS OF AUTHORITARIANISM

An attempt to pursue this kind of policy was made in the USSR in 1988-90. Its most conspicuous element was the constitutional reform of 1988 which provided, in particular, for political representation of public organizations at the Congress of People's Deputies. Why has this policy failed and resulted, moreover, in the disintegration of the state?

To answer this question, it is necessary to examine how the new social elites that emerge in the course of the reforms affect policy-making in conditions of authoritarian rule and in the case of representative democracy.

Under representative democracy various social groups may affect policy-making through a system of political parties represented in the national legislature or, if the regime is a presidential republic, through the election of the president. The role and participation of elites in these processes will depend on the extent to which they prove capable of controlling their respective social groups and of representing those groups' interests.[4] In conditions of representative democracy certain

---

3 Compare Migranyan 1990, p.7:

> The transition from an 'ideal' totalitarian system to a democracy cannot be made in one big leap - the initial one. As the first steps are made to loosen the totalitarian grip on the spiritual and, subsequently, the economic life of society, as various forms of non-state ownership are made legal, society tends to become increasingly complex, giving rise to numerous conflicting interests. The latter's growing polarization increases the possibility of chaos and the eventual collapse of the political system that is being restructured. It is therefore vital that while the complicated process of moulding and reinforcing civil society is going on in the economic and spiritual spheres, strong authoritarian rule should be maintained in the political sector, so as to impose certain restrictions on the present stage of democratic change.

> The above argument was first stated in Migranyan 1989. This controversial article caused an extensive polemical debate, which a number of prominent political writers of the time joined in: for this, see *Literaturnaya gazeta* 1989 (33, 38, 39, 42, 52) (articles by Ye. Ambartsumov, L. Batkin, I. Klyamkin, A. Kron, A. Migranyan and others, in Russian); see also Pospelovsky 1990.

4 For classical works on the problem of elites, see Mosca 1939; Pareto 1968; Michels

types of elite may experience crises because of their inability to express and protect the interests of the social groups from which they draw their support. An example of a crisis of this kind is provided by the situation in some American or British trade unions. But, generally speaking, elites feel secure under representative democracy. Elections allow them a degree of influence on the administration, since any government risks losing the election if it pursues a policy that impinges upon too many group interests.

Social elites are much less secure under authoritarianism.[5] Their influence on the state authorities is not institutionalized and usually depends on personal connections. This breeds both unrestrained corruption and permanent lack of confidence in the future. The natural response to this challenge is to form Mafia-type clans that fight for power unrestricted by any rules. The main argument against authoritarianism as a transitional phase between totalitarianism and democracy is essentially that the alleged 'transitional phase' is nothing but a dead end that allows for no way out: to extirpate the clans that unite 'independent' social elites and state bureaucracies under authoritarian regimes seems far more difficult than to establish representative democracy 'by decree' under totalitarianism or by way of a revolution that would destroy all power structures whatsoever.

An authoritarian regime will therefore face a dilemma: it must either draw on populism in its war on corruption, which would inevitably mean a war against corrupt elites as well, or it must content itself with being a mere instrument of these cliques, serve their interests and suppress popular movements that seek to prevent this usurpation of power by the arrogant elites. Outwardly a regime of this kind will not differ very much from totalitarianism, although in essence they are certainly different: rather than being dominated by the state, various, and sometimes rival, corporative elites become the state's master. This is a kind of 'totalitarian pluralism' that does not

---

1949; among more recent studies, see Lasswell *et al.* 1952; Prewitt and Stone 1973; Putnam, 1976; for a review of literature on elites in Russian, see Ashin 1985.

5　The thesis that the legitimacy of authoritarian regimes rested, to a considerable degree, on the masses' negative attitude towards existing elites was commonplace in the political science of classical antiquity and of the Renaissance: see, for example, Aristotle 1952, pp.506–7; compare Machiavelli (1972, p.84): 'The people also, seeing that they cannot resist the rich, give their support to one man and make him prince, so that with his power he will protect them'.

exclude either private property or a developed economy: it is compatible with both.

It has only one flaw, but it shares it with totalitarianism: both suppress freedom; however, this also means suppression of creative activity, and hence of scientific, technological and cultural development. A temporary success may be possible, but the price to be paid will be high: the nation will have to depend on other countries that follow different - namely, democratic - ways, for everything pertaining to the highest accomplishments of human reason. Whether there are any social or moral reasons to prefer this kind of regime to the more familiar totalitarianism is highly doubtful.

Such regimes can exist on certain conditions, and can even win outside support for reasons of political expediency - for example, when two superpowers compete for influence over the Third World. However, after this bipolar system has ceased to exist, and while the West is consolidating its influence in the political and economic fields, the prospects for these regimes are much less favourable.

WHY DID *PERESTROIKA* FAIL?

Let us return, however, to the situation in the Soviet Union. What can be said about the failure of *perestroika* in the light of the considerations discussed above?

As noted above, the principal features of the policy pursued by the reformist leadership of the CPSU were: (1) setting the 'corporative' elites (the academic, literary, industrial and the like) against the central party-state bureaucracy and granting the former certain privileges and authority; (2) likewise setting republican political elites against the central apparatus; (3) attempting to play the resulting balance to their own advantage; (4) denying the 'new elites' that emerged in the course of economic reforms (mainly, in the cooperative movement) and in the course of democratic development (as a result of *glasnost'*) access to real power positions and trying to bring them under effective control; (5) barring political pluralism and the formation of political parties independent of the official state leadership; (6) working out complicated constitutional arrangements in order to keep under control the process of democratization and the activities of the 'liberated' corporate elites; (7) maintaining the old regime's repressive system as a reserve.

These basic features were distinctly observable in the activities of the Congresses of People's Deputies. On the whole, the policy described above fitted well with the model of 'enlightened authoritarianism'. Why, then, did it fail?

The policy of *perestroika* was based on a fundamental and easily discernible idea that determined all its various features outlined above. This idea was that of effecting a transition from a totalitarian to a Western-type modern state, while leaving in power the old elite, formed under conditions of 'real socialism'. Such a policy would have stood every chance of success in the 1960s, when this elite had not yet lost effective control over the society and while the memories of Stalinist nightmares were still alive. By the end of the 1980s and after twenty years of 'stagnation', however, real control over social development had been lost, and the old elite did not enjoy a thread of legitimacy. Where it still managed to preserve real power, it was the power of clans and based on corruption.

The outcome of *perestroika* was total defeat. Corporate elites – captains of industry and directors of collective and state farms – gave up whatever concern they might have had for increasing industrial and agricultural output and set to expanding their own privileges and engaging in 'wild privatization'. This *prikhvatization*, as it has been popularly styled (the neologism is derived from the verb *prikhvatit'* – 'to seize'[6]), was accompanied by the deterioration of established economic ties and by a resulting decrease in output. At the same time the managerial elites effectively barred the emergence of an alternative market economy. National political elites extended their claims far beyond what the reformers had ever expected of them. Starting with the idea of 'regional self-financing', devoid of any economic sense whatsoever and intended, indeed, to boost the regional elites' economic power, rather than some kind of economic reform, they soon demanded political independence as well.

One of the most fatal consequences for *perestroika* was the sequence of elections in 1989 and 1990, held first on the central

6 The effect is further amplified by the word's other phonetic, albeit not semantic, associations, such as *prikhvosten'* ('hanger-on' or 'stooge') and *prokhvost* ('scoundrel').

(Union) and then on the republican level. From the standpoint of preserving as much power as possible in the hands of the old elite, the order made sense. It allowed for the election to the central institutions of power to take place immediately after the Constitutional amendments were enacted and while democratic and 'market' forces had still had no time to form independent political movements and parties. But the disastrous result was the disintegration of the Soviet Union. As has been shown above, the helpless *Sobor* type of Union legislature soon lost legitimacy, while its republican counterparts, elected a year later under more democratic conditions, felt themselves far more secure in this respect and dared to defy the 'conservative communist Centre' and proclaim their own sovereignty. And after the August *putsch* expunged what remained of the Centre's legitimacy, the republics did not hesitate to abolish it once and for all.

A major role in these developments was played by Gorbachev's stubborn refusal to establish a party of his own to replace the CPSU, which he was still supposed to be leading but over which he was gradually losing day-to-day control. Although the Communist Party proclaimed itself 'the initiator of *perestroika*', it was an open secret that not only a considerable part of its functionaries (especially in the provinces, away from the watchful eye of the top authorities), but many of its rank and file as well were suspicious of the reforms, not to say hostile to them. In the circumstances Gorbachev's attempt to play, in his newly acquired capacity as the first president, the role of 'mouthpiece of the people at large' – invoking, indeed, the traditional image of 'our father, the tsar' – served only to confuse his supporters and throw them into disarray.

Might that outcome have been avoided? To write an 'alternative history' is not an easy task, of course, particularly as the grounds for such a pretentious undertaking are usually somewhat shaky. So much of what happened was due to a coincidence of accidental circumstances, and in any case so many factors that influenced the events of 1989–91 remain unknown and it is difficult to say when they will be made public, if at all. But it would be totally unscholarly to abandon any such attempt completely.[7] And perhaps the decisive argument for

---

7 It is often argued that 'history has no subjunctive mood'. This widespread argument is, however, absolutely wrong. History apparently does not have and cannot have two different indicative moods, but it does have the subjunctive one. If we lack knowledge

why 'historic alternatives' to the policy of *perestroika* must not be ignored is the present situation in Russia. This situation is in many respects analogous to the one the Soviet Union faced in 1988, and if the 'general guidelines' of the policy of *perestroika* are adhered to once again, Russia may well suffer a similar fate.

A MISSED ALTERNATIVE

What was then the alternative that might have helped stabilize the situation in the USSR in 1988? We shall not consider here the obvious possibility of returning to the totalitarian state, since that policy could hardly be regarded as a means of stabilization. It would have at best prolonged the life (or the agony) of the regime by a few years to end in a still more violent social outburst.

The real alternative presents itself as follows. (1) Introduce a constitution for direct implementation that would omit any reference to consequential legislation and, even more pertinently, to subordinate acts. This would have permitted the central government to take advantage of all the resources then available for carrying out a radical constitutional reform at the earliest opportunity. That constitution would have had to provide for political pluralism, for a parliament formed on the basis of multi-party elections and remaining in permanent session, for human rights and freedoms, and also for property rights. (2) Carry out a simultaneous reform of the military by creating a professional army, enhancing the role of the middle-rank officers, many of whom proved susceptible to the democratic spirit of the time, and restricting the influence of the conservative generals. (3) Carry out a legal reform to check the arbitrary rule of the executive and take normal business activity from under the jurisdiction of the criminal code. (4) Hold elections first to the local and regional assemblies and then (after approximately a year) to the All-Union

---

of the alternatives that once faced our predecessors, we shall never be able to understand what happened, and even less *why* it did. If a historian refuses to discuss alternatives, his or her picture of the past will necessarily be a distorted one. It will be an artificial composition, unrelated to reality. A reality without alternatives is not the genuine reality that existed in the past. Hence any explanation based on the former is bound to be inadequate. The past was full of alternatives, and even though it is not easy to analyse them, they must not be left unexamined.

legislature. This sequence would have allowed for a multi-party system, however frail at first, to evolve at that early stage. An established (and legalized) multi-party system would have had a considerable effect on the Union-wide election in the following year. The 'old elite' was sure to win the local and republican elections, but with little or no progress made in a year and provided the democratic opposition were given time to consolidate itself, this opposition would have won the election to the all-Union parliament. In such circumstances the disintegration of the Union would have been impossible, since it would have implied political regression. If it had been a case of the 'democratic Centre' withstanding the conservative regional elites (rather than vice versa), separatism would have meant forming a bloc with reactionary forces, whereas centralist tendencies might have enjoyed widespread democratic support. Whether that would have been a lasting arrangement and the nationalist and separatist feelings could have been appeased for long may be questioned, of course. However, the respite might have proved long enough to accomplish, at least, the most pressing reforms, before disintegration of the country and the ensuing chaos made the reformers' task still more difficult.

The conflict between the ideas of 'federalism' and 'unitarism' has been characteristic of practically all revolutions that have happened in the course of the last two hundred years.[8] Which idea would eventually emerge as the dominant one depended largely on which was supported by the leading revolutionary movement: the example of the French Revolution is most illuminating in this respect.

Had some such programme been carried out at the appropriate time, we would probably now be witnessing a democratic Union of Sovereign States enjoying political and economic stability, rather than a Commonwealth that is afflicted by national conflicts and is approaching an economic disaster and most of whose constituent 'independent states' are still ruled by their old communist elites.

Perestroika lagged behind the changes that were going on in the minds of the people and it brought the society and the state to a condition of economic and political chaos. The only reasonable reformist policy is to anticipate the changes in social consciousness.

8   See Jaurès (1969–72) **5**, Ch.9; Hamilton *et al.* 1961.

Such a policy would be fraught with great personal risks for the reformers, of course, but as the summer of 1991 was to show, *'perestroika'* harboured dangers no less serious.

The paradox of the situation in mid-1992[9] is that nothing of the radical programme outlined above had been realized by the Russian democrats upon their accession to power. Matters stood no better in the other successor states that emerged on the territory formerly occupied by the Soviet Union. However, nowhere was the political situation as reminiscent of the situation in the USSR on the threshold of the dramatic events of *perestroika* as it was in Russia. The Federal Treaty, the sovereignty of the constituent republics, a declining economy, the delayed agrarian, legal, constitutional, military reforms and, last but not least, the continuing lack of organized mass support for the policy of reform – all these problems are capable of bringing about another disaster unless urgent steps are taken to transform Russia into a modern democratic state.

TRADITIONAL CULTURE AND THE PROSPECTS FOR TRANSFORMATION

This study has demonstrated that the most important single obstacle to the transition from a totalitarian to a democratic society is the incompatibility of the new forms of social life and the new political institutions with the political culture of the nation. The inference is not particularly novel, as a matter of fact: it fully conforms to the *a priori* assumptions and predictions of political scientists. It would be odd, indeed, to expect the masses of a population that has never had any democratic experience and is, moreover, burdened with false impressions concerning the nature and the potential of democracy to master quickly the culture of democratic behaviour and to acquire immunity to its temptations and 'infantile disorders'.

However, the results of our study suggest a far greater conservativeness in the old political culture than one would normally have expected. The overnight changing of political slogans and professed values – accompanied, moreover, by the sudden emergence and

9   The bulk of this book was completed in May 1992.

almost universal spreading of the hitherto unpractised forms of mass political behaviour such as rallies and strikes and a variety of coercive actions (transport blockades and the like) – could not help creating an impression that 'the process had started'.[10] It had indeed, even though not as quickly as it seemed, and perhaps not quite in the direction that had been intended. It has become evident that political cultures contain layers that are far more stable and far more conservative than political values or habits of political behaviour. These consist, first and foremost, of complexes of socio-ontological patterns that set systems of 'coordinates' used to appraise both individual political situations and personal and collective behaviour within them. In this capacity, the socio-ontological attitudes, unless they undergo substantial changes themselves, not only limit the range of permissible innovations in values and operational experience but create prerequisites for the wind's subsequent return 'according to its circuits' (Eccles.1: 6): the Russian people may yet reap the whirlwind of their own history.

We have established the continuity of social ontology within the framework of national political culture from the old pre-revolutionary times until the recent *perestroika* years. We have seen how the Soviet political culture was able to absorb the most important elements of the traditional culture by interpreting them in a different ('Bolshevik') way and casting them in a new ('Soviet' or 'socialist') mould. We have further witnessed how the hybrid thus created started to break up into its original components under the influence of changed circumstances and how from under the burden of the revolutionary and post-revolutionary accretions the mentality of *sobornost'* has been gradually emerging on to the surface of political life in its traditional form. We have not forgotten that this type of political mentality has already paved the way for totalitarianism on one occasion – despite the different ideological and party prejudices of those who shared in it. We must not, therefore, allow ourselves to be seduced by the apparent affinity of the populist rhetoric of *sobornost'* and the language of democracy. The lesson of Russia's history must be learnt: namely, that a modern democratic society will not emerge unless the political mentality of *sobornost'* is overcome.

10 Mikhail Gorbachev's characteristic expression.

9 *Post Scriptum:*
The 'Candlelight Congress'

> We cannot fall in love again with those
> whom we have really ceased to love
> once.
> — F. de La Rochefoucauld, *The*
> *Maxims.*

The Fifth Congress did not end this story. On 17 March 1992 a group of People's Deputies of what had become the former USSR held a so-called Sixth Congress. The Congress was to be convened in the Kremlin, as appropriate, but since the initiative was not welcomed by the Russian authorities, the deputies met in Voronovo, some 50 miles southwest of Moscow. The semi-illegal character of the meeting and the dramatic atmosphere around it were emphasized by lack of electricity in the assembly hall: the Congress took place by the light of candles. What a blessing for future historians of a romantic disposition!

Given the situation in which the Congress was held, one should not, perhaps, allow oneself to be too ironical. However, *le choix oblige.* The Congress turned out to be a perfect exemple of *sobornost'*. A quorum was lacking, and although the organizers reported several hundred deputies to have assembled in Moscow, only some twelve dozen reached Voronovo: in the atmosphere of secrecy that reigned around the Congress some were left unaware of the destination and some were lost en route. However, the lack of a quorum did not embarrass those present, who apparently believed they had sufficient authority to act as they did. If the press is to be relied on (for no proceedings have been published and it is not even known whether any official record was kept at all), eighteen resolutions were passed in the course of 44 minutes.[1] No discussion was held; as for the drafts, the deputies were said to have read them on their way to Voronovo, in the buses.

However, another event was intended to become the apotheosis of *sobornost'*. It also was scheduled to take place in the Manège Square on 17 March, the day of the Congress and, incidentally, the first anniversary of the 1991 referendum on 'the preservation of the renewed Union'. This happening was styled 'the nation-wide *Veche*' and was to demonstrate the people's solidarity with the Union deputies, to confirm the results of the referendum and, above all, to elect General Albert Makashov, one of Boris Yeltsin's rivals in the previous year's presidential election, as the new Russian president. It did not go as far as the election, however: the participants confined themselves to nominating General Makashov as their candidate for the presidency and to proclaiming him 'the Head of the nation-wide movement for renewal of the Motherland'. But the very intention of electing a president of a multi-million nation right there in the square – without any superfluous formalities and by the vote of a few dozen or even a few hundred thousand volunteers,[2] authorized by no one but nevertheless holding themselves to be genuine exponents of the popular will – could appear only in minds permeated with the ideals of *sobornost'*. The circle seems about to close. Is there any escape from it?

---

1 See Ivanov-Smolensky 1992; Tregubova 1992.
2 The organizers reported that some 350,000 people had taken part in the rally; the Moscow militia estimated the number of the participants as 70,000: see Krasnikov 1992).

Bibliography

Aberbach, J., R. Putnam and B. Rockman (1981), *Bureaucrats and Politicians in Western Democracies*, Cambridge, MA: Harvard University Press.

Adorno, T. and M. Horkheimer (1972), *Dialectic of Enlightenment*, New York: Herder & Herder.

Alker, H. and B. Russett (1965), *World Politics in the General Assembly*, New Haven, CT: Yale University Press.

Arendt, H. (1958), *The Origin of Totalitarianism*, Cleveland, NY: Meridian Books.

Aristotle (1952), *Politics* in *The Works of Aristotle*, vol.2, Chicago, IL: Encyclopedia Britannica.

Arrow, K. (1951), *Social Choice and Individual Values: (Cowles Commission Monograph 12)*, New York: Wiley.

Artyushkin, V., A. Belyayev, Y. Sandler and V. Sergeev (1990), 'Neural Networks Ensembles as Models of Interdependence in Collective Behavior', *Mathematical Social Sciences*, 19.

Ashin, G. (1985), *Sovremennye teorii elity: Kritichesky ocherk (Modern Theories of Elites: A Critical Essay)* (in Russian), Moscow: Mezhdunarodnye otnosheniya.

August (1991), *Avgust-91 (August '91)* (in Russian), Moscow: Politizdat.

Averintsev, S. (1977), *Poetika rannevizantiiskoi literatury (Poetics of Early Byzantine Literature)* (in Russian), Moscow: Nauka.

Bakunin, M. (1972), *Statism and Anarchy* in S. Dolgoff (ed.), *Bakunin on Anarchy*, New York: Knopf.

— (1989), *Gosudarstvennost' i anarkhiya (Statism and Anarchy)* (in Russian) in *Filosofiya. Sotsiologiya. Politika (Philosophy, Sociology, Politics)*, Moscow: Pravda.

Balzer, H. (ed.) (1991), *Five Years That Shook the World: Gorbachev's Unfinished Revolution*, Boulder, CO: Westview.

211

Baranov, A. and V. Sergeyev (1988), 'Natural-Language Argumentation and the Logic of Practical Reasoning' (in Russian) in *Myshlenie, kognitivnye nauki, iskusstvenny intellekt (Thinking, Cognitive Sciences, Artificial Intelligence)*, Moscow: Nauka.

Berdyaev, N. (1947), *The Russian Idea*, London: Geoffrey Bles.

— (1972), *The Origin of Russian Communism*, Ann Arbor, MI: University of Michigan Press.

Binnendijk, H. (ed.) (1987), *National Negotiations Styles*, Washington, DC: Foreign Service Institute, US Department of State.

Birch, A. (1971), *Representation*, London: Pall Mall.

Bulgakov, S. (1991), 'Heroism and Selfless Devotion' (in Russian) in *Vekhi. Intelligentsiya v Rossii (Landmarks: The Intelligentsia in Russia)* (in Russian), Moscow: Molodaya gvardiya.

Burlatsky, F. (1988), 'On Soviet Parliamentarism', *Literaturnaya gazeta*, 16 June.

Carr, E.H. (1950), *A History of Soviet Russia: The Bolshevik Revolution, 1917–1923*, London: Macmillan.

Chaadayev, P. (1991), *Lettres philosophiques* in *Polnoe sobranie sochineniy i pisem (The Complete Works and Letters)* (in French and Russian), vol.1, Moscow: Nauka.

Cherepnin, L. (1978), *Zemskie sobory Russkogo gosudarstva v XVI–XVII vv. (The Zemskie Sobors of the Russian State in the 16th–17th centuries)* (in Russian), Moscow: Nauka.

Constitution (1985), *Constitution (Fundamental Law) of the Union of the Soviet Socialist Republics. Adopted at the Seventh (Special) Session of the Supreme Soviet of the USSR, Ninth Convocation, on 7 October 1977*, Moscow: Novosti Press Agency.

Constitution (1988), *Konstitutsiya (Osnovnoy zakon) Soyuza Sovetskikh Sotsialisticheskikh Respublik. S izmeneniyami i dopolneniyami, vnesyonnymi Zakonom SSSR ot 1 dekabrya 1988 goda na vneocherednoi dvenadtsatoi sessii Verkhovnogo Soveta SSSR odinnadtsatogo sozyva (Constitution (Fundamental Law) of the Union of the Soviet Socialist Republics. With Amendments and Supplements introduced by the Law of the USSR of 1 December 1988 at the Extraordinary Twelfth Session of the USSR Supreme Soviet of the Eleventh Convocation)* (in Russian), Moscow: Izvestiya.

CPSU in Resolutions (1983), *Kommunisticheskaya partiya Sovetskogo*

Soyuza v rezolyutsiyakh i resheniyakh s"ezdov, konferentsii i plenumov TsK (The Communist Party of the Soviet Union in Resolutions and Decisions of Its Congresses, Conferences and C.C. Plenary Sessions) (in Russian), Moscow: Politizdat.

Dahl, R. (1982), *Dilemmas of Pluralist Democracy: Anatomy vs. Control*, New Haven, CT: Yale University Press.

— (1985), *A Preface to Democratic Theory*, Berkeley and Los Angeles, CA: University of California Press.

Davydov, A. (1990), 'The First Stage is Coming to an End: More Mandates that Aspirants' in *Proryv v demokratiyu (Breakthrough to Democracy)* (in Russian), Moscow: Izvestiya.

de Gaulle, C. (1954), *Mémoires de guerre. L'Appel: 1940–1942*, Paris: Librairie Plon.

First Congress (1989), *Pervy S"ezd narodnykh deputatov SSSR: Stenografichesky otchyot (First Congress of the USSR People's Deputies: Proceedings)* (in Russian), 6 vols, Moscow: Izdatel'stvo Verkhovnogo Soveta SSSR.

First Congress (1990), *Pervy S"ezd narodnykh deputatov RSFSR (First Congress of the RSFSR People's Deputies)* (in Russian), (Bulletins 1–51), 16 May–22 June, Moscow: Verkhovny Sovet RSFSR.

Fisher, G. (1980), 'International Negotiations: A Cross-Cultural Perspective', [no place of publication given]: Intercultural Press.

Fourth Congress (1991), *Chetvyorty S"ezd narodnykh deputatov SSSR: Stenografichesky otchyot (Fourth Congress of the USSR People's Deputies: Proceedings)* (in Russian), 4 vols, Moscow: Izdatel'stvo Verkhovnogo Soveta SSSR.

Gidaspov, B. (1989), 'Report of the Credentials Commission' (in Russian) in *First Congress* (1989).

Gorbachev, M. (1987), 'New Year Address to the Soviet People: Soviet TV Broadcast of 31 December 1986' (in Russian) in *Izbrannye rechi i stat'i (Selected Speeches and Articles)*, vol.4, Moscow: Politizdat.

— (1988a), 'October and *perestroika*: The Revolution Continues (Report at the Joint Jubilee Meeting of the CPSU Central Committee, the USSR Supreme Soviet and the RSFSR Supreme Soviet on the Occasion of the Seventieth Anniversary of the Great October Socialist Revolution in the Kremlin Palace of Congresses on 2 November 1987' (in Russian) in *Izbrannye rechi i stat'i*, vol.5, Moscow: Politizdat.

— (1988b), 'The Party of the Revolution is the Party of *Perestroika*: Speech at a Meeting with Party Veterans, Participants in Revolutionary Events, Shock-Workers of the Five-Year Plans and Members of the Leningrad Party Organization *Aktiv* on 13 October 1987' (in Russian) in *Izbrannye rechi i stat'i*, vol.5, Moscow: Politizdat.

Gozman, L. and L. Etkind (1989), 'From the Power of the Cult to the Power of People' (in Russian), *Neva*, no. 7.

Gurevich, A. (1984), *Kategorii srednevekovoi kul'tury (Categories of Medieval Culture)* (in Russian), Moscow: Iskusstvo.

— (1990), *Srednevekovy mir: Kul'tura bezmolvsvuyushchego bol'shinstva (The Medieval World: The Culture of the Silent Majority)*, Moscow: Iskusstvo.

Habermas, J. (1987), *The Philosophical Discovery of Modernity*, Cambridge, MA: MIT Press.

Hamilton, A., J. Madison and J. Jay (1961), *The Federalist Papers*, New York: Mentor Books.

Hardy, D. (1977), *Petr Tkachev: The Critic as Jacobin*, Seattle, WA, and London: University of Washington Press.

Hayek, F. von (1976), *The Road to Serfdom*, London: Routledge & Kegan Paul.

Hegel, G. (1975), *Lectures on the Philosophy of World History. Introduction: Reason in History*, Cambridge: Cambridge University Press.

Heidegger, M. (1971), *Poetry, Language, Thought*, New York: Harper & Row.

Herzen, A. (1924–28), *My Past and Thought: The Memoirs of Alexander Herzen*, New York: Knopf.

— (1956), 'The Russian People and Socialism: An Open Letter to J. Michelet' in A. Herzen, *From the Other Shore* and *The Russian People and Socialism*, London: Weidenfeld & Nicolson.

Hobbes, T. (1980), *Leviathan*, Harmondsworth: Penguin.

Ivanov-Smolensky, G. (1992), 'A "Historic" Congress in the Sovkhoz of "Voronovo"' (in Russian) in *Izvestiya*, 17 March.

Jaurès, J. (1969–72), *Histoire socialiste de la Révolution française*, 6 vols, Paris: Editions Sociales.

Kamensky, Z. (1980a), *Moskovsky kruzhok lyubomudrov (The Moscow Circle of Lyubomudry)* (in Russian), Moscow: Nauka.

— (1980b), *Russkaya filosofiya nachala XIX veka i Shelling (Early 19th-century Russian Philosophy and Schelling)* (in Russian), Moscow: Nauka.

Karpenko, I. (1990a), 'Before the Repeated Election' in *Proryv v demokratiyu (Breakthrough to Democracy)* (in Russian), Moscow: Izvestiya.

— (1990b), 'The Election of the USSR People's Deputies has Begun' (in Russian) in *Proryv v demokratiyu.*

Kazhdan, A. (1968), *Vizantiiskaya kul'tura (Byzantine Culture)* (in Russian), Moscow: Nauka.

Kliger, S. (1989), 'Publicism–88 as an Object of Inquiry: Sociological Commentary' (in Russian) in *V svoyom otechestve proroki? Publitsistika perestroiki: luchshie avtory 1988 goda (Prophets in Their Own Country? Social and Political Journalism of Perestroika: The Best Authors of 1988)*, Moscow: Knizhnaya palata.

Krasnikov, E. (1992), 'The Communist Idea is Dead' (in Russian) in *Nezavisimaya gazeta*, 18 March.

Lasswell, H., D. Lerner and C. Rothwell (1952), *The Comparative Study of Elites: An Introduction and Bibliography*, Stanford, CA: Stanford University Press.

Law on Elections (1988), *Zakon Soyuza Sovetskikh Sotsialisticheskikh Respublik o vyborakh narodnykh deputatov SSSR (Law of the Union of the Soviet Socialist Republics on Elections of the USSR People's Deputies)* (in Russian), Moscow: Izvestiya.

Lenin, V., *Polnoe sobranie sochinenii (PSS) (Complete Works)* (in Russian), Moscow: Politizdat, various years.

— (1961), *What Is To Be Done? Burning Questions of Our Movement* in *Collected Works*, vol.5, Moscow: Foreign Languages Publishing House.

— (1964a), 'Can the Bolsheviks Retain State Power?' in *Collected Works*, vol.26.

— (1964b), 'Constitutional Illusions' in *Collected Works*, vol.25.

— (1964c), 'Declaration of Rights of the Working and Exploited People' in *Collected Works*, vol.26.

— (1964d), 'Draft Decree on the Right of Recall' in *Collected Works*, vol.26.

— (1964e), 'Political Parties in Russia and the Tasks of the Proletariat' in *Collected Works*, vol.24.

— (1964f), 'Speech at the First All-Russia Congress of the Navy on 22 November (5 December), 1917' in *Collected Works*, vol.2.

— (1964g), 'Speech at the Meeting of the Petrograd Soviet of Workers' and Soldiers' Deputies on 25 October (7 November) 1917' in *Collected Works*, vol.26.

— (1964h), *The State and Revolution: The Marxist Theory of the State and the Tasks of the Proletariat in the Revolution* in *Collected Works*, vol.25.

— (1964i), 'The Tasks of the Proletariat in the Present Revolution' in *Collected Works*, vol.24.

— (1964j), 'Theses for a Report at the 8 October Conference of the Petrograd Organisation, also for a Resolution and Instructions to Those Elected to the Party Congress' in *Collected Works*, vol.26.

— (1964k), 'Theses on Constituent Assembly' in *Collected Works*, vol.26.

— (1965a), 'Draft Programme of the RCP(b)' in *Collected Works*, vol.29

— (1965b), *The Immediate Tasks of the Soviet Government* in *Collected Works*, vol.27.

— (1965c), *One Step Forward, Two Steps Back: The Crisis in Our Party* in *Collected Works*, vol.7.

— (1965d), 'Report on Ratification of the Peace Treaty' in *Collected Works*, vol.27.

— (1965e), 'Rough Outline of the Draft Programme' in *Collected Works*, vol.27.

— (1965f), 'Speech at a Joint Session of the All-Russia Central Executive Committee, the Moscow Soviet and All-Russia Trade Union Congress on 17 January 1919' in *Collected Works*, vol.28.

— (1965g), 'Speech at the Moscow City Conference of the RCP(b) on 18 January 1919' in *Collected Works*, vol.28.

— (1966), 'Our Foreign and Domestic Position and the Tasks of the Party' in *Collected Works*, vol.31.

Literaturnaya gazeta (1989), various issues.

Livy (1965), *The Early History of Rome*, Harmondsworth: Penguin.

Lossky, N. (1991), *Kharakter russkogo naroda* (*The Character of the Russian People*) (in Russian) in N. Lossky, *Usloviya absolyutnogo dobra* (*Conditions of the Absolute Good*), Moscow: Politizdat.

Lotman, Yu. (1973), 'Canonical Art as Information Paradox' (in Russian) in *Problema kanona v srednevekovom iskusstve Azii i Afriki* (*The Problem of Canon in the Medieval Art of Asia and Africa*), Moscow: Nauka.

Machiavelli, N. (1972), *The Prince, Selections from The Discourses and Other Writings*, London: Fontana/Collins.

Mannheim, K. (1956), *Ideology and Utopia*, New York: Harvest Books.

March, J. and J. Olsen (1989), *Rediscovering Institutions: The Organizational Basis of Politics*, New York and London: Free Press.

Marcuse, H. (1964), *One-Dimensional Man*, Boston, MA: Beacon Press.

Marx, K. (1976), *Economic and Philosophic Manuscripts of 1844* in K. Marx and F. Engels, *Collected Works*, vol.3, New York: International Publishers.

— (1979), *The Eighteenth Brumaire of Louis Bonaparte* in K. Marx and F. Engels, *Collected Works*, vol.11, Moscow: Progress.

— (1983), 'Letter to J. Weydemeyer of 5 March 1852' in K. Marx and F. Engels, *Collected Works*, vol.39, Moscow: Progress.

— and F. Engels (1976), *The German Ideology: Critique of Modern German Philosophy According to its Representatives Feuerbach, B. Bauer and Stirner, and of German Socialism According to Its Various Prophets* in *Collected Works*, vol.5, New York: International Publishers.

Materialy plenuma (1989), *Materials of the Plenum of the Central Committee of the CPSU, 15–16 March 1989* (in Russian) (Moscow: Politizdat, 1989).

Medvedev, R. (1989), *On Stalin and Stalinism: Historical Essays* (in Russian), *Znamya* (1-4).

Michels, R. (1949), *Political Parties: A Sociological Study of the Oligarchical Tendencies of Modern Democracy*, Glencoe, IL: Free Press.

Migranyan, A. (1989), 'A Long Way to the European Home' (in Russian), *Novy mir*, no.7.

— (1990), *Perestroika as Seen by a Political Scientist*, Moscow: Novosti.

Minsky, M. (1985), *The Society of Mind*, New York: Simon & Shuster.

Mirrors (1989), *Zerkala (Mirrors)* (in Russian), Moscow: Moskovsky rabochii.

Mosca, G. (1939), *The Ruling Class*, New York: McGraw-Hill.

Nersesyants, V. (ed.) (1985), *Istoriya politicheskikh i pravovykh uchenii: Drevnii mir (History of Theories of Politics and Law: The Ancient World)* (in Russian), Moscow: Nauka.

Nesterov, F. (1980), *Svyaz' vremyon: Opyt istoricheskoi publitsistiki (The Bond of Times: An Essay in Historical Current Affairs)* (in Russian), Moscow: Molodaya gvardiya.

Nicolson, H. (1942), *Diplomacy*, London: Oxford University Press.

Orlov, A. (1989), *Tainaya istoriya stalinskikh prestuplenii (The Secret History of Stalin's Crimes)* (in Russian) in *Ogonyok* (nos 46ff).

— (1991), *Tainaya istoriya stalinskikh prestuplenii (The Secret History of Stalin's Crimes)* (in Russian), Moscow: Avtor.

Ortega y Gasset, J. (1932), *The Revolt of the Masses* (New York: Norton.

Pareto, V. (1968), *The Rise and Fall of Elites: An Application of Theoretical Sociology*, Totowa, NJ: Bedminster Press.

Parshin, P. and V. Sergeyev (1990), 'Conceptual Reconstruction and Conflict Resolution: Further Reflections on the Caribbean Crisis' (Paper presented to the 1990 ISA Annual Convention in Washington, DC).

Party Worker (1991), *Spravochnik partiinogo rabotnika, 1990 (Party Worker's Handbook, 1990)* (in Russian), vol.30, Moscow: Politizdat.

Plato (1966), *The Republic*, Cambridge: Cambridge University Press.

Pleshakov, K. and D. Furman (1989), 'The General and the Particular in the Sociopolitical and Ideological Development of the PRC and the USSR' (in Russian) in *Mirovaya ekonomika i mezhdunarodnye otnosheniya (World Economy and International Relations)*, no.12.

Polybius (1984), *The Rise of the Roman Empire*, Harmondsworth: Penguin.

Popper, K. (1971), *The Open Society and Its Enemies*, Princeton, NJ: Princeton University Press.

Pospelovsky, D. (1990), 'Totalitarianism – authoritarianism – democracy?' (in Russian) in *Knizhnoe obozrenie (Book Review)*, no.20.

Prewitt, K. and A. Stone (1973), *The Ruling Elites: Elite Theory, Power, and American Democracy*, New York: Harper & Row.

Putch (1991), *Putch: Khronika trevozhnykh dnei* (*The Putsch: A Chronicle of the Troubled Days*) (in Russian), Moscow: Progress.

Putnam, R. (1976), *The Comparative Studies of Political Elites*, Englewood Cliffs, NJ: Prentice-Hall.Rabinowitch, A. (1976), *The Bolsheviks Come to Power: The Revolution of 1917 in Petrograd*, New York: Norton.

Robespierre, M. (1957), 'Sur le gouvernement représentatif' in *Textes choisis*, vol.2, Paris: Editions Sociales.

— (1965), 'Speech at the Convention on 16 November 1792 in *Izbrannye proizvedeniya* (*Selected Works*) (in Russian), vol.2, Moscow: Nauka.

Rousseau, J.-J. (1974), *The Social Contract*, in *The Essential Rousseau*, New York: Mentor Books.

Russell, B. (1920), *The Practice and Theory of Bolshevism*, London: Allen & Unwin.

Second Congress (1990), *Vtoroi S"ezd narodnykh deputatov SSSR, 12–24 December 1989: Stenografichesky otchyot* (*Second Congress of the USSR People's Deputies: Proceedings*) (in Russian), 6.vols, Moscow: Izdatel'stvo Verkhovnogo Soveta SSSR.

Sergeyev, V. (1985), 'Artificial Intelligence as a Method of Studying Complex Systems' (in Russian) in *Sistemnye issledovaniya, 1984* (*Systems Studies, 1984*), Moscow: Nauka.

— (1986), 'The Structure of Political Argumentation in Thucydides' Melian Debate' (in Russian) in *Matematika v izuchenii srednevekovykh povestvovatel'nykh istochnikov* (*Mathematics in the Study of Medieval Narrative Sources*), Moscow: Nauka.

— (1987), 'Patterns of Understanding of Political Development' (in Russian) in *Uchyonye zapiski Tartusskogo gosudarstvennogo universiteta* (*Transactions of Tartu State University*), 751.

— (1991), 'Precedent Logic and Building of International Order: Using the Past to Construct the Future (Exemplification and Models of Pre-Understanding)' (Paper presented to the 1991 ISA Annual Convention in Vancouver).

— and A. Baranov (1990), 'Some Features of the Contemporary Political Discourse in the USSR' (Paper presented to the Third Soviet-American Seminar on Interdependence in Berkeley, California).

— and V. Tsymbursky (1990), 'Cognitive Models of Decision-making in Application to Political Science and History' (in Russian) in *Kompyutory i poznanie* (*Computers and Understanding*), Moscow: Nauka.

Simon H. (1957), *Administrative Behavior*, New York: Macmillan.

— (1991), *Models of My Life*, New York: Basic Books.

Sixsmith, M. (1991), *Moscow Coup: The Death of the Soviet System*, London and New York: Simon & Schuster.

Slusser, R. (1987), *Stalin in October: The Man Who Missed the Revolution*, Baltimore, MD, and London: Johns Hopkins University Press.

Spinoza, B. (1951), *A Political Treatise* in *The Chief Works by Benedict de Spinoza*, vol.1, New York: Dover Publications.

Stalin, I. (1941), 'Contribution to Questions of Leninism' (in Russian) in *Voprosy leninizma*, Moscow: Politizdat.

Third Congress (1990), *Vneocherednoi Tretii S"ezd narodnykh deputatov SSSR: Stenografichesky otchyot* (*Extraordinary Third Conress of the USSR People's Deputies: Proceedings*) (in Russian), 3 vols, Moscow: Izdatel'stvo Verkhovnogo Soveta SSSR.

Tkachev, P. (1976a), 'The Eve and the Next Day of the Revolution' (in Russian) in *Sochineniya* (*Works*), vol.2, Moscow: Mysl'.

— (1976b), '"Nabat": The Magazine's Programme' (in Russian) in *Sochineniya* (*Works*), vol.2, Moscow: Mysl'.

Tolstoy, L. (1904a), *My Confession* in *The Complete Works*, vol.13, London: Dent.

— (1904b), *War and Peace* in *The Complete Works*, vol.5–8, London: Dent.

Transition (1991), *The Transition to Democracy: Proceedings of a Workshop National Research Council*, Washington, DC: National Academy Press.

Tregubova, E. (1992), 'The Congress of the USSR People's Deputies Has Successfully Come to an End' (in Russian) in *Nezavisimaya gazeta*, 18 March.

Troyan, S. (1990), '"Reliable People" in the Assembly Hall' (in Russian) in *Proryv v demokratiyu* (*Breakthrough to Democracy*), Moscow: Izvestiya.

Tucker, R. (1987), *Political Culture and Leadership in Soviet Russia: From Lenin to Gorbachev*, New York: Norton.

Twelfth Session (1988), *Vneocherednaya dvenadtsataya sessiya Verkhovnogo Soveta SSSR (odinnadtsaty sozyv), 29 noyabrya – 1 dekabrya 1988g.: Stenograficheksy otchyot (Extraordinary Twelfth Session of the USSR Supreme Soviet (Eleventh Convocation), 29 November – 1 December 1988: Proceedings)* (in Russian), Moscow: Izdatel'stvo Verkhovnogo Soveta SSSR.

Verba, S. (1987), *Elites and the Idea of Equality: A Comparison of Japan, Sweden and the United States*, Cambridge, MA: Harvard University Press.

Voslensky, M. (1991), *Nomenklatura: Gospodstvuyushchii klass sovetskogo obshchestva (Nomenklatura: The Ruling Class of Soviet Society)* (in Russian), Moscow: Sovetskaya Rossiya and MP 'Oktyabr'.

Walicki, A. (1991), 'Morality and Law in Theories of Russian Liberals of Late 19th–Early 20th Century' (in Russian) in *Voprosy filosofii* (8).

Weber, M. (1958), *The Protestant Ethic and the Spirit of Capitalism*, New York: Charles Scribner's Sons.

Weeks, A. (1968), *The First Bolshevik: A Political Biography of Peter Tkachev*, New York: New York University Press; London: University of London Press.

Zenkovsky, V. (1953), *A History of Russian Philosophy*, 2 vols, New York: Columbia University Press; London: Routledge & Kegan Paul.

Index